VOICES OF SPORT

Other Books by Maury Allen

Marv Albert
Jack Brickhouse
Fred Capossela
Ken Coleman
Bill Currie
Don Dunphy
Win Elliot
Frank Gifford
Marty Glickman
Curt Gowdy
Ernie Harwell
Russ Hodges
Dan Kelly
Lindsey Nelson
Chris Schenkel
Ray Scott
Vin Scully
Jim Simpson
Bill Stern
Chuck Thompson
Bob Wolff

with MAURY ALLEN

voices of sport

An Associated Features Book

GROSSET & DUNLAP
A NATIONAL GENERAL COMPANY
Publishers • New York

PHOTO CREDITS

12, 101—ABC
23, 79, 123, 181, 193—UPI
24, 35—Los Angeles Dodgers
36, 228, 239—NBC
55—Mike Sirico
56—WHN
67—George Kalinsky
68—Camera 5 (Ken Regan)
80—Detroit News (Kilpatrick)
91—Courtesy Ernie Harwell
92—Courtesy Curt Gowdy
102—Courtesy Ken Coleman

112—Courtesy Chuck Thompson
124—Mutual Broadcasting System
135—Courtesy Don Dunphy
136—Courtesy Marty Glickman
146, 156—Radio Station KSFO
158, 169—Radio Station WGN
170—Radio Station KMOX
   (Lewis Portnoy)
182—Courtesy Bill Currie
194—Look Magazine
218, 227—Courtesy Freddie Capossela

Published simultaneously in Canada
Printed in the United States of America

To Teddy: The loudest and sweetest voice of them all.

Introduction

THE father and the nine-year-old son sat together on the shedding rug in a small apartment in Brooklyn and stared into the face of the floor radio. The drama of the night came quickly from the voice of Don Dunphy as he called the blows in the first Louis-Conn fight.

When it was over, when Conn was counted out, there was no doubt in the mind of the father, who should have known better, or the son, who was too young to know, that they had really "seen" a great fight.

Years later the father and the son did "see" a magnificent moment in sports when Bobby Thomson cracked Ralph Branca's pitch into the left field stands for the pennant. No matter that a son wouldn't eat his dinner, despite the father's assurance that "next year would be better," or a mother who couldn't really understand this nonsense. It was the sound of the announcer's voice calling out a pennant for the Giants that lingered through all the years.

There were other voices: Bill Stern on Saturday afternoons bringing excitement for two steady hours, and Marty Glickman from the Garden with the "swish" of college basketball or from Yankee Stadium with a touchdown pass at a Giants game.

Then there was that day when the boy had grown to manhood and the radio was in an Army barracks in Tokyo at 4:00 A.M. and all the others kidded him about Brooklyn and forced him to wager a month's salary—$98.60—on his team. Johnny Podres got the last out for the Dodgers and all Brooklyn exploded in joy. From 10,000 miles away, through the miracle of radio, it was vivid and clear and totally memorable.

Soon the emotional thrill of sports, the pure, unselfish drama of athletic competition, the stripping away of all the world's anguish, became the consuming passion of this young man's life. He wrote of the drama and the deeds, the failures and the frustrations, the entire scope of sports and its vital presence on the horizon of American life.

This book was born, really, on those days long ago when young men stared into the floor radios and were brought close to the scene by the vocal skill of the radio reporter. Add all that to the closeness of the television picture, from the small box sets first seen so unattainable through store windows to the brightness and warmth of green grass and blue skies and gold uniforms on a color set.

This book, then, is for all the young men who were brought across the country to huge and exciting ball parks, to football fields and boxing rings, to golf courses and race tracks by the Voices of Sport.

And it is also for those men of magic who sat above the action to bring clearly and concisely the sounds and the smells and the sights of sports to young and old across this land, to crowded city apartments and wide open farm lands, to small country villages and military outposts, to any place on this earth where a small boy could sneak a radio into his history class on an October day and be reprimanded by a teacher and then requested to turn it up so all could share the drama of the game.

In some small way this book is a hearty thank you and a congratulatory well-done for all the voices who carried the drama of the playing fields to so many homes.

This esteemed roll of voices has covered the gamut of sports in all its magnificence from a unique perch above the action, part of it, yet away from it, content only in carrying the story to the listener for his personal pleasure and for his emotional attachment to an event.

For all the young men who shared a radio with their fathers or sat on a couch for the Saturday afternoon football game on television, may this book be our way of thanking the Voices of Sport for lending us their eyes and ears.

Maury Allen
Dobbs Ferry, N.Y.

Contents

VOICES OF SPORT

Lindsey Nelson is backed up by Red Grange.

1

Tackled by the Bench

LINDSEY NELSON

Literate, personable, articulate Lindsey Nelson is one of the major voices in the history of American sports broadcasting.

Nelson came out of the University of Tennessee to bring accuracy and drama to the broadcasting of college football, professional football, baseball, basketball, tennis and golf to the American public.

His assignments have included the National Open Golf Tournament eight times, the Army-Navy football game eleven times, the Rose Bowl four times, the Cotton Bowl nine times, the Sugar Bowl five times as well as NBA championships, NIT championships, national tennis titles and the Davis Cup.

After seven seasons of describing the ups and downs (mostly falldowns) of the New York Mets, Nelson was thrilled by the success of the Mets in 1969. He has been describing Mets games, with former home run slugger Ralph Kiner and Broadcaster Bob Murphy, since the team was established back in 1962. He had the master skill of laughing with the Mets instead of at them as they struggled to

1

find success in those early trying years.

He was able to handle the comedy of the Mets from 1962–1968 with the same restrained professional poise as he handled their excitingly dramatic turnaround to the pennant and the World Series.

Nelson has been a warm, soothing voice on the air in one-time-or-another partnership with such bombastic talents as Leo Durocher, Fred Haney, Joe Garagiola, Jackie Robinson, Gene Sarazen, Jim Crowley and Frankie Albert. He remembers well Durocher's on-the-air penchant for speaking his mind, a major ingredient in Leo's charm.

"We were doing this game and Leo was describing the possibilities. There was a man on first and Leo said, 'Lindsey, there's no way this guy will steal in this spot. Whoops, there he goes.' Things like that couldn't faze Leo."

Nelson began his broadcasting career describing college games at the University of Tennessee, where he was graduated with a BA degree in English. He served four and a half years with the Ninth Infantry Division during World War II, with three years in North Africa and Europe, and received battle stars for seven campaigns.

Among his wartime friends were authors Ernest Hemingway and Maxwell Anderson, famed wartime correspondent Ernie Pyle, and a fellow officer in the 9th Division from Fort Bragg to VE Day, William C. Westmoreland.

In 1951, he received his first national exposure as a sportscaster for the Liberty Broadcasting System, where he did major league baseball and college and pro football. He was the voice of the New York Yanks of the NFL, the franchise which became the Baltimore Colts. In 1952, he joined NBC and was the major sports voice of that network for 10 years. He now does Notre Dame football games as well as post-season games and does professional football games for CBS-TV.

Nelson broadcast NBC's weekly baseball coverage for five years, did the All-Star games and the World Series and served as manager of sports for NBC.

He has broadcast almost every game of the Mets for the nine years of their existence and was one of the major figures in their champagne splashdowns as they were winning the pennant and the World Series in 1969.

Nelson lives with his wife, Mickie, and their two daughters, Nancy and Sharon, on Long Island.

He considers the triumph of the Mets an outstanding sports thrill but he remembers one game even more as the most fantastic afternoon he ever spent in the broadcasting booth. This was when Lindsey was with

Red Grange at the Cotton Bowl on January 1, 1954. It was the day Nelson proved to Grange and all the sports world that he knew the rules.

Lindsey Nelson

I SPENT New Year's Eve with the rule book and Red Grange.

This was the night before the Cotton Bowl, Alabama vs. Rice, on January 1, 1954, and I sat in my room with Grange in the Adolphus Hotel in Dallas going over last-minute preparations for our NBC telecast of the game the next day.

Grange and I had never worked together on a telecast and there were many small details to be discussed. I was to do the play-by-play and Grange, old number 77 of the Fighting Illini, was to do the color on the game.

I had arrived in Dallas five days earlier to watch the teams work out, to talk with some of the players and the coaches, to familiarize myself with the broadcasting setup in the Cotton Bowl. A couple of days later Grange had arrived directly from Detroit, where he had seen the Lions beat the Browns, 17-16, for the National Football League championship.

"Did you hear about the play?" Red asked.

"Which one?"

"Layne and Walker," he said.

I had missed the game and Grange explained what had happened. Bobby Layne, playing quarterback for the Lions, had passed off to halfback Doak Walker. Then Walker, in trouble, had run around and passed downfield to none other than the quarterback, Bobby Layne. Confusion had followed. Layne was finally ruled an ineligible receiver and the play was called back. Detroit won the game anyway on a Layne pass but the weird play had caused much conversation at the game.

"Here's the rule, Lindsey," Grange said. "We better prepare ourselves for it if it comes up again."

We continued our discussion of the rules, trying to cover ourselves for any emergency, no matter how unlikely. There are few things as embarrassing to a broadcaster as being caught with his preparation down, especially in something as basic as the rules.

"Did you ever see a guy come off the bench and make a tackle?"

"No," Grange said, "what happens if he does?"

I held the rule book in my hand and discussed the rule with Red. It was quite clear. This was the most unlikely happening in a football game. Come off the bench? Ridiculous. But the rule-makers, being careful men, had provided a rule to cover the eventuality. It was clearly in the book.

"This is one instance in a football game," I said, "when a referee can actually award a touchdown."

We discussed the rule for quite some while, agreed it could never happen, went over final plans for the game and went to the hotel dining room for our New Year's Eve dinner. Our revelry would have to wait. New Year's Day was going to be a very busy afternoon for us.

I got up early and went down for a leisurely breakfast the next day. There was plenty of time before Red and I would leave for the Cotton Bowl. I had a second cup of coffee and read *The New York Times*. The lead story on the front page was about a place in Asia called Vietnam. On January 1, 1954, General Henry Eugene Navarre, commanding officer of the French Union Forces in Indochina, addressed his troops in Hanoi and told them, "I fully expect victory in the long war against the Communists in six months."

I turned from the front page to the sports pages. I read the story previewing the Cotton Bowl between Rice and Alabama, looking for any piece of news I might have missed or any tidbit I could use on the air. There was nothing but the usual pessimistic quotes from the coaches, Red Drew of Alabama and Jess Neely of Rice.

Red and I got into a cab, told the driver to take us to the Cotton Bowl and settled back to begin one of the oddest days I have known in broadcasting.

A few minutes before the game we studied our depth charts from our broadcasting booth on the west side of the double deck stadium. There were 75,504 people settling into their seats as the bands massed at the middle of the field. The crowd stood at attention as they played the National Anthem.

Rice will be kicking off to Alabama and defending the north goal to our left with Alabama at the south goal to our right. The crowd is on its feet and there's the kick . . . the 1954 Cotton Bowl is underway.

Alabama couldn't move with the ball and punted to Rice. The Texans weren't able to move it either in the early minutes of the first quarter and they kicked back to the Crimson Tide. Alabama took over the football on its own 22-yard line and came out for its second drive.

The Alabama quarterback was a soft-spoken, handsome junior from Montgomery, Alabama, named Bryan Bartlett Starr. He was eight days shy of his 20th birthday and had not had a spectacular college career. He did not have a spectacular afternoon that day either, but was to figure in a key play. He was to have, of course, a spectacular career as the quarterback of the Green Bay Packers in their golden years under Vince Lombardi.

Now Starr led the Alabama team downfield in the first drive of the afternoon. He kept the Crimson Tide on the ground most of the drive, passing short occasionally to keep the Rice defense loose. He worked downfield three, five, six yards at a time.

Alabama drove the ball almost to the Rice goal. It was third down, late in the first quarter, just a foot to go for a touchdown. Starr called the play in his huddle. Alabama came out quickly to the line of scrimmage.

Starr over the ball checking the Rice defense. A give to Tommy Lewis over the right side of the line . . . touchdown, Alabama . . . Bart Starr hands off to fullback Tommy Lewis and the Crimson Tide leads, 6-0, with three minutes left in the first quarter.

The extra-point kick was missed and Alabama led, 6-0, as it kicked off to Rice. The Owls couldn't move against the tough Alabama defense and had to kick again. The punt was partially blocked and Alabama had the ball on its own 45. Starr took them downfield again. Now it was a first down on the 25. Alabama fumbled on the next play and Rice had the ball on its own 21.

Until this point Alabama, keying on flashy Dicky Moegle, a lithe, swift Rice halfback, had kept the Rice offense in check. Now Alabama was ready defensively as Rice moved to the line of scrimmage.

The handoff to Moegle . . . he breaks to the right . . . eludes one tackler . . cuts upfield at the 40 . . . he's all alone . . . Dicky Moegle . . . nobody near him . . . Moegle at the 20 . . . Moegle going in for a Rice Touchdown . . . Dicky Moegle, a 19-year-old junior halfback from Taylor, Texas, raced through the entire Alabama defense and scores for Rice. The run covered 79 yards and the score is tied, 6-6. Here's Leroy Fenstemaker in for the extra point try . . . the kick is up . . . and . . . good. Rice leads, 7-6. Red.

"Lindsey, Moegle showed the speed we had heard about. He got a hole in the right side of the Alabama line, knifed through it quickly and busted loose all by himself. He's tall and thin and doesn't look like he has the kind of speed but once he got past the Alabama secondary he was gone. Rice leads, 7-6. One minute left to play in the first quarter."

Behind for the first time in a game they were favored to win, Alabama took the kickoff, raced 23 yards downfield and had a first down on its own 46. Starr drove Alabama into Rice territory and with a long pass had a first down on the Rice five-yard line.

First and goal for Alabama. Two minutes gone in the second period. Starr over the center calling the play . . . a handoff to the quarterback . . . fumble . . . Rice ball. Rice has recovered Bart Starr's fumble.

The quarterback of Alabama, destined to become one of the great quarterbacks in football history, had trouble with the handoff and dropped it less than five yards from the Rice goal line. Now, instead of having a shot at the go-ahead score, Alabama was back on the defensive.

Rice was in the huddle five yards into its own end zone. They had to move the ball quickly out of the shadow of their own goal. They decided to go again to their key man, Dicky Moegle.

Rice was lined up in a tight T formation. They were on the five-yard line on the east side of the field, 95 yards away from a touchdown. Alabama was bunched close defensively, looking for the short power burst to get Rice out from its own territory. Moegle was at the right halfback position for Rice.

There's the handoff to Moegle . . . he cuts through the right side of the Alabama line . . . he's loose at the 20 . . . he's moving toward the sideline . . .

Rice had called the same play that had worked for the touchdown. Moegle had sprung free again after a quick handoff. This time he cut toward the sideline for more running room instead of toward the middle of the field, where the Alabama defenders were coming from. Now he was racing down the opposite side of the field from us. The television cameras had him zeroed in perfectly and I followed his progress as he charged down the field toward another touchdown.

I glanced quickly at the Alabama defense. Not a man was within 20 yards of him. There was only one possible tackler, a slow moving tackle named Ray Crawford, angling toward Moegle from the opposite side of the field. Crawford was moving at a sharp angle in an attempt to head off Moegle before he could get into the end zone. I reasoned quickly that if Crawford were to catch Moegle it would happen somewhere along the ten-yard line of Alabama. Moegle had that much room to cut before Crawford's angle could be a factor. In my mind, I made an instant decision. Moegle would race past Crawford easily and go in standing up for his second touchdown.

Moegle is free at the 35 . . . he's racing down the sidelines . . . he's at midfield . . . he's at the Alabama 40 . . .

I was just about to tell the twenty-five million people watching the game that Dicky Moegle had scored his second touchdown, this one a brilliant burst of 95 yards and Rice was now leading, 13-6.

Then it happened. I can't remember how. Nobody can. It was too quick. Moegle was racing down the sidelines, roaring to a touchdown, stepping quickly, his legs churning, his lithe body gracefully spreading distance between himself and the helpless pursuers.

In an instant, he was down. Flat. On the ground. His body writhing in pain. Gasping for breath. My God, had he been shot?

There had been 75,000 people cheering, roaring, rooting, hoping for him to score, or hoping, if they were Alabama rooters, for him to run out of bounds accidentally, or trip on a yardstripe, or step in a hole.

None of this happened. Yet, he was down.

Moegle is down on the Alabama 38-yard line. I don't know how he got there but he's down. He had covered 57 yards without a hand being laid on him. Now he is down on the Alabama 38. Just hold on.

At first it was a blur in the action. Then I could see him clearly. A figure in an Alabama uniform, no helmet on his head, retreating quickly to the Alabama bench, forcing his way behind the bench-warmers, moving backwards out of the play. He would move backwards out of the play but forward into fooball history.

The coaches had all raced to the spot as Moegle was helped to his feet. A crowd had gathered around him now of coaches, Alabama players, Rice players, officials, fans, trainers, some police and sideline helpers. Nobody quite knew what they were looking for.

In the stands there was an oppressive silence, as if 75,000 people had at once lost their ability to talk. They were stilled by the sudden turn of events, silenced by the striking blow to Moegle from somewhere, from someone, from something.

In those few moments of doubt I had not the slightest idea what had happened. One instant Moegle was running for a touchdown. He was alone. The nearest tackler was 20 yards away and I had concluded he could not catch the runner. In the next instant, Moegle was down. Had he been shot? Had he tripped? Had the Alabama player without the helmet anything to do with it?

Finally, the referees began pointing to the Alabama bench, to a

7

figure who had tried to disappear into a crowd of his teammates, to the offensive fullback of the Alabama Crimson Tide named Tommy Lewis, who had scored his team's first touchdown and had been waiting impatiently on the sidelines for Alabama to get the ball again as his team's defensive unit was on the field.

Now the situation began to clear. Tommy Lewis, the Alabama fullback, had watched Moegle roar toward him on the way to a score, had leaped off the bench, rushed onto the field and caught Moegle with a jarring blind side tackle. The 12th man on the field, the man who knocked Moegle down, was the unhelmeted figure who had been seen backing sheepishly off the field a few seconds before.

Lewis, the 19-year-old hard-running fullback for Alabama, had interfered with the play by crashing Moegle to the ground. The officials had spotted him and now they stood near the Alabama sidelines with the opposing coaches discussing the play.

In the booth, a grin crept over Grange's face. He quickly recalled our long and detailed conversation New Year's Eve. It had centered on two major points of interest in the rule book. The first pertained to the quarterback as an eligible or ineligible receiver, as Bobby Layne, in the NFL championship game, had been. The second pertained to the very situation, this impossible situation, that had just been unfurled before our eyes.

"Lindsey," Grange said, "what about this play?"

Red held out his hand, palm up, as if to motion to me that the ball was all mine and I could do with it as I wished. Under normal circumstances I might have choked. But with the rule fresh on my lips from our session the night before, I began with utmost confidence.

The rule clearly states that if a play is interfered with by an act palpably unfair, such as a 12th man coming off the bench as we have just seen here, the referee has the power to award a touchdown. If the referee rules that the runner would have scored, he can now give Rice six points. They are still discussing it across the field.

The referee in charge was Cliff Shaw. He stood in the middle of a group of officials with the two head coaches and their assistants. It wasn't so much an argument as a discussion in which everybody was willing to learn and listen. Then Shaw nodded his head, all parties seemed to agree and he raced downfield toward the Alabama goal. He carried the ball over the goal line and dramatically raised his hands straight over his head in the well-known football sign. Shaw was awarding Rice a touchdown.

As the rule states, Shaw is awarding a touchdown to Rice. Moegle is being given credit for a 95-yard run and there is no further penalty on the play.

Lewis, the alternate captain of the Crimson Tide, stood with his head down along the sidelines. He watched Shaw raise his hands over his head for the score. He shook his head and walked back to the Alabama bench. There was nothing else for him to do at the time.

The rule had been clearly explained to the television viewers and now Grange and I smiled at each other as we broke for a commercial.

"Red, it couldn't have been better if we had rehearsed it," I said.

Grange just shook his head. He still didn't believe he had seen such a strange play.

The game finally resumed as Leroy Fenstemaker kicked the extra point and Rice led, 14-6.

Moegle scored another touchdown later in the game, this time on a run of some 34 yards, and this time without interference from the sidelines and very little from the field, as Rice pushed its lead to 21-6. A final-period score by Rice gave them the Cotton Bowl victory over Alabama, 28-6.

As soon as the final gun sounded, reporters rushed to Lewis for some explanation of his tackle. He could offer none. He was just a very sad young man.

"I just looked at Moegle on the ground and I kept telling myself I didn't do it, I didn't do it, and I knew it wasn't so. I knew I did," he said.

Lewis hung his head as he tried to explain his actions. "One minute I was sitting on the bench just thinking what I would do the next time I got into the game and the next minute I was off the bench and racing at him. I hit him a hard tackle and he was down. I'm too emotional. I guess I'm just too full of Alabama. He just ran too close to our bench and before I knew what I was doing I had him tackled. Then I jumped up and got off the bench. I kept telling myself I didn't do it but I know I did."

Moegle said he never saw Lewis coming.

"If I had," he said, "I would have stiff-armed him or side-stepped him or something. I was looking straight ahead at the goal and glancing sideways at the one guy who had a shot at me. He was still 20 yards from me as I crossed midfield. I knew that I was going all the way again. No one could lay a hand on me. The next thing I knew, I was on my back and gasping for breath," Moegle said.

There were no stop-action films on television in 1954 but game films clearly revealed that Lewis had come from the bench, crossed in front of Moegle and nailed him full speed just at the middle of the Alabama bench.

If nothing else, the tackle had been crisp and hard. Lewis had come off the bench illegally but he had, at least, not made a complete fool of himself by missing the tackle. In fact, there were people who thought he had shown some of the innocent idealism of college football, the emotions of the game and the discipline of his training. He was a crimson-shirted player from Alabama and when he saw the white-shirted Moegle from Rice, he went after him.

Lewis was a guest the following Sunday on the Ed Sullivan Show. He got loud cheers as films of his feat were shown. Moegle didn't get any cheers. He had his three touchdowns and his team had the Cotton Bowl win.

Red Grange and I discussed the play long into the night. We were amazed at how our hard work and devotion to duty in studying the rule book had paid off so quickly. Barely 12 hours after we had finished studying the book and examining the rules we had used the explanation of the play on the air.

The next day I flew to the NCAA meetings. Matty Bell, the coach of Southern Methodist University, was leading a discussion of the rules. He congratulated me on knowing the rules so thoroughly and being so quick in being able to cite the exact rule on the air in such a once-in-a-lifetime situation.

Of course, I would never let on that Red Grange and I had discussed that very rule for a long while the night before I was ever called on to discuss it on the air before 25,000,000 viewers.

That was the first NBC telecast Red Grange and I had ever worked together and we received much favorable comment and many awards from critics for our coverage of that game.

Several years later Red Grange sent me a copy of his autobiography. I opened the book and looked at the inscription Red had written on the first page.

"To Lindsey Nelson," he wrote, "The first guy who knows the rules."

Oddly enough, there was an epilogue for me. It came on the air, on CBS-TV in 1962 at the Yale Bowl.

Yale was playing Princeton, and Terry Brennan and I were doing the TV commentary. A Yale quarterback named Ed McCarthy, No. 17, took a snap from center, flipped the ball back to his fullback who was trapped near the sideline. The fullback looked for a receiver, found one in the end zone and lofted a soft pass. I can still see that big No. 17 coming up to meet the football, and as he nestled it to his bosom and fell to the turf of the end zone at the north end of the Yale Bowl, I'm sure I was the only guy there whose thoughts were of the Adolphus Hotel in Dallas, Texas. I could hear Red Grange saying that the T-quarterback was an ineligible receiver. And I said on the air that Ed McCarthy was an ineligible receiver. However, the officials didn't seem to hear me because they signalled touchdown and the teams lined up for the extra point.

Our director wasn't sure, either, so he punched up a shot of the Princeton coach, Dick Colman, who wasn't bothered about Yale having scored on an illegal play. I asked Terry Brennan to pick up the rulebook in my attaché case on the floor and read the rule to our audience. He did. At his apartment in Manhattan, CBS sports veep Bill MacPhail wasn't sure. He admitted he didn't know the rules that well. All he knew was that he had an announcer who kept saying it was an illegal touchdown, but he doubted that his announcer knew something that the officials, players and coaches didn't—and nobody else had made a move to do anything about the score.

It was not until the next morning that a confirmation appeared when Kenny Smith wrote in the *New York Mirror*, after checking with the game officials, "Fifty thousand people left the Yale Bowl yesterday without knowing that they had seen an ineligible receiver score a touchdown, but the television audience had been told."

The *Mirror* Sports Editor, the late Dan Parker, wrote: "Didn't Lindsey Nelson vindicate his entire craft, frequently charged with second guessing, with his description of the illegal Yale touchdown at the Bowl on Saturday?"

It happened in November, 1962, at the Yale Bowl in New Haven, Connecticut, but it had begun for me with Red Grange at the Adolphus Hotel in Dallas, Texas, on New Year's Eve of 1953.

The next year, the NCAA Football Rules Committee made the T-quarterback an eligible receiver.

*A couple of regulars on the golf circuit:
Chris Schenkel and Arnie Palmer.*

2

In the Rough with Arnie

CHRIS SCHENKEL

Slender, debonair Chris Schenkel, singled out by President Richard Nixon as his favorite sports broadcaster, has come a long way from his modest beginnings as a high school announcer in his hometown of Bippus, Indiana.

The American Broadcasting Company sportscaster has covered just about every major sporting event there is from bowling to basketball, from prize fighting to the Olympics. He is equally at home in the violent world of football and the quiet drama of golf.

Working with former Oklahoma coach Bud Wilkinson, Schenkel brings college football to millions of people every Saturday afternoon on the NCAA Game of the Week.

Schenkel began his career as a sports announcer in basketball-mad Indiana. He moved from the games in Bippus to college games on the campus of Purdue University at Lafayette, where he graduated in 1943 with a major in radio broadcasting. He learned his trade while working for small salaries at local radio stations around Indiana.

In 1943 Schenkel entered the Army in

World War II and was discharged as a First Lieutenant in 1946. He resumed his sportscasting career on various stations in the Midwest before taking a job in Providence, R.I. He moved on to Boston, where he was exposed to big-city broadcasting for the first time.

His first big break came in 1952 when he was signed by Dumont Television and the New York Football Giants. Then he subbed for Ted Husing on the Monday night fights. Chris was hired as a one-night replacement for Husing and stayed on the show for six years. Husing retired due to failing health.

Schenkel's association with the Giants lasted 13 pleasant years, the golden years of Giant football.

"I like to think," laughs Schenkel, "that the decline of the Giants and my leaving them had no connection."

Schenkel then became the sportscaster on the NCAA football games which week after week hold the attention of more than thirty million viewers.

In addition to the NCAA football, Schenkel's credits include the National Basketball Association Game of the Week, including the stirring New York Knicks' championship, the Professional Bowlers' Tour, ABC's major golf tournaments, Major League Baseball and the Olympics. Schenkel is also a frequent contributor to ABC's "Wide World of Sports."

The versatile broadcaster covered championship fights including Patterson-Johansson and Cooper-Clay, and racing's Triple Crown.

His smooth, poised delivery has won accolades from listeners and critics across the country.

Schenkel, who has put in hundreds of thousands of miles covering sports for more than two decades across the country and around the world, lives in New York with his wife Fran and their three children.

Here, Schenkel relives a dramatic, yet painful day on the golf course of the Olympic Country Club in San Francisco. It is June 20, 1966, at the National Open and Schenkel is at the microphone.

Chris Schenkel

ON a beautiful, clear Wednesday afternoon in June we arrived at San Francisco's International Airport for an exciting event.

The National Open Golf Tournament was scheduled to begin the next afternoon at the Olympic Country Club in San Francisco. This would be the first major TV colorcast of a golf tournament and I hoped the players would provide some drama for me to describe on the ABC cameras.

On Thursday morning as the tournament began I walked the entire course to familiarize myself with each hole. We would be doing some broadcasting from the holes, but we would be doing most of it from a control point and off the monitors so we could catch as much of the action as we could. My broadcasting partner was Byron Nelson, and Jim McKay and Bill Fleming of ABC would be on the course. All of the big names of golf—my pal Arnie Palmer, Jack Nicklaus, Billy Casper, Champagne Tony Lema, Dave Marr, Ben Hogan, Phil Rodgers and most of the others—would be competing for the $25,000 first-place prize.

Palmer and Nicklaus, who had shared domination of golf in the '60s, would be watched the most. They were the big names, the colorful characters, the personalities who could sell the tournament to the viewing public.

The course was in marvelous shape with the greens lush and rich, the trees in the rough cut tight, the air crisp and invigorating off the ocean, the occasional fog usually lifting by early afternoon.

After the first two rounds on Thursday and Friday it was evident that Arnold Palmer was at the top of his game. He moved ahead to a quick lead and seemed destined to break the course record. Arnie's Army moved closer, pressing the ropes, challenging the guards on each stroke Arnie took. As the golf ball left his driver for each hole, they would race like a swarm of giant ants down the fairways to the greens for a good view of Palmer's final attack on each hole.

"I don't mind them closing in like that," Palmer explained to the sportswriters. "I'd probably do the same thing myself if I wanted to see some great golf."

As Arnie finished his Friday round well in the lead, we made a dinner date for that evening. Arnie, his pilot, Darrell Brown, Byron Nelson and I would have dinner together at one of San Francisco's showplace restaurants, The Blue Fox. It was a marvelous evening with Arnie in great humor, Byron telling some marvelous stories and Darrell and I improving our golf game just listening to these two guys.

On Saturday Arnie renewed his attack on the course, driving and slashing and putting incredibly well, leaving the rest of the field well behind. As night fell over San Francisco Saturday, Arnold Palmer held a seven-stroke lead on his nearest rival, Billy Casper. Palmer seemed intent on breaking the course record and shattering the opposition.

Sunday would be our major televising day. We would be on the air longer that day than any other and expected to spend most of the afternoon zooming in on Arnie, on Arnie's Army and on Billy Casper as they played together for the final 18 holes of the tournament.

Early Sunday morning we were ready to go. Our equipment was in place from the 10th hole through the 18th as the crowds grew larger and larger to see if Arnie could cut a few more strokes off par. Palmer had already won the Open once, in 1960 at Cherry Hills. Casper had also won it once, in 1959. Palmer had come close twice before losing in a playoff to Jack Nicklaus at Oakmont in 1962 and to Julius Boros at Brookline in 1963.

Palmer seemed as certain of winning a tournament, as he teed off that Sunday morning, as a golfer can ever be. He was seven strokes up, playing beautifully and hardly seemed to have any competition. Arnie's Army was beaming broadly. Their man was putting on some show.

Casper, who entertained the sportswriters by describing his exotic menu of buffalo meat and other rare weight-reducers, was playing steady, conservative golf. Not brilliant but good. Going into the final day, it looked like he would finish a comfortable second, well ahead of the slumping Nicklaus.

More than 15,000 persons crowded onto the course as Palmer lined up his first drive of the last day of the tournament.

Arnie's Army pressing against the ropes as Palmer prepares for his drive. He addresses the ball . . . now he's ready . . .

WHISH. . . . The noise of Palmer's clubhead crashing against the golf ball had a unique ring. You could almost hear the power and the contact in the stroke as he put his arms, his legs, his hips and that tremendous athletic body against the small ball. The ball sailed far and true, some 250 yards, almost on the middle of the fairway as Palmer began that Sunday as he had left off on Saturday, simply destroying a golf course with his brilliant game.

There was little to indicate there would be any change in the pattern of the tournament as Palmer and Casper finished the first nine holes together. Palmer had a five on the sixth hole but other than that had continued his masterful play. He shot a 32 for the nine holes while Casper had a 36.

Now as Palmer moved to the tenth hole he led Casper by seven strokes with nine holes to go. There had been no warning signs that the golf match was just about to begin.

Here we are at the tenth. . . . Palmer with a seven stroke lead . . . hits a beautiful drive well down the fairway . . . some thirty or forty yards from the green . . . still rolling . . . near the rough . . .

The ball went down a small incline and landed in the rough. Arnie would have to blast out to get a straight shot to the green. As was his style, he would not baby the ball. He would hit it hard, trying for the most distance he could get, not worrying about the possibilities of mis-direction. This time he was caught by a tree. Arnie slashed at the ball and caught an overhanging branch. The force of the iron was shot and the ball landed well beneath the green. Arnie's third shot made the green some 12 feet from the pin.

Palmer over the ball . . . gets his feet into position . . . the gallery is still . . . Arnie steadies the putter . . . now he's ready . . . ooohh . . . the ball hit the side of the hole and just rolled by . . . . Arnie drops it in . . . for a five . . . that was the first bad putt all afternoon for Arnold Palmer.

Casper was on the green in three, some six feet from the hole and calmly dropped the putt. He had put a slight dent in Arnie's huge lead but only eight holes remained. To win, Casper had to make up seven strokes in eight holes. He needed six strokes in eight just for a tie. He was being asked by his fans to do it against the master, Arnold Palmer, in one of Palmer's hottest tournaments up until this time. It was a bad bet.

On the 11th both Palmer and Casper parred the hole with fours. They each parred the 12th with threes. Now Arnie led Casper by six strokes with only six holes to go. There was little hope for a victory party of buffalo meat that night.

On the par three 13th Palmer was on the green in two. He had a long, sloping putt to the right for his par. He studied it, moved back and studied it again. The crowd was sensing that Arnie might be tiring. He had played so well, so brilliantly for so long, that now the putts were starting to look longer than they were.

Palmer, bent low against the cup, his putter held loosely in front of him, his eyes on the curve and the slope. Now he moves back to the ball and readies himself for the putt . . . he rolls it up there . . . short . . . the ball stops inches from the cup . . . Arnie holes out for a four.

Now Casper was being noticed more. Quietly he had cut a stroke from Palmer's lead and now could cut another. He was about ten feet from the pin on the left side. He tugged at his hat and moved to the ball.

The putt is downhill to the right . . . Casper has been putting well all afternoon . . . now he is ready again . . . the ball is rolling . . . in . . . Casper has a three on the thirteenth . . . he trails by five . . . five holes to go.

Now for the first time there seemed a chance. The tough holes were coming up. The 14th had some tricky bunkers, the 15th had a wooded area, the 16th was a huge hole, some 604 yards, the 17th had a rough, the 18th had trees. The crowd hustled to the 14th as Casper drove clean down the fairway. Palmer matched the drive. Each made the green with his second shot, Palmer some 30 feet away on the right, Casper a little less on the left. Neither could sink the long putt. Each took a par four.

Here we are at the 15th, a par three, 370-yard hole . . . a bunker on the left . . . a rough to the right . . . Palmer driving . . . hooking a little to the left . . .

Palmer was a little more than halfway down the fairway. The crowd had rushed down quickly as he walked to the ball. They were becoming excited as Palmer walked quickly with that rapid, certain pace, his brown hair blowing in the slight breeze, his head up, his eyes searching out the white golf ball. He climbed the slight incline as the cameraman moved closer and he selected a seven iron from his bag. Now he would try to drive the ball over a bunker on the left to the green. If he could make this shot well and get his par he would be almost unbeatable with only three holes to go.

Palmer stands over the ball . . . the shot is high to the left . . . it's going to be short of the green . . . and into a bunker . . . Arnie is in the bunker on the left side . . . the crowd is gasping in agony.

Casper had hit a marvelous shot to the right on the green some 25 yards from the pin. He was on the green in one and Arnie was in a bunker in two.

Palmer is always at his most dramatic in the toughest spots. Like the true champion he is, he attacks the course most vigorously when he is in trouble. He was in bad trouble now as he stood at the base of the bunker.

. . . a brilliant shot by Arnie . . . the ball crashing out of the bunker rolling toward the pin . . . still rolling . . . finally stopping some seven or eight feet from the pin . . . straight in front of it . . . Arnie has a chance for a par three if he can sink this putt . . . he stares at the ball . . . looks at the hole . . . moves to get a better

*angle . . . now he is over the ball . . . the putt . . . rolling . . . oh
. . . off to the left.*

Palmer had overshot the hole and missed the putt. He shook
his head and looked at the skies. He was disgusted with himself.
As he dropped the putt in I thought back to how casual, how funny,
how good-humored he was at dinner Friday night. He was a good
friend of mine and I was struggling to maintain my objectivity. I
wanted to walk up to Arnie after he missed that putt and cheer
him up.

Now Casper sunk his long putt for a birdie two. Arnie had a
bogey four and the lead of seven strokes had dwindled to just three
as they walked to the 16th. We watched all the drama from our
TV monitor behind the 18th green—the control point. What was
there to say, really? Arnie's lead was slipping away and he could
see it happening. He had to steady himself for the final three holes.

The 16th was the hole I will always remember. Arnie will probably remember it the rest of his life, too. It was 604 yards of mon-
strous fairway and green, a dogleg left, a large tree jutting out like
some hungry monster anxious to swoop up anything hit its way,
a long, hilly green, a beautiful hole to look at, a shocking hole to
play.

*Palmer looking down the fairway . . . the drive is long to the
left . . . hits a tree down there . . . is bouncing off . . . rolling away
from the fairway . . . a tough break for Arnie.*

Casper's drive was much shorter and much straighter. He was in
the middle of the fairway on the par four hole. Arnie was lost in
the woods. The ball was finally discovered resting in the rough on
the left side, some 300 yards from the hole at an impossible angle
to the green. Palmer went to his three iron to crack out of the deep
brush. The ball stung the bottom of some trees, grazed a branch
again and came to rest at the edge of the rough, still some distance
from the center of the fairway.

This made the crowd restless. Arnie was slipping down before
their eyes and they kept pushing closer and closer for the better
look. Casper's second shot got him on the edge of the green. Arnie
was in deep trouble.

Now he used his nine iron to drive the ball out of the rough and
finally on the fairway. He had used three strokes to get within 300
yards of the pin. There was no more room for error. If Arnie was
to save himself from complete disaster on this hole he had to come
up with a couple of brilliant shots.

He almost did.

Palmer took his number three wood and drove the ball some 250 yards to the right of the green. Unfortunately for Arnie, the ball rolled a little too far and came to rest smack in the middle of another bunker. On the 16th hole, famed for its rough on the left and bunker on the right, Arnie had managed to catch both. He blasted out of the bunker on his fifth shot and rested some four feet from the cup. Casper had birdied the par five hole as Arnie stood over the ball for his putt.

Arnie has done well to be in this position on this hole. If he makes the putt it will give him a six and a one-stroke lead with two holes to go. Now he's taking his time, studying the putt carefully, moving back from the ball. The crowd watches closely . . . the putt . . . drops . . . in.

The crowd let out a huge cheer and Arnie smiled for the first time in several holes. He had bogeyed with a six but he could still win with two good holes. The crowd sensed that after taking two bogeys on two holes, Palmer would be equal to the challenge of the 17th and the 18th.

The 16th hole would be the talk of the tournament and Arnie would laugh about it later and say, "It was the greatest six I ever had."

The par-four 17th was another dangerous hole, a rough on the left, a rough on the right, 415 yards of hilly terrain. Arnie had to keep his lead here or go into the 18th with all the pressure of the final hole. Palmer led by just one stroke with the last holes to go. He had taken two bogeys in the previous two holes as Casper had shot two birdies. The big lead had dwindled away to just one stroke as the late afternoon sun moved behind the San Francisco hills.

Palmer on the 17th . . . hits a short drive . . . sailing toward the left rough, bouncing in there and disappearing in the brush. . . . Another bad drive by Arnold Palmer.

Now the pressure was on Arnie again. The man who almost single-handedly had revolutionized the game and popularized golf was on the threshold of a shocking setback. He had led by seven strokes in the National Open with nine holes to go. Now he led by a single stroke.

Arnie with a six iron . . . hits one off the end of the club . . . into the rough on the right side.

Palmer had shot his way out of one problem into another. With the crowd streaming for the hole and the police holding them back and the officials watching closely, the cameras caught Arnie's face as he set up for his third shot. There was anger and unhappiness and frustration on his face. He couldn't believe what was happening. Casper was on the green with a short putt to go. Palmer had hit a wedge to within seven feet of the pin. Now the pressure was on him again as Casper sank his putt.

Arnold Palmer has to sink this putt to hold his one-stroke lead. . . . He is off to the right and above the pin . . . he hits the ball . . . it is falling away. . . . Arnold Palmer has missed the putt. . . . Now he drops it in and has taken his third straight bogey. Casper shot a par four on this 17th and now after 71 holes the National Open is all tied between Arnold Palmer and Billy Casper. Each has a 274. Casper has made up seven strokes in eight holes. The National Open, and the $25,000 first prize, might be settled on this next hole. If the tie isn't broken, there will be a playoff tomorrow afternoon.

Now it was all hanging on the 18th. Palmer had three straight bogeys while Casper had two birdies and a par on the last three holes. While all the attention focused on Palmer because he had the huge lead at the start of the day, the popularity and his own army, Casper had played steady, impressive golf all afternoon. Palmer's fives and sixes wouldn't have meant much if Casper wasn't keeping his shots down at the same time. As the pressure built, Casper proved equal to it.

Now on the 18th, with the score tied at 274, Palmer drove down the fairway and Casper followed almost in the same spot. Both were on the green in two, Palmer to the right, Casper more to the left. The third shots got them close and each man withstood the enormous pressure to sink the putts for par fours.

The afternoon was over. Palmer and Casper had tied and Casper was the hero of the day with his magnificent come-from-behind show.

In the press tent both players tried to explain the events of the afternoon. Neither really could.

"I hit some balls into the rough," said Palmer, "and when you do that you aren't going to win too often. Maybe I should take up eating buffalo meat."

Palmer had just blown a big lead but now he could relax and laugh about it as he kidded with the press. He wouldn't have to hit a golf ball for 24 hours.

Byron Nelson and I had dinner together that night. We never even asked Arnie. We were sure he would be too busy preparing himself for the playoff 18.

"It's going to be awful hard for Arnie," said Nelson. "When you lose a lead like that it is hard to forget it so quickly."

Nelson was right. Arnie just wasn't the same man the next day. They were all even through 12 holes. Then Casper sank a marvelous putt of 35 feet for a birdie on the 13th. It took the steam out of Arnie.

Palmer missed an eight-foot putt on the 14th and took a birdie. Casper parred the hole. Palmer two-putted the terrible 15th, the same hole that had given him the trouble the day before, and was three strokes down with three holes to play.

The tournament ended for Palmer with a 73, three over par. Casper shot a 69, one under, to win the 1966 National Open at Olympic Country Club.

Casper won $26,500 and Palmer earned $14,000 for finishing second.

As I think about it now I remember Arnie straining and struggling and pushing to salvage something from the 16th, that man-eating 604-yard hole, with its trees and its roughs and its bunkers. He came out of the jungle with a six—"the best six I ever had"—and I wondered about it later. I guess it showed Arnie's true greatness.

Most of us would have come out of it with a 12. But few of us would have, like Arnold Palmer, come out of it laughing.

Arnie's Army watches Palmer hit from the trap in the 1966 U.S. Open.

Vin Scully

3

Next Year Comes to Brooklyn

VIN SCULLY

It was a drab Dodger game in the Los Angeles Coliseum on August 24, 1960. Vin Scully was filling in the duller moments with stories and anecdotes and revealing flashes of information. He began talking about the umpiring team. He leafed through the record book and cited a few facts about umpire Frank Secory. He mentioned Secory's age and noticed that the umpire was born on August 24, 1912.

"Well, what do you know about that?" Scully said. "Today is Frank Secory's birthday. Let's have some fun. As soon as the inning is over I'll count to three and on three everybody yell, 'Happy birthday, Frank!'"

With the park filled with transistor radios, Scully said, "Ready? One, two, three." And the crowd roared, "Happy birthday, Frank!" Secory looked up, astounded, and the crowd sat back bubbling with self-satisfaction. Scully's people had responded to his call.

Few announcers have had as much impact in a town as Vin Scully has had in Los Angeles. He came from Brooklyn with the Dodgers in 1958 and carried the gospel of Dodger baseball to Sunset Strip, to Hollywood, to Pacific Palisades, to the sun-drenched porches and smog-filled streets of Los Angeles. Scully was Los Angeles' first link to Major League Baseball. They could ask for no better teacher.

Scully was born in New York and grew up as a New York Giant fan in general and a Mel Ott fan in particular. He attended Fordham Prep in the Bronx, served two years in the Navy and returned to Fordham University where he began his broadcasting career. His first job was in Washington, D.C.

Washington, famed for being first in war, first in peace and last in the American League, could dull a man's appetite for the game. Scully almost lost all interest in the sport.

"Nothing," says Scully, "could kill your interest in baseball faster than three years of the Senators."

While Washington's baseball performance went mostly unnoticed, Scully's broadcasting at WTOP, the CBS flag station, did not. His smooth delivery, his warm, resonant voice, his impeccable grammar, his erudite description of football on the CBS roundup show and his good humor came to the notice of Dodger owner Walter O'Malley in Brooklyn.

Giant fan Scully became the third Dodger announcer in 1953 with Red Barber and Connie Desmond in Barber's Catbird Seat high above home plate in Ebbets Field.

He was hired to do the 1953 World Series with Mel Allen when Barber balked at the token fee. Scully was 25 years old when he broadcast his first Series game.

"Take care of my boy," O'Malley told the veteran Allen.

"I remember throwing up violently over breakfast," said Scully. "The other thing I remember about the 1953 Series was yelling on the air that Whitey Ford had left third base too soon on a fly ball after Commissioner Ford Frick had reminded us not to umpire. Thank God Ford turned and went back to third. It probably saved my career."

Scully's career has included Sandy Koufax's four no-hitters, the 104 steals by Maury Wills and two of the three perfect games in baseball since the broadcasting era began: Don Larsen's World Series gem and Koufax's perfect game against the Cubs in 1965.

Now Scully describes another day he will never forget. It is October 4, 1955, the day the agony ended.

Vin Scully

THE seventh game of the 1955 World Series. The Dodgers would have another chance. They had made a sickening habit of losing the World Series to the Yankees and they would send a 23-year-old lefthander named Johnny Podres to the mound in Yankee Stadium. It was impossible to be confident.

It was shortly after 7:00 o'clock when I awoke from a fitful sleep, opened the curtains at our home in Bogota, N. J., and examined the clear, blue sky. It was a beautiful fall day and I could see that weather would be no factor in the game. The sun might be troublesome in left field, as it always is in the Stadium, at this time of year. I wondered who Walter Alston would play in left field, the one position where the Dodgers didn't have a regular who excelled. The Dodgers had George Shuba or Jim Gilliam or little Sandy Amoros, a peppery guy who had been playing a lot of late-inning defense when Gilliam, an infielder by trade, was in left field in Alston's platoon.

My mother, an excitable, red-headed woman, was more nervous than I was. She had become a fanatic Dodger fan since I had started broadcasting the club's games in 1953 and now prepared breakfast for me with one eye on the boiled eggs and one eye on the clock. It was nearly six hours before game time but she didn't want me to be late.

With one motion, she placed my eggs on the table and our dog Blackie's food in his tray on the kitchen floor. It was a wonder she didn't give me the dog food and Blackie the eggs the way she was moving.

At 10:15 I turned on the motor of my car, pulled out of our garage, moved on to the street, headed over the George Washington Bridge and drove eagerly down the Major Deegan Highway for Yankee Stadium. I listened to the car radio but I didn't hear very much. I kept thinking how nice it would be for the Dodgers, for all of Brooklyn, for my mother, if they could finally win one. I thought about Carl Furillo and Jackie Robinson and Pee Wee Reese and Gil Hodges and Roy Campanella and all the others who had played so brilliantly for so many years in Brooklyn and had always been denied this final prize.

From over the rise on 145th street, Yankee Stadium looked huge and awesome. There was a mystique about The House That Ruth Built that defeated as many teams as the Yankees did. As I drove closer to the park the building seemed so huge, so inspiring, so difficult to conquer. I thought of Ebbets Field, small and friendly, warm, comfortable, so different from Yankee Stadium. If only the final game could be played there. I knew the Dodgers would certainly win. Now I could only hope. I could not feel secure.

The gates were already open and the kids in the bleacher line moved quickly into the park, carrying their lunches in brown paper bags, waving banners, smiling at the police, holding their extra sweaters in their arms if the day were to suddenly turn colder. It was a school day and I laughed when I thought how many kids had written notes to their teachers about the demise of their dear, departed grandmas.

"Hi, Vin," said the guard at the press gate.

"Beautiful day, isn't it?"

"Sure is. Who's going to win?"

I didn't answer that one. I just smiled and waved and walked into Yankee Stadium. I thought only about doing my best on the air, not making any mistakes like the Ford thing in 1953 and hoping for the best.

At 12:00 o'clock in Bogota, my mother put the leash around Blackie's neck and took him for a short walk. She wanted to make sure he wouldn't need to go out after the game started. She was going to spend the afternoon watching me describe the Dodger victory on television. She just knew it. Just in case, she cheated a little and whispered a silent prayer.

Most of the Dodgers were dressed as I walked into the clubhouse at Yankee Stadium. They didn't seem any more nervous than they were for any big game during the season. They were aware of the tradition of Dodger losses. Most of them had been with the club since 1947 when the Dodgers came to the forefront of National League teams. The Yankees had beaten them that year and again in 1949, 1952 and 1953. Only Reese had played on the Dodger team that lost to the Yankees in 1941, the Series remembered for Mickey Owen's miss of Hugh Casey's strikeout of Tommy Henrich.

Doc Wendler, the trainer, worked over Podres' arm as he did with every starting pitcher before every game.

"Good luck, John."

"Thanks, Vin. Good luck to you."

Podres was a cool one, a handsome lefthander from the tiny up-state New York town of Witherbee, who had come out of the minors to win a place in the Dodger rotation. He had already beaten the Yankees once, relying heavily on his tantalizing change-up.

Podres got off the table and walked into the clubhouse. He sat down, finished putting on his uniform and waited for the signal to begin his warmup pitches.

"Any problems, Doc?"

"No, Vin. Everybody's ready for this one. They'll have all winter to get over any aches and pains."

"Hey, Vin, look at this."

I turned to see Carl Erskine standing with a telegram. He handed it over to me and I read the message. It was a wish for a Dodger victory from Erskine's friends back home in Anderson, Indiana. Carl took the telegram back from me and placed it on the bulletin board of the clubhouse. None of the Dodgers seemed to look up at it. They were busy dressing, busy with their own thoughts, busy with the mission at hand.

I went into the press room under the stands at Yankee Stadium, sat down with some of the Brooklyn writers, wondered at how their stomachs could take a full dinner while mine could barely handle a cup of coffee, and checked the lineup card. There were no surprises. Gilliam was in left field in the Dodger lineup. I was certain if the Dodgers got ahead that Alston would send Amoros out to left field. The Dodgers had gotten off to a fantastic start that season and Alston hardly ever seemed to make a wrong move.

Many people believed the Dodgers of 1955 were the best team Brooklyn ever had. It was a veteran team and that had to help them today as the pressure of the seventh game grew. The Yankees had a veteran team also and they had been winning World Series games with regularity. I thought the law of averages might finally catch up with them. As a professional I quickly discounted that. Podres just had to be good.

At 12:45 my mother brought Blackie into the house after another walk, turned on the television set while a staff announcer was saying, "Stay tuned for the seventh game of the 1955 World Series between the Brooklyn Dodgers and the New York Yankees," and poured another cup of coffee. She was sure the announcer had mentioned the name of the Yankees louder than he had the name of the Dodgers. She was sure he was showing favoritism.

Mel Allen was talking to some fans behind the broadcasting

booth as I sat down to write the lineups on my card.

"Well," said Allen, "DiMaggio was more graceful. He could chase a fly ball without you knowing it. Mickey probably had greater speed when he first broke in but didn't move like Joe did in the outfield."

Now he turned to me. "Hi, Vinnie, howya doin?"

"Fine, Mel, just about all set."

Allen turned back to the kids. "See y'all later." Then he sat down. "How about that?" said some kid. It was one of Mel's favorite phrases, his trademark to Yankee fans. He laughed as we waited for the time to go on the air.

Allen studied the monitor in the press box, looked up at the director, who was holding the earphones tight to his head, and watched for his finger. Now it moved downward toward Mel. "Good afternoon, everybody," he said, in his warm, Alabama drawl, "and welcome to Yankee Stadium."

Mel was to do the first four and a half innings of the game and I was to do the final four and a half innings. These arrangements had been set up by Commissioner Frick and as Mel went on the air I wondered if my nervousness would build even more as the seventh game went on.

I could almost hear my own heart pounding as Mel said, ". . . and now, ladies and gentlemen, our national anthem." The huge crowd stood silently and I lifted my head to study the signs on the bleacher walls, to look out past the Stadium to the apartment house roof beyond, filled with people, to watch the subway cars creep slowly past centerfield as if the motorman wanted to catch an inning or so, to wonder if this would be a good day for the Dodgers.

Almost with the first pitch, my stomach settled down. I had been doing Dodger baseball for three years now and I felt comfortable in my ability. This was my second World Series and though I still had some normal nervousness, I wasn't a 23-year-old like Podres. I was certain he had to be more nervous than I.

The game was scoreless until the Dodger half of the fourth inning. Roy Campanella was the batter. This was an odd-numbered year and Campanella had good seasons in the odd-numbered years—1951, when the Dodgers lost the playoff to the Giants when Campy was out with an injury; 1953, when he was the league's MVP, and now again in 1955. Campanella lined a ball into the left field corner for a double and the Dodgers had a threat. I marked it down on my scorecard and Allen said, "The batter is the dangerous Gil Hodges."

Hodges had gone the entire 1952 World Series without a hit. In a burst of emotion the applause had grown louder each time he came up as the fans encouraged him to break the slump. He started the 1953 season in the same slump. Finally, on a hot day, a Brooklyn priest had cancelled his service by saying, "It's too hot for church today. Let's all go home and pray for Gil Hodges." Hodges quickly came out of his slump and had one of his best years.

Now, having another good year, he lined the next pitch to left field and the Dodgers led the Yankees, 1-0, in the seventh game of the 1955 World Series.

My mother missed the run. With Campanella on second and Hodges coming to the plate, she couldn't stand the suspense. She picked up the leash, put it over Blackie's neck, opened the door, walked around the block and returned to the television set to hear Allen say, "At the end of four innings, it's the Dodgers one and the Yankees nothing."

The Dodgers went out in the top of the fifth and Allen said, "And now to carry you the rest of the way, here's Vin Scully."

"Hi, everybody, thanks Mel. The Dodgers lead the Yankees, 1-0 as we start the bottom half of the fifth inning."

In Bogota, my mother moved to the coffee pot again. She looked at Blackie and shook her head. Her little boy Vinnie was on the air and Blackie would just have to wait.

In the sixth inning Reese singled off the lefthanded curve ball of Tommy Byrne. Now the batter was Duke Snider. With the Dodgers ahead, Alston was playing for another run, especially with the left-handed Snider batting against the lefthander Byrne. Snider put down a perfect bunt to the mound. Byrne quickly moved in, picked it up, threw to Bill Skowron at first base. As Skowron moved for the ball, Snider raced by him and brushed his outstretched hand and the ball trickled to the ground.

Both runners are safe. The Dodgers have men on first and second and Campanella is the batter.

I wondered if Campanella would bunt in this spot. I thought back to 1953. Campanella had come into a Series game with a bad hand. I reminded the listeners of that fact and Campanella had immediately bunted instead of swinging away with his bad hand. I felt very smart. The next time Campy was up I quickly pointed out his bad hand. He promptly hit a ball into the upper deck. I did not feel so smart.

Now Campanella did bunt the runners along. Carl Furillo was walked and Hodges was up again. Bob Grim was the relief pitcher.

My mother loved Gil Hodges. He was one of her favorite Dodgers. Her nerves just couldn't handle the situation. She grabbed the leash, grabbed Blackie and marched out of the door.

Hodges swings and there's a fly ball to centerfield. Cerv is getting under it, Reese is tagging at third, Cerv makes the catch and throws toward third base, the Dodgers lead 2-0.

Now my heart seemed to be pounding a little faster still. It was the bottom of the sixth, Podres still working smoothly on his shutout, the Dodgers in command of the game.

George Shuba had batted for Don Zimmer in the top half of the inning and now Gilliam moved in from left field and Sandy Amoros went out to play left field.

Billy Martin walked to start the Yankee half of the sixth and Gil McDougald bunted for a base hit. The Yankees had the tying runs on base and the pattern seemed familiar. The Dodgers had always been able to come close. Would it just be close again?

Yogi Berra was the hitter as Podres studied Campanella for the sign. Podres wanted to pitch Berra away so that he couldn't pull a ball into the nearby right field seats. Amoros moved a couple of steps into the left field corner.

Berra swings and there is a fly ball toward the left field corner, Amoros going over, going over. . . .

I remembered seeing Amoros moving toward the line in left field and now as I watched the ball going out there my mind quickly registered the fact that he was a left-handed thrower. The glove would be on his right side, in the direction Berra's fly ball was falling away from him, as he churned his little legs toward the sinking baseball.

Going over . . . he makes the catch. Now here comes his throw to Reese, over to Hodges . . .

I could see McDougald at second base. He was almost on the bag when Sandy caught the ball. He turned quickly and headed back for first base and then he stumbled. He stepped into a small hole or a spike mark or something but he broke stride. Now he was sliding back into first base as Hodges was stretching.

McDougald slides . . . he's out . . . a double play.

Podres got out of the inning and the Dodgers came to bat in the seventh. They failed to score. Now it was the Yankees in the seventh. No score.

In Bogota, my mother found the leash again, found Blackie, opened the door, walked around the block, whispered another prayer for the Dodgers and came back in time to hear me say, "At the end of seven innings, Brooklyn two and the Yankees nothing."

The Dodgers go out in the eighth. Now it is the Yankees in the eighth. Podres throws a strike. And the crowd cheers, this Yankee crowd, this crowd that had rooted all game for the Yankees now seemed to turn against the home team and turn toward the Dodgers and toward the young lefthander on the mound.

The Yankees went out in the eighth against Podres.

At the end of eight innings, the Dodgers two and the Yankees nothing. . . .

The Dodgers went out in the top of the ninth and the crowd started cheering Podres as he walked to the mound for the bottom of the ninth. I sat in the booth and thought about all the years of frustration, all the times I had seen the Dodgers play, all the years they had lived without ever winning a World Series, all the people in Brooklyn who never lost heart, who kept saying, "Wait 'till next year."

Two out, nobody on for the Yankees, the Dodgers lead 2-0, Hank Bauer is the batter . . .

In Bogota my mother panicked. She had the leash in her hand, but Blackie was hiding. My mother sat down in her chair, took a deep breath and faced the inevitable. She would have to listen to the final out. She debated turning off the set for an instant and then decided against it.

Bauer swings, a ground ball to Reese at shortstop, the throw over to first . . .

Pee Wee tried to aim it. The ball sank as it sailed to Hodges at first. It didn't seem to have enough carry. Hodges stretched those long legs of his, bent as far as he could go and leaned toward short.

Bauer is out and the Dodgers win, 2-0.

The crowd exploded in glee. I let the noise rise to its crescendo. Then I took a deep breath and said . . .

Ladies and gentlemen, the Brooklyn Dodgers are the champions of the world.

The Dodgers had finally won a World Series and I was close to tears. The crowd was still roaring its approval and in Bogota my mother wept unashamedly as we broke for a commercial. I stood up and started to make my way out of the press box.

"Aren't you going to say goodbye?" asked Mel Allen.

I was too stunned to talk. I said goodbye to Mel and made my way down to the Dodger clubhouse. The scene was pandemonium. Grown men were being urged by photographers to kiss each other, and champagne poured over heads. The joy and laughter was everywhere and Johnny Podres, the man who had pitched the

Dodgers to their first World Series win, looked glassy-eyed and giddy without a drink ever passing into his lips. I shook hands all around and thought that this one day, this one game, this one victory made up for all the heartache of the years gone before.

I went home to Bogota, congratulated my mother and Blackie for making it through the day, cleaned up, picked up a date and drove over to Brooklyn for the victory party at the Bossert Hotel. As soon as we passed through the Brooklyn Battery Tunnel the streets were alive with people shouting and cheering and laughing. The streets were covered with newspapers and confetti and torn telephone books. We drove to the hotel, parked and walked toward the entrance.

My date couldn't believe the scene. I was recognized by the fans and as we walked through the door we were applauded.

"I've never gotten a standing ovation before," my date said.

The party went well into the early morning hours and we finally drove back to Manhattan to stretch out the joy of the Dodger championship in Toots Shor's restaurant. We sat with Mr. and Mrs. Buzzie Bavasi. Somebody came over and gave Buzzie a copy of the *Daily News*. The general manager held up the newspaper and I saw the huge headline.

It said: **THIS IS NEXT YEAR.**

The only Dodgers left
from the 1955 championship team:
Coach Jim Gilliam, Vin Scully
and Manager Walter Alston.

Jim Simpson and Bob Hope at the Super Bowl.

4

Broadway Joe's Super Bowl

JIM SIMPSON

Jᴜᴍ Sɪᴍᴘsᴏɴ's big broadcasting break came in 1952 when the Navy allowed him to freelance the 1952 Olympic Games from Helsinki, Finland, for CBS.

"I was in the Navy at the time," the good-looking NBC sportscaster recalls, "and I was covering the activities of the Navy personnel in the Games. CBS asked me if I could give them some radio reports. The Navy said I could do it as long as it didn't interfere with my daily schedule for the Navy."

Simpson had plenty of experience for the assignment. His broadcasting career began as a 15-year-old in Washington, D.C., on station WINX.

"I was in high school at the time and I did a sports show on that small station. We covered everything from ball scores to hunting and fishing tournaments. We must have had, oh, five or six listeners."

Simpson, who is 43, was born in Washington and spent most of his early career in the nation's capital. After service in the Coast Guard during World War II, he worked at

Jim Simpson

Channel 9 in Washington as his first television exposure. There were two other well-known broadcasters there at the same time, Gene Klavan, radio personality on New York's WNEW, and Walter Cronkite, the famed CBS newscaster.

When the Korean War broke out, Simpson went on active duty with the Navy, which led to his big chance at the 1952 Olympics. He has since covered three more Olympiads on radio and television.

After his release from the Navy in 1953, Simpson went back to Washington and worked at Channel 5, and returned to reporting for CBS.

Simpson went to work for the American Broadcasting Company in 1960 and teamed with Jim McKay on the highly successful Wide World of Sports show in 1961. In 1964 he moved over to NBC, where he now handles college football games, professional football, skiing, golf and baseball.

He teams with Sandy Koufax on the NBC weekly back-up baseball game and is a member of the World Series and All-Star Game teams.

"I used to think of myself as an athlete," said Simpson, "until I started working with somebody like Koufax."

The former lefthanded pitcher for the Dodgers and the veteran broadcaster have made a comfortable team on NBC's baseball schedule.

Simpson also worked as one of NBC's professional football experts beginning with the early years of the American Football League and is now teamed with former New York Giant Al DeRogatis on the telecasts of the American Conference of the National Football League.

Simpson makes his home in Bethesda, Maryland, with his wife and their five children.

Here he recalls the drama of the most shocking football upset of all time. It is January 12, 1969, and Jim Simpson is in a unique spot for him—along the sidelines—at the Super Bowl game in the Orange Bowl in Miami, Florida. There are 75,377 people in the stadium determined to see if Joe Namath can put his money where his mouth is. It is Super Sunday—the Baltimore Colts, the pride of the National Football League, against the New York Jets of the upstart American Football League.

Jim Simpson

"We're going to win this game. I guarantee it."
—Joe Namath

I HAD read those words in a newspaper in Mobile, where I had been all week preparing for the North-South game I was to do on NBC on Saturday. As soon as the game was over I was to fly to Miami to work the sidelines for the Super Bowl.

It was impossible not to think of the boast Joe Namath had made. But was it really a boast? I had watched the AFL since its earliest days and I was certain the Jets were a fine team and certainly Namath was the finest quarterback ever produced in the league. Would he be good enough to beat the Baltimore Colts?
I believed he was.

There was a conflict of spirit as I thought about the game. I had been a National Football League fan all my life. I had been weaned on the Washington Redskins and even though I could never attend, since I was working AFL games on Sundays, I held season tickets to the Redskin games and my wife and sons would go or we would give them away.

As the game approached I remember arguing about the merits of the Jets against the Colts with my son, Bret, 16. He was a Redskin fan, an NFL fan, and he was certain, as most people that day were, that the NFL champions would wipe the ground up with the Jets.

I had worked with former football players like Kyle Rote and Al DeRogatis and I respected their opinions. They had convinced me that the AFL champions could win.

"Check with Mr. DeRogatis or Mr. Rote," I told Bret, "you know they wouldn't say it if they didn't believe it. They think the Jets can win. They really do."

Bret and I went over the teams man by man, matching positions and my argument seemed to grow stronger. The quarterbacks, the key men, were Earl Morrall and Joe Namath, with an outside chance that injured Johnny Unitas would get in the game.

I told Bret what Al DeRogatis had told me. "If the Jets can get Morrall out of the pocket," Al said, "the Jets can win."

The Colts had good running backs in Tom Matte and Jerry Hill, splendid receivers in Jimmy Orr, Willie Richardson and John Mackey, maybe the best tight end in football. But the Jets had Matt Snell and Emerson Boozer and a fine blocker in Billy Mathis. Tight end Pete Lammons and flankers Don Maynard and George Sauer could catch the football.

The Colts won the NFL title on defense but the Jets were solid there also with Gerry Philbin, an outstanding defensive end, and a good pass rush.

And Bret would always say, "What about Bubba?"

Bubba Smith, the 6-7, 295-pound defensive tackle of the Colts, was a team all by himself. He had spent a spectacular college career at Michigan State being urged on by fans with the resounding cry of "Kill, Bubba, kill." The words had rung in the ears of many quarterbacks as they were pounded to the earth by this huge, fierce man. If the Jets were to win he had to be kept off Joe Namath. Dave Herman, the tough, offensive guard of the Jets, would have the chore of attacking Bubba. The outcome of the game might depend on their personal battle.

I had come in from Mobile and now I was on the sidelines at the Orange Bowl as Curt Gowdy, Kyle Rote and Al DeRogatis were to do the play-by-play and the color from the booth. I would watch the game from the sidelines and do a half-time show and the post-game show. I was so close to the players and the sidelines, as the Colts kicked off to the Jets, I could almost hear them breathe.

I had come on the field just before the game began. I had covered the AFL all season and it was hard not to be rooting for them. I also felt a strong affection for Weeb Ewbank. I had broadcast the games of the Baltimore Colts when Weeb coached the team and now he was back in a championship game with the Jets. If his team won, he would be the first pro football coach in history to win championships in both the NFL and the AFL. I knew Weeb was busy with his preparations but I walked up to him just before the kickoff. I just wanted to greet him and wish him well.

"How are you, Weeb?"

"Everything's fine," he said.

I looked straight into his eyes for a reading. This man was not putting on an act. He was telling the truth. He felt that he was ready for the biggest game of his life.

"How's it going to be, Weeb?"

"I'm telling you," he said, with some force, "everything's going to be fine."

There was a ring of confidence in his voice. This was not a man given to brash statements. He was a conservative, low-key person, who went about his chores in a business-like manner. He just knew his team was ready and he just wanted me to know it.

The Baltimore kick boomed in the air and the Jets took over for the first play of the 1969 Super Bowl. Namath bent low over the center, took the snap from John Schmitt and handed off to fullback Matt Snell. The burly fullback from Long Island cracked the left side of the Colts' line for three yards. The crowd buzzed and oohed at that. The Jets had moved some on the first play. The Colts were mortals. They had given ground to a charging fullback.

Namath, trying to establish his running game before he put his heralded arm to work, gave the ball back to Snell on the very next play. The fullback crashed through the same spot, behind the driving blocks of tackle Winston Hill and guard Bob Talamini, and gained nine yarsd and a first down. As the left side of the Baltimore line fought him to the ground, safetyman Rick Volk came up to help in the tackle. Snell put his helmet down and tore into Volk's middle as he was being dragged down from behind. Snell popped right up. Volk lay dazed on the rich, green grass of the Orange Bowl. The Jets had inflicted the first knockout punch.

It may have been that play, that very moment, that the afternoon pattern was set. It was only the second play of the game but the Jets had made a first down, cut the Colts' line in two and injured one of their starting defensive backs. It was all there for the crowd, and more importantly, the Baltimore bench to see.

I walked up and down the sidelines like a nervous cat. I followed each movement of the game for more signs that the Jets were the equals of the Colts. I wanted the Jets to win, but more importantly, I didn't want them to be embarrassed. There had been so much talk of the inferiority of the AFL, so many put-downs of these fine football players that I knew the question of respect was as much in the mind of the players as the question of winning.

Now the Colts had the ball for the first time. John Mackey caught Morrall's screen pass and ran over safetyman Jim Hudson for 19 yards. This was what the NFL people called the Mickey Mouse league defense. But this was John Mackey, not some average tight end. He had run over a lot of NFL backs in his time. The Colts made a couple of more first downs before Larry Grantham and Gerry Philbin began putting pressure on Morrall and chasing him out of the pocket.

I remembered Al DeRogatis saying, "If the Jets can force Morrall out of the pocket they can win."

Weeb Ewbank had told his team in one of their last meetings, "Morrall is no threat when he's forced to scramble."

Now the Jets were forcing him to do that. The Colts stalled and Lou Michaels, who had gotten into a shouting match with Namath a few days earlier at a Fort Lauderdale night spot, came in to try a field goal from the 27. It missed. The Jets had the ball again.

Namath completed a swing pass to Bill Mathis for 13 yards and a first down. Now he was ready to show them what all the excitement in the AFL was about, what had earned him $400,000, what had brought the AFL to this game. Namath was about to pass long.

I watched Don Maynard split right. I could see him bent over, loose, nonchalant, as Namath called the count. Then Maynard was off, racing by cornerback Bobby Boyd, being picked up by safetyman Jerry Logan, flying by him as he broke into the open some 35 yards downfield. Now Namath let go of the ball and I leaned forward to watch that perfect spiral sail down the right side of the field.

Maynard had come into the game with a bad leg. Now, an instant before he reached up for the ball, he stumbled ever so slightly. It threw him off stride just a fraction. The ball hit his outstretched fingertips and bounced away.

The Jets hadn't scored but they had scared the hell out of the Colts with Namath's long bomb. This was the arm and the play they spent the rest of their long afternoon worrying about. Namath hadn't completed this particular pass to Maynard but he had won the first battle in the psychological war. He had shown the Baltimore defense what the Jets were all about.

The first period ended scoreless but the Jets controlled the early minutes of the second period. With Matt Snell ripping the Colts' line and Namath hitting George Sauer, as the Colts leaned toward Maynard, the Jets drove to the 21. Then Namath hit Snell with a pass over the left side for 12 yards and a first down on the nine.

On the next play Snell gained five to the right side. Then Namath, playing his hot hand, sent Snell back to the left side of the Baltimore line for the first score of the game, a driving four-yard gain. Jim Turner kicked the point and at 5:57 of the second quarter the American Football League led the National Football League for the first time in a Super Bowl. The score was 7-0.

Now the first half was ending. I was thinking about the half-time show. We would have Bob Hope on as our guest. I had worked with Hope during the Bob Hope Desert Classic golf tournament and I knew that he was a real football fan. I also knew that he was a National Football League fan and the 7-0 halftime score would be as much a shock to him as it was to most everyone else in the ball park that day.

Curt Gowdy, Al DeRogatis and Kyle Rote were finishing the play-by-play and comments on the first half as Hope walked on to the field.

The famed comedian was wearing a double-breasted sports jacket and a sporty checked hat. He looked beautiful in living color. He was also stunned by the game. With a few seconds to go before we were on the air, he confessed, "You know, there has been some betting on this game. If this keeps up a few of my friends will have to start new careers."

I laughed at that and thought of all the NFL fans across the country who were trying to figure out what was happening. Of course, they had the consolation of knowing that in previous years the other two AFL representatives, Kansas City and Oakland, had each folded in the second half of their Super Bowl games. But the party of the second part each time was Green Bay and the Colts didn't look like Green Bay at this moment.

The signal came from the booth and we were on the air. *This is Jim Simpson on the sidelines with the score 7-0 at halftime in favor of the New York Jets and our guest is Bob Hope. Bob, what about these Jets?*

"They have just been fantastic, amazing, incredible. *It's hard to believe it. They are playing better than anybody thought they would. Actually, they have dominated the game even though the score is only 7-0. If Namath connects on a couple of those long ones it could get higher.*"

Hope and I chatted some more about the game, discussed the golf tournament and were anxious to see if the pattern would continue in the second half.

. . . now back to Curt in the booth.

The two teams were back on the field for the second half. The Jets certainly looked as determined as they had in the second half. The Colts appeared more tense, more concerned. After all, they had not scored, they were trailing by a touchdown and the Jets were gaining more confidence in their game after each play.

In the third quarter the Jets went ahead, 10-0, when Jim Turner kicked a 32-yard field goal and moved the score to 13-0 when Turner kicked another from the 30.

By now Johnny Unitas began loosening up along the sidelines. The Jets had rushed Morrall out of the pocket and into confusion. The veteran, who had guided this fine team most of the year as

Unitas nursed a sore arm, had lost his poise. Johnny Unitas was about to come in to see if he could save it.

The morning of the game I had sat with Al DeRogatis and discussed this very point. We knew that Unitas could play if he had to but couldn't throw long. The Jets would give him the short pass and defend against the long one. They would make sure all his receivers stayed in front of them.

Unitas got into the game but showed little in his first series of downs. The Jets got the ball back, drove down field and moved toward the Colts' goal again.

The gun sounded for the end of the third period. The Jets led, 13-0, and the best quarterback on the field was Namath, not Unitas. With 1:34 gone in the last quarter, Jim Turner booted another field goal and the score was 16-0.

In a conservative game, this was a rout. I felt confident that nobody ever again would be kidding me about doing the AFL games. I was certain the Jets would win and the AFL would finally gain parity with the NFL.

Unitas was still trying to salvage something from the game. At least he would spoil the shutout. With three minutes and 19 seconds left in the game, Unitas sent Jerry Hill over left tackle with Tom Matte, one of the few Colts who played a game he could be proud of, throwing the key block for the score. The Colts had finally got on the board against the league that was supposed to have no defense. It took the Colts 56 minutes and 41 seconds of the third Super Bowl to do it.

Unitas had one more chance for a score but the pass was tipped away by Larry Grantham. In seconds the game was over.

The Jets, the incredible, wonderful, fantastic Jets, led by Joe Willie Namath, had pulled off football's most stunning upset, 16-7, over the pride of the NFL.

As the crowd exploded and the Jets ran off the field to their dressing rooms, Milt Woodard, the president of the American Football League, came rambling over toward me. He was to be our first post-game guest. The wives of the victorious Jets players were to be our second guests.

An NBC assistant had looked at me earlier and asked, "Where are the Jets wives sitting?"

"I don't know," I said, "just get up in the stands and holler, 'I'm from NBC and we are looking for the wives of the Jets players.' They'll hear you. They'll find you."

Now Woodard was coming over with a group of pretty young

ladies not far behind them. I would interview Milt first and then switch to the wives before going back to the booth where Curt and Kyle and Al would sign off this spectacular game.

"Milt," I said, "congratulations."

"We did it. They said we couldn't do it but we did it."

His face was lit up with a huge smile and just the trace of a tear of joy or sweat or emotion running down his cheeks. His white hair glistened in the late afternoon sun and I can't remember ever seeing a happier face in my life.

"Milt, they called this a Mickey Mouse league and made fun of it but I think we should let the victory speak for itself. I don't think we should resort to any of that pettiness that has been thrown at this league. Let's just make it a great day for the Jets and for the AFL."

Woodard nodded and the signal came from upstairs.

This is Jim Simpson on the field and we have with us one of the happiest human beings in the world at this moment, Milt Woodard, the president of the American Football League. Milt, congratulations.

"Jim, thank you very much, and on behalf of everybody in the American Football League I want to congratulate both coaches and both teams for a fine football game and to tell you just how proud we are of the showing of our team. The Jets are true champions."

Milt and I discussed the game for several minutes and the AFL president never gloated over the victory as well he might have. It was a warm interview and I always felt Milt Woodard, a man who had taken much needling and much abuse over the years from people who wanted to downgrade his league, acted with much class that afternoon when he could have told sixty million listeners, "I told you so."

Then came the Jets wives. All the joy was there. They were radiant and attractive in their new dresses and large corsages. They all explained the pleasures of the victory in so many different ways. They all felt happy at the win, happy they would never again have to make excuses for their husbands playing in the "other league," happy to be sharing in this incredible sports story.

One very attractive young lady, the last to come on camera, showed how much the game meant, how they had worked up and waited for this moment.

"I'm Mrs. Dave Herman," said this young lady, with a warm, slow, smile. "My husband played opposite Bubba."

Win Elliot

5

Match Race

WIN ELLIOT

WIN ELLIOT, who is the anchorman on CBS Radio Network's Sports Central USA weekend broadcasts, is almost as famous for his family as he is for the major events in so many sports he has covered.

Elliot lives with his wife and their ten children ("Count 'em," says Elliot) in a large home in Westport, Conn. A family that size keeps a man moving to bring in the groceries and Elliot has been in the broadcasting business steadily for 32 years.

He began his diversified and illustrious career on the air after winning an audition with Radio Station WMEX in Boston in 1937.

Elliot gravitated to broadcasting after an athletic career at the University of Michigan. He won varsity letters in hockey and in track and field and graduated from the university with a bachelor of science degree in zoology.

The Boston break came soon afterwards and he has been on the air ever since except for a stay in the Maritime Service during World War II.

Elliot was one of the few sportscasters to

broaden his base of operations with other interests. In the golden era of radio he was heard on such shows as the very popular quiz program, "Quick as a Flash," "Country Fair," and "Break the Bank."

He also moved from radio to the television version of "Break the Bank" and did such other television programs as "Tic Tac Do" and "Win with a Winner." While he was doing these shows he was continuing to work in sports which was, and remains, his main area of interest.

After he started his broadcasting career in Boston he covered the games of the Boston Red Sox and the Boston Bruins. He moved to New York after World War II and has covered a wide range of sporting events including the Triple Crown of racing and other racing events of national scope, the Stanley Cup and regular-season hockey games, college and professional football, track and field, boxing, golf, soccer, horse and dog shows, rodeos, bowling and even billiards tournaments.

Now it is August 31, 1955, and Win Elliot stands in the infield at Washington Park in Chicago as the spectators begin to sense the excitement of the day.

Once and for all, they will know which is the better horse, Swaps or Nashua.

Win Elliot

THE Dodgers were running away with the pennant race in the National League and Brooklyn was yawning through the summer waiting for another battle with the hated Yankees. The Dodgers were the best in the National League. The Yankees were the best in the American League. There was little to argue about until October.

But in horse racing they were arguing. They were arguing every day since the first Saturday in May, since the day Swaps, the big chestnut California-bred horse had come out of the West to win the Kentucky Derby, beating the highly regarded Nashua and the field with incredible ease.

William Woodward, Jr., who had made his fortune in Wall Street, thought he had the best horse in the world in Nashua. He had been proven wrong in the Derby as he watched Swaps destroy his horse in the most prestigious race in the sport.

Eddie Arcaro, the best jockey riding, had climbed down off Nashua's back, dust and mud on his face, to look forlornly as Woodward bowed his head in defeat.

"Hey boss," he said kindly, "what are we going to do about that horse?"

He nodded at Swaps as Rex C. Ellsworth, the cowboy from Arizona, patted his big horse and watched the garland of roses being placed on his neck.

Woodward had all the money a man could want to have. He had some beautiful horses at his farm and his pride and joy was Nashua. Nashua had everything but a Derby win. Woodward thought he had the better horse.

After the Derby, Nashua raced at the best tracks in the East, sweeping race after race, dominating the racing picture except for the lone Derby defeat.

Rex Ellsworth bred cow ponies. He treated the Thoroughbred he owned with all the roughness and freedom of another cow pony. Swaps had prospered under this handling and had come from California to win every race he had entered that year, including the Derby.

Nashua was clearly the best of the East. Swaps was clearly the best of the West. Swaps was clearly the best of all since he had beaten Nashua fair and square in the Derby.

But Woodward had faith in his horse. He wanted one more chance, he wanted one more opportunity to get the two three-year-olds on the same track and find out if the Derby had not merely been an accident.

Nashua had lost to Swaps in the Derby but took the other two jewels in the Triple Crown, the Preakness in Maryland and the Belmont Stakes in New York. Swaps, meanwhile, had stayed out West, winning the California Stakes, the Will Rogers Stakes and several other races in an unbeaten season.

Early in August it happened that Swaps would be coming East to race in Chicago. Nashua would be going West to race in Chicago. Could they get together again?

Benjamin F. Lindheimer, executive director of Arlington Park, was sitting in his office one day when the telephone rang. The caller was movie actor Don Ameche.

Ameche was an ardent racing fan and horse owner. He knew Woodward. He knew Ellsworth. He knew Lindheimer. He was the only man who knew all three vital participants in the drama.

"Ben," began Ameche, "could we arrange a match race between these two horses?"

Lindheimer didn't have to ask Ameche what two horses he was talking about. The names of Swaps and Nashua were on everybody's lips and when the two horses arrived in Chicago separately to race in the area all sorts of speculation began in the press.

One Chicago headline writer asked, "Is Swaps Ducking Nashua?"

"The idea is ridiculous," said Ellsworth, "if we can find a time and a place and the conditions are right we will certainly race him again."

Chicago seemed like the place. The time could be in the next two weeks. That's how long both horses would be in Chicago. Only the conditions had to be right.

Lindheimer decided that a match race between these two brilliant horses would be a natural for the final day of his August program at Arlington Park. He solved all the conditions. The track would put up $100,000 in a winner-take-all race.

I was assigned by the Columbia Broadcasting System to do the color on the race with Jack Drees handling the television running of the race and Bryan Field doing it over radio.

The race was to be run on a Thursday afternoon, the seventh race in a nine-race program, going off sometime between 5:00 and 5:30 in Chicago and 6:00 and 6:30 in New York—just late enough to catch people at home after a summer day at the offices. Sunny Jim Fitzsimmons, the trainer of Nashua, had just turned 81, but was still working as hard as a man could possibly work in getting Nashua ready for the race.

"I can't ever remember wanting to win a horse race more," said Sunny Jim.

Meshach Tenney, training Swaps, was certain his horse would be in excellent shape for the race.

"He's beaten everybody he's run against this year including Nashua," said Tenney. "I don't see any reason why he shouldn't continue doing just that."

There would be no other horses in the race. The two owners had drawn for post positions and Nashua would start on the inside post. Swaps would start two stalls away so there would be no possibility of contact between the two horses as they broke from the gate. They would each carry 126 pounds, the same as the Derby weight, over the mile and a quarter course.

On the morning of August 31, 1955, I felt the butterflies in my stomach. I knew this was a big one. The attention of the entire racing public turned to this race and anybody who had ever seen a race or read about one seemed to have an interest in the outcome. Two champions were going to settle the dispute head to head. This was the way it should be in sports.

I got to the track early and checked out all the working conditions with our crew and staff. This was one race we wanted to take no chances with.

Unlike any other race I had ever worked, the horses would be saddled on the infield in full view of the public and the betting would fluctuate as people saw some little something that would change their minds.

"Who do you like?" a fan asked in front of the two-dollar window.

"I like them both," he answered, "but how can you make any money that way?"

That was how most people felt. They liked both horses. They were both champions, both capable of running away with the race and each had great followings among the fans.

That they had raced once before seemed to be the single most significant factor. Swaps had beaten Nashua in the Derby and now the tabulators were indicating that the betting public thought it would happen again.

Before the race went off, there had been $174,737 bet. The public had backed Swaps, the California favorite, with $107,359 while $67,378 was bet on Nashua. Swaps was the favorite at 3-10 as the windows closed and Nashua was 6-5.

Good afternoon everybody, Win Elliot here from Arlington Park, some 25 miles from Chicago, where Swaps and Nashua are about to settle the long argument in a match race over this beautiful mile and a quarter track. But first, a word from Tums. . . .

As soon as the studio commercial was finished and everyone was prepared to settle all their problems with Tums if they had the wrong horse, the cameras focused on me again.

Eddie Arcaro will be on Nashua and Willie Shoemaker will be riding Swaps. The purse will be $100,000 winner-take-all.

Then the trainers and the grooms helped the jockeys into the saddle. You could almost sense that the horses were anxious to go. They never once looked around to see if there were any other horses on the track. It was as if they knew they were the stars of this show all by themselves.

"Four minutes to post time," said the track announcer, "you have four minutes."

It hardly seemed enough time to study these horses again and decide once and for all which horse was best. Would it be the horses deciding the race? Or the jocks? What about the trainers? Or maybe simply the luck of the owners.

I stood in the infield as the horses went on the track and began loosening up. I talked to Sunny Jim and to Meshach. I interviewed Ellsworth and I interviewed Woodward. There wasn't much to say now. It was just time to be nervous. The victory statements would come later with the disappointments of defeat.

The horses are approaching the starting gate. Eddie Arcaro on Nashua is being led into the inside post position with Willie Shoemaker on Swaps being led in just to his right in the third stall. Both horses are calm. Neither is moving.

The clang of the gate. The huge rush of noise from the stands. The sight of dust and dirt flying. The electricity racing through the old track. Nashua and Swaps. Swaps and Nashua, together again, alone, to settle it once and for all.

The first moments in the race are most important. The pace is set out of the gate. Somebody has to catch somebody. Which horse would it be?

I remember Nashua coming out of the gate, looking like Pegasus, the winged horse, flying through the air, Arcaro's whip cracking down on him, the horse climbing forward, his hooves barely touching the ground as he jolted out of the gate. Swaps came out just as hard but Shoemaker was shocked that his horse hadn't been first. He had always, until this time, been first.

We stood in the winner's circle watching the two horses race down the first quarter of a mile of the track. Mr. Fitz had difficulty seeing the race so his groom described it to him.

"He's ahead by a length now, Mr. Fitz, and moving good. Don't you worry none. He'll win it."

Now Swaps had recovered from the great start of Nashua and was driving forward. The winner of all his races as a three-year-old, he seemed to sense that he would need just a little extra if he was to catch this horse. Nashua was ahead by a length. Now Swaps came on, Shoemaker whipping him forward, and they were only a half length apart at the turn.

"Six furlongs to go, Mr. Fitz," said the groom, "they're pretty close together but he still has him."

Nashua had slipped back and Swaps had come on. Nashua led by just a neck as they moved around the far side of the track. The fans were all on their feet shouting and waving the horses onward.

The noise was deafening as the two beautiful animals struggled for command with about half a mile to go.

"He's stretching it out, Mr. Fitz, he's stretching it out."

Now less than half a mile remained in the race. Nashua had begun to open up more space between himself and Swaps. Now a length, a length and a half, now two lengths. Now it was three.

"Don't worry, Mr. Fitz, he's got it going good now. He's way out there. He's opening up more, he's opening up more."

Nashua had begun to thunder down the stretch toward the finish line. Swaps was far back now, some five lengths, then six, laboring under the effort, not answering to the pleading whip of Shoemaker, running out of steam, finding the distance and the competition and the dust and the noise not to his liking any more.

Suddenly there was the finish line, just in front of us, Nashua crossing it easily, looking as if he was just picking up a head of steam, looking as if he was ready to run another race, any distance, against any opposition, any day.

And then Swaps across the line, his fans standing stunned along the rail, tearing up programs, looking down on the ground, shaking their heads, trying to figure out why they didn't put their money on Nashua, already studying the charts for the next race.

The winner was Nashua over Swaps by six and a half lengths in the time of two minutes, four and one-fifth seconds, Arcaro over Shoemaker, Woodward over Ellsworth, Sunny Jim Fitzsimmons over Meshach Tenney, all the backers of the society horse over the backers of the cowboy horse this day.

Sunny Jim stood next to me now in the winner's circle, his face broken out in a huge smile, his old eyes twinkling in the summer sun, his body suddenly more erect, more alert, as a result of what had just happened.

"I have some great days and great times in this business," he said, "but this . . . this is just wonderful . . . just wonderful . . . this has to be the thrill of my life. I said before I can't remember a race I wanted to win more and I can't. This is just wonderful."

And the old man put his hand to his eyes and brushed away a tear. It had come down to this one race and the old man had been a winner. The years slipped off him as he stood there enjoying the pleasure of victory.

Now the horses were approaching the winner's circle and Ellsworth went out to meet his horse and his jockey and find out why he no longer had an undefeated horse. Shoemaker bounced off the horse and threw his whip to the groom. He walked forward to meet Ellsworth as I moved over for my interview with the losing jockey and the losing owner while the winners stood in the circle for pictures.

"I don't know what happened," said Shoemaker, "I think maybe . . ."

Then Shoemaker stopped. He spotted me moving in with microphones and whatever it was he wanted to say he didn't want to say it on television before millions of people. There was something on his mind but it would be told to Rex Ellsworth in the privacy of their own meetings.

There was some talk later that Swaps had hurt his leg in the race and so Nashua was able to run away from the California horse. Nashua's victory was too clean, too total, too magnificent to be tainted with any hint of beating a hurt horse.

On that afternoon, in those few minutes, Nashua was the best horse in the world, the only horse in the world, and no injury, no uncertain conditions of the track, no mistakes by a jockey or crowd noises or bad diet could take that from him. The two horses had met on the race course and had settled the matter that afternoon the way it should have been settled, horse to horse. Swaps had won the Derby and Nashua had won the match race. Now they were even and forever to remain so.

There was no happier man that afternoon than William Woodward, Jr., the proud owner of Nashua. He didn't have the Derby in his stable but he had the Preakness and the Belmont and now the greatest match race ever run.

Woodward and his wife stood in the winner's circle, a happy, smiling couple, riding as high in the world at that instant as two people can ever be who have devoted their lives to the raising and breeding of horses.

A few months later William Woodward was dead, shot to death in his own home by his wife, who mistook him for a late night prowler.

The shock and tragedy of this event filled the newspapers for many, many days and no story failed to mention the name of Nashua, the horse William Woodward loved so dearly.

On that afternoon of August 31 in Arlington Park, Nashua beat Swaps and William Woodward had been the proudest owner in racing.

Win Elliot with Sunny Jim Fitzsimmons.

Marv Albert

6

A Crown for the Knicks

MARV ALBERT

As a fuzzy-cheeked 20-year-old, Marv Albert was broadcasting professional hockey and basketball games from Madison Square Garden. At 27, he is probably the youngest announcer of major league sports in the country with his stirring accounts of New York Knicks basketball and New York Rangers hockey.

At 14, Albert put the first nail in the Dodgers' coffin in Brooklyn. He was an office boy for the Dodgers and was entrusted with their tickets when the club played several games in Roosevelt Stadium, Jersey City, as the first step in the eventual move from Brooklyn across the country to Los Angeles.

"I carried the tickets with me on the subway. If I never got there," Albert says, "maybe they never would have moved out of Brooklyn."

Albert began his office boy career with the Dodgers as the result of a meeting with Dodger vice president Fresco Thompson at a time when Marv was appearing on a panel radio show for youngsters at Ebbets Field.

When the Dodgers moved to Los Angeles,

Albert, like all other Brooklyn employees, received a "Dear Marv" letter from Walter O'Malley, the Dodgers' owner.

"He offered everybody in the organization the same job they had in Los Angeles. I still have the letter."

Not too many 14-year-olds could move on their own to Los Angeles so Albert went back to broadcasting his games on tape in the basement of his Brooklyn home.

After graduation from Abraham Lincoln High School, he entered Syracuse University and began his sports broadcasting career over Mutual station WFBL, doing the Syracuse baseball games among other assignments.

Albert, who had obtained a job as the ball boy for the Knicks after his Dodger job ended, became friendly with broadcaster Marty Glickman, who hired him to do statistics at Knicks and Rangers games. This led to an on-the-air association and eventually the full-time Knicks and Rangers broadcasts.

There is probably no broadcaster in America with a more hectic fall schedule than Albert's. He does regular sports shows on station WNBC, broadcasts the Knicks and Rangers at home and away, does TV and radio commercials and has done New York Yankee pre-game and post-game shows.

The young broadcaster lives with his wife, Benita, and their young son, Kenny, in Long Island.

Here it is May 8, 1970, and Albert will be high above the basketball floor at Madison Square Garden. It is the Knicks vs. the Los Angeles Lakers. Neither has ever won the NBA title. They will play this night until somebody does.

Marv Albert

IT had come down to this, the final night of the National Basketball Association championship series. The Knicks and the Los Angeles Lakers were tied at three games apiece.

Los Angeles was always winning its division and losing to the Celtics in the championship round. Now the Celtics were old and tired and Bill Russell was retired. The Lakers only had to beat the young and energetic New York Knickerbockers. It was to be no easy task.

The series had been a strange one. Jerry West had fired in a fantastic one-handed shot as time ran out in the third game to tie it for the Lakers. The shot, estimated to be anywhere from 55 feet to 90 feet depending on the estimator, had tied the game. Still, the Knicks went on to win in overtime.

The Lakers, with West playing with an injured left thumb, had won the fourth game to tie the series. The Knicks, playing without Willis Reed in the second half (he had injured his hip), won the fifth game to go one-up.

The Lakers had been brilliant in the sixth game in Los Angeles and seemed on the threshold of finally breaking the jinx and winning the championship. Still they had their doubts.

"If we beat the Knicks," said Elgin Baylor, "the Celtics will probably be out there somewhere waiting for us."

The Celtics still haunted the Lakers, but that was only a ghost of defeats past. All L.A. had to do was beat the Knicks this one basketball game to end the agony.

The Knicks had never won an NBA title but they hadn't really come very close in their 23 years in the league. Now it was different. They had swept through their division, had turned in a masterful 18-game winning streak, and had played the kind of basketball that sent Garden fans into ecstasy.

"The 19,500 people in this building who watch us play," said Bill Bradley, "aren't fans. They are participants."

The big question of the night was Willis Reed. Could he play on that severely injured hip? If he did play, would it matter, considering his condition and considering his opposite number, Wilt Chamberlain.

Shortly after noon on the day of the game I finished lunch with my wife and son and headed for Madison Square Garden. I was about to interview Willis Reed. I wanted to have an answer, if I could, for the listening audience on my radio shows on WHN at 5:30 that evening. Willis looked tired and discouraged by the pain as we chatted while the equipment was being set up. If I had to guess at that instant, I would have guessed the Knicks would be playing the championship game that night without him. But there is more to a man than physical strength. Courage is a hard thing to measure. Willis had it in abundance. Finally, we got down to the questioning.

"What about the hip, Willis? Can you play tonight?"

"Marv," he said, "I'll be out there tonight even if I have to do it on one leg."

That was the answer I expected to hear. If humanly possible, Willis would be on the court. At his physical best, Reed had to battle hard to contain Chamberlain. In his present condition it would be a rugged task. I was glad I would be high up in the broadcasting booth. I didn't want to be in the middle when these huge men went at it together.

I took a cab back to the station at 400 Park Avenue and began writing and putting together my three sports shows. The Knicks and Lakers would be starting at 7:30 and I would be able to do the 5:30 show live and then tape the next two shows to give me enough time to get to the Garden and prepare for the broadcast. I had a good, solid interview with Willis, the hottest news of the day.

I finished the 5:30 show, piled my papers into my briefcase and set out for Madison Square Garden. I was thinking about Willis, about my preparations, about a dozen other things as I started down the elevator.

At least I didn't have to think about my station break. This time it would be automatic and I would be correct. The fifth game had given me some trouble. I was doing all the Knick games over WHN. We did the fifth game over WNBC because of a conflict with the Yankee baseball game and when it came time to make my station break, I said, as I had for so many years, "You are listening to Knicks basketball over WHN." As soon as the words were out of my mouth, my statistician, Bob Meyer, gave me a shot in the ribs that almost knocked me over. I didn't know if he was just being funny or decided he didn't like me any more. It was a few seconds before I realized what I had done. Then it dawned on me and I apologized to the radio audience and mostly to NBC for cheating them out of a station break.

I would have no such problems for the seventh game. We were back on WHN and if I was too excited to think about such things my reflex action would help me this time around.

Now the cab was rolling down Park Avenue, turning crosstown and rushing toward the Garden. I wasn't nervous but I checked my watch. It was 6:15 and I had plenty of time. As we turned down Seventh Avenue I breathed a lot easier. The Garden was in walking distance now. Even if the unforeseen happened, I would still make it. I sat back in the cab and relaxed. It was the last bit of relaxing I would have for the rest of the night.

The Garden was alive with excitement as I headed for the press elevator. The crowds were everywhere, in the aisles, pushing toward the seats, climbing the back stairs, rushing, moving, trotting to get to their spots before the great show was to begin. I got out of the elevator and walked into the press room. My wife Benita was to meet me there with my score sheets.

She had been an usherette in Shea Stadium when I met her and is one of the finest basketball fans ever produced in New York. Her job for the playoff broadcasts was to make up the scorecards with the names and numbers. It was done in orange, brown and green crayon and I could peek at the sheets during the broadcast if I needed it. You don't like to take a chance during a championship game so I wrote everything down. I even wrote down, "This is Knicks basketball on WNBC." I just forgot to read it.

"Do you have the scoresheet?"

"Yes, I do," said Benita, "but they aren't in the right colors."

That would be a bad break for the Knicks. We had all become superstitious during the championship. Everything had to be done as it was the day before. Benita had made up the cards each day in orange, brown and green crayons. Now there were no crayons of those colors.

"What happened to them?"

"Kenny hid them," she said.

There was no telling where an active two-year-old might hide some crayons, so Benita didn't waste the time looking. She made up her cards in blue and I hoped the Knicks would be equal to the challenge. So far, in this incredible season of 1969-1970 they had been equal to every other challenge.

Coach Red Holzman's wife, Selma, had worn the same dress for every game of the series and she was in it again. I was sure Selma's dress would have more powerful magic than Kenny's lost crayons.

Shortly before 7:00 o'clock I left the press room after wolfing down a couple of sandwiches and drinking a Coke. There just wasn't time for dinner with this hectic pace. Maybe there would be more time afterwards. I took the elevator up to the broadcasting booth which hung from the top of Madison Square Garden some 200 feet in the air or 28 Wilt Chamberlains standing on each others' shoulders. The teams would take the floor shortly for their warmups and I would begin to check shoulders, haircuts and round backs. I could tell the players by the way they walked and moved rather than their numbers. It was much easier that way.

This was going to be the last Knicks basketball game broadcast over WHN. The Knicks were shifting to WNBC and it would be the final night in the booth for Tom Franken, my engineer. He had been the engineer for Red Barber's broadcasts back in Brooklyn and had been around the sports scene for many, many years. Bob Meyer, my statistician, who also reminded me of what station I was on, was in the booth as we went over our last-minute preparations. We read all our commercials, checked our statistics and got all our cue cards lined up. The Los Angeles Lakers crew, in the booth next to me, were finishing their preparations.

"Do you see him yet?"

I had asked Bob Meyer to alert me as soon as Willis took the floor. I wanted to get an idea of his condition. As the Knicks began their warmup shots on the floor there was no sign of Willis. He had said he would play. I had told the radio audience he would. Now he was making me sweat.

With three minutes to go before air time I put on a head set and listened to the final three minutes of Bill Codare's disc jockey show from the station. He played his final song, signed off and I could hear the introductory music being played on the air. We were ready.

Good evening, everyone, this is Marv Albert from Madison Square Garden . . . the New York Knickerbockers and the Los Angeles Lakers in the seventh game of the NBA championship series. The teams are tied at three games each and the winner of this game . . .

As I said the words I thought back to the Knick teams I had known in the late 1950s. There were some fine individual players like Carl Braun and Harry Gallatin and Dick McGuire and Richie Guerin but there had never been that big center to lead them to a championship. This time there was the big center, Willis Reed, but at this instant he was under the stands at Madison Square Garden being treated.

Reed had received a cortisone shot and carbocaine to dull the pain in his hip. No one knew if he would be ready to play.

The Knicks had been shooting for ten minutes when the chant began in the stands. "We want Willis, we want Willis," they shouted, echoing the sentiments of everybody connected with the Knicks in any way at all. The Knicks had won the fifth game when Willis had to leave with his injury but had been crushed in the sixth game when he had never dressed. Their chances without him didn't seem very good.

Now five minutes remained before the game as the Knick players began peeling off their warmup jackets. Some stayed on the floor shooting. Some sat on the bench. All eyes seemed to be on the alleyway between the stands toward the Knicks' dressing room.

First there was a muffled sound. Then a large rumble of noise. Then a huge roar. Then Bob Meyer poked me again. I was staring straight down at the floor and didn't need the poke. There he was, huge Willis, 6-10, and 240 pounds, walking slowly, carefully across the Garden floor to the basket where the Knicks were taking their final shots.

As the crowd discovered him it let out a huge, sustained roar that may have shaken the building to its very foundation. Bill Bradley had said it best. It wasn't filled with 19,500 fans. It was filled with 19,500 participants.

Across the floor the Lakers stopped to watch Willis walk on to the floor. Wilt Chamberlain and guard Keith Erickson had started to smile at the sight. They were not surprised. Wilt knew it all along.

"I know what kind of an athlete Willis is," said Chamberlain. "I anticipated that he would start."

Willis moved behind the foul line and took a ball in his hands. He bounced it once, twice, then let it fly toward the rim.

Yes. Willis has hit his first practice shot from 15 feet away. The crowd is going wild. Here's his second one . . . yes. Willis is two for two in warmups and the Knick fans are beside themselves with joy.

It was the first time I could ever remember broadcasting a practice shot with such emotion. There was only one other night that approached it. The first time Bill Bradley ever put on a Knicks uniform in his first professional game in 1967 the reaction was similar. They cheered every move he made that night, from his warmup shots, to taking off his jacket, to kneeling at the scorer's table, to scoring his points. This was the same. Every move of Willis' was watched. Every move was tied to Knicks history.

It was almost game time and my mind wandered for an instant back to my days as Knicks ball boy. I grew up in the era of their disasters as they lost big games season after season and never could win a title. Now they were this close. It would be cruel for them to fail now. But what of the Lakers? They had come so close so often. Would this be the night the agony ends for them?

Public address announcer John Condon's voice was rising as he introduced the Knicks to the crowd. The cheers grew louder and louder and louder. Then he came to Reed. The sound of his voice was drowned by the noise. Willis walked to the floor, took a few steps toward the rest of the team and turned back. He would save every step he had for the game.

Willis is at the center of the court, shakes Chamberlain's hand and now we are ready. The ball is up, here we go, controlled by the Lakers, Willis never even jumped.

The ball was bounced around and the Knicks came up with it at center court. Bill Bradley got it over to Dave DeBusschere who threw it to Reed just off the side of the key.

Willis left-hands it up . . . YES. . . . Willis Reed has hit his first shot. The Knicks lead, 2-0.

"All I was thinking about," Bill Bradley said later, "was the defense Willis could add to us. He had to contain Chamberlain. We weren't thinking of offense. Now he hits that first basket. What a lift."

The Lakers came back down the floor and Jerry West, brilliant as always, whisked a pass into Chamberlain under the basket. Before Wilt could turn and stuff, Willis was on him. He was on him a little too closely and a foul was called.

Wilt on the line, the fans beginning to get on him . . . he studies the basket . . . the shot is up . . . and . . . missed . . . rebound DeBusschere.

The pattern was set, maybe right at that very instant. Reed, playing on a sore hip, barely able to walk, let alone run, had pushed his first shot from the field through the basket. Chamberlain, who had played marvelously two nights before as the Knicks failed to hold him down, had missed his first free throw. Chamberlain had made a sensational recovery from knee surgery but it hadn't changed his free-throw shooting. He still was not a good free-throw shooter and proved it as he missed the next shot.

Now the Knicks led, 2-0, with Los Angeles having the ball. They moved down court quickly and tested Reed. Chamberlain backed toward the basket, got the ball, turned and stuffed a layup through the hoop to tie the score at 2-2. It was the last time all night the Lakers would know such wealth.

The Knicks got the ball back and Bradley made a foul shot.

The significant battle was underneath, between Wilt and Willis. In the sixth game, with Willis out, Chamberlain had moved at will toward the basket. With Willis in, even moving slowly on a bad leg, Chamberlain couldn't move quite as well. He was involved with Reed's presence on the floor as much as he was involved in making his shots.

The Knicks have the ball on the right side . . . it goes to Willis . . . he shoots . . . YES. . . . Reed is two for two from the floor . . . the crowd is on its feet . . . The Knicks lead, 5-2.

The momentum was all for New York. Reed's presence had inspired them and demoralized the Lakers. He had come on the floor, limping, managed to get off two quick shots, had already pushed Chamberlain away from the basket and was the key man in the Knicks' attack again as he had been all year.

Before long, it was a rout.

Walt Frazier, working as hard on offense as he always does on defense, had a steal for a basket and converted the foul. The Knicks led, 10-2.

Then all of the Knicks caught fire, Bradley, DeBusschere, Dick Barnett, Frazier and the bench, Mike Riordan, Cazzie Russell, Dave Stallworth, and finally, Nate Bowman, who relieved Reed to the thunderous applause of the crowd. They knew they had seen what courage really was.

The Knicks led by 14 at the quarter and by 27 at the half. They were outscored 27-25 in the third quarter and by 30-19 in the last quarter. By then it didn't matter. The Knicks had pushed so far ahead it was just a question of the seconds running out on the clock.

Now there are 55 seconds to go . . . 55 seconds before the Knicks become the champions of the world . . . 54 . . . 53 . . . 52 . . . now there are 10 seconds left . . . 9 . . . 8 . . . 7 . . . 6 . . . 3 . . . 2 . . . 1 . . . there's the buzzer . . . the Knicks have won the NBA championship . . . by a score of 113-99. The New York Knicks have beaten the Los Angeles Lakers four games to three.

The crowd was on the floor, reaching out to pound the players, to capture some of the joy of the moment, to bask in this reflected glory . . . to be part of the New York scene again, as the Jets had started it and the Mets had continued it, and now the Knicks had sustained it.

I had not prepared anything special to say for the night because the Knicks had said it all. They had busted open the league early with the 18-game winning streak and had turned on the whole city, and a lot of the country, to their brand of exciting basketball.

I raced downstairs to get into the Knicks' dressing room to do a locker room show. The Knicks were drinking beer and being happy as I arrived there but there was none of the bedlam that had characterized the Jets and the Mets. Perhaps the Knicks knew they would win it all along.

The Knicks, as the season had worn on, had become the team of the people. They had been able to translate what so many people felt and knew about the game into the action on the court. In a way, they played the schoolyard basketball that all New York knew, with movement and excitement and flair, and all the fans could identify with it.

They had some special fans in the dressing room like the actor Dustin Hoffman. Cazzie Russell greeted Hoffman with an imitation of Hoffman's character of Ratso from Midnight Cowboy. Still, with all the noise and all the excitement and all the forced frivolity, it was a private victory of the players and coach Red Holzman, who had worked so long and so hard to bring this victory to New York.

After the dressing room cleared, I shook hands with each of the players, and thanked them for an exciting season. They had provided more excitement than any team in recent memory.

I left the dressing room and took the elevator upstairs to the press room. Benita was waiting for me, her scorecard filled with x's and o's as she kept track of every basket and free throw. All of the players were there and their wives, too. As each player walked in, the people in the room stood as one and gave them a standing ovation.

It was Dave DeBusschere's wife who stood first when Dave appeared and led the standing ovation for her favorite Knick. At that moment, it wasn't a wife cheering a husband, it was a Knick fan cheering her favorite player.

Soon Red Holzman came in and Selma Holzman led the cheering for him. Again everyone in the room stood and cheered and laughed with Red. He had brought forth a miracle in a little more than two years on the job in rebuilding the team, fitting in all the parts and remaking it in his own image.

As the night went on the players drifted out to celebrate the victory in their own ways with their own friends. Soon the press and the other broadcasters and all of the people who had been in the press room were drifting out.

I hated to leave. I wanted to talk about this night as long as I I was thinking about how far the Knicks had come and how long ago it seemed since I was the ball boy of the Knicks. More than a million people had listened to this game on radio, the largest local radio audience of all time, and now it was all over. It had happened. The Knicks had won a world championship and I didn't even have to come in the next day to count the basketballs.

*Walt (Clyde) Frazier gets
a hero's interview from Marv Albert
following the Knicks' wrap-up of NBA crown.*

Frank Gifford

7

Vince and His Starr

FRANK GIFFORD

Handsome Frank Gifford, the triple threat CBS broadcaster, who is equally at home as an interviewer, a color man or a commercial announcer, has been one of the giant figures on the sports scene since his college days at USC.

Gifford, who has just turned 40, has been scoring touchdowns or reporting about them for more than two decades, and was one of the few college All-America players to get even better in the professional ranks.

He began his spectacular football career at Bakersfield High in California. He moved on to Bakersfield Junior College, where he gained Junior College All-America honors, and then continued his exploits at USC.

Despite the coming of the age of specialization in college football after World War II, Gifford was a triple threat back at USC who could run, pass and placekick with equal skills. He was USC's punter as well, caught passes and played defensive halfback.

Gifford co-captained the West team against the East in the Shrine game and the North against the South in the Blue-Grey Classic and

Frank Gifford

played 60 minutes in each game in his senior year at USC.

In 1952 he turned down a fabulous money offer from the Canadian Football League to sign with the New York Giants as their number one draft choice.

He set four career records in 12 seasons with the Giants including the team's all-time scoring mark (484 points), most touchdowns (78), most passes caught (367) and most yards gained (5,434). He also set a record for most passes caught in a single game with 11.

Gifford played both ways in 1953 for the Giants, made the Pro Bowl as a defensive back that season and came back in 1954 to make it as a running back.

In 1956 he was named the league's Most Valuable Player and played in the Pro Bowl for six straight seasons. Gifford played on five Eastern Conference championship teams with the Giants and one league title team in 1956.

He was injured in the final game of the 1960 season, by a brutal tackle by Chuck Bednarik of the Eagles, and retired.

"I worked for CBS radio in 1961 and scouted for the Giants," he said. "When the next season came around I thought I could still play for a few more years despite what people said."

Skeptics said Gifford was risking serious injury by coming back to football but he proved them all wrong. He added three more seasons to his brilliant career, this time as a flanker back, and finally retired after the 1964 season.

While still a player, Gifford worked for CBS and did the colorcast of the 1962 Gator Bowl as well as the 1964 NFL championship game.

"As long as the Giants weren't playing in the game," he said, "I was involved in the championship broadcasts."

Gifford has had professional training as an actor. He was under contract to Warner Brothers at one time and made several movies.

"I still might consider a movie if the right thing came along at the right time," he says.

The right thing could well be the "Frank Gifford Story," since few athletes in football history have had as spectacular and dramatic a career as Frank Gifford.

He describes the most thrilling football game he ever saw. It is December 31, 1967, almost New Year's Eve, Green Bay, Wisconsin.

Frank Gifford

THE phone rang in the hotel room and I sleepily reached out from under the covers to get at it before it rang my ears off.

"Good morning, Mr. Gifford," said the sweet voice of the operator, "it's seven o'clock and it's thirteen degrees below zero."

I knew then it wasn't going to be the most pleasant afternoon I had ever spent on a football field.

We had arrived in Green Bay on Friday to do the championship game between the Green Bay Packers and the Dallas Cowboys. Weather was always a factor in Green Bay at this time of year so we quickly went out to Lambeau Field to inspect the conditions.

Vince Lombardi, who had been a coach with the Giants when I was a player, and had now gone on to his brilliant career at Green Bay, was quick to point out that he had taken care of all the possibilities. He showed the field to Jack Buck and me just before the Friday practice.

"We have these coils under the ground," said Vince. "If the weather should turn colder we will just increase the power. There's no problem. The field will be in excellent shape as long as it doesn't snow. The forecast is for clear and dry. The field won't be frozen. The heating system will take care of that."

We watched the Packers work out. Then we watched the Cowboys loosen up on the field. They seemed pleased that the temperatures were moderate for Green Bay at this time of year. It was cold, all right, maybe twenty degrees or so, but it was reasonable for a football game.

By Saturday it had even gotten a little warmer with the late afternoon sun pushing the temperature to near thirty degrees. It was obvious that the championship of the NFL would be settled on the field between the Packers and the Cowboys with no consideration given to the weather. The better team was going to win and that was that.

Early Saturday evening there was a shift in the wind and the cold began to creep into Green Bay. Still, as we went out for dinner Saturday night, the temperatures were well above the 20 mark. For Green Bay that was a tolerable temperature.

I had played in some cold championship games. I knew the feeling. In 1956 we beat the Chicago Bears, 47-7, in Yankee Stadium with the temperature under 20 the whole game and the wind whipping at our faces hard enough to make you cry.

Even worse than that, especially because we lost, was the 1962 championship game. Green Bay beat the Giants, 16-7, as Jerry Kramer kicked three field goals with the temperature at 15 degrees and the wind reaching 30 miles an hour most of the time on the field. Every pass had a chance to be blown out of Yankee Stadium and every tackle had a chance of cracking somebody in half.

The broadcasting booth in Lambeau Field was enclosed by a thin window but it didn't do much when the temperatures got under 20. As I went to bed Saturday night I realized there was all the chance in the world that Sunday morning would be a lot colder than 20.

Then the hotel operator called and gave me the bad news. I couldn't believe it could get as cold as 13 below.

I turned on the radio just in time to hear the weather forecast. The high for the day wasn't expected to be any better than ten degrees below zero. It seemed an outrage to call a temperature like that a high.

All I could think of as I got dressed was having plenty of hot coffee in the booth. We would need a lot of it to drink and we would need a lot more of it to put our hands around just to stay warm.

I had played in enough cold championship games and seen enough others to know how to dress for them. I had the heaviest socks, sweaters and coat I owned ready for the battle. Then came a horrible thought: Can any amount of clothes, no matter how heavy, do anything to defend you from 13-below-zero weather? At that moment I couldn't help but think of my college days at USC when we thought sixty degrees was a cold day for a football game.

As soon as I got to Lambeau Field I went down to examine the playing surface. The field was hard but it wasn't completely frozen. Lombardi's electric wires had done some good. I wondered if they would be working now.

"We won't have the wires on during the game," somebody from the Green Bay staff told me, "the cold is too intense. If we tried to increase the electricity to warm up a field this cold, we would increase the power just enough to blow up the ball park."

The cold was almost inhuman. But there was one consolation. It was perfectly still in the air. There was not much wind that day and I knew then the Packers and the Cowboys would still settle the game on the field. It really wouldn't matter to the guys playing. The electricity of the game and their own activity on the field would keep them warm enough. It was the guys who weren't playing and the rest of us who would have the tough day.

Jack and I had some quick coffee in the press room, went over some final plans for the game with our crew and headed upstairs to the booth.

I had on a thick pair of woolen gloves but everything was bitingly cold, the chairs, the booth, the microphones, the monitors, the programs and the pencil. Several of the writers had suggested championship games should be played in warm weather sites and I thought then just how nice an idea that seemed to be. Los Angeles or Miami seemed so much better a place to be that moment than Green Bay, Wisconsin.

Good afternoon, ladies and gentlemen, and welcome to the National Football League championship game at Green Bay, Wisconsin . . . the temperature is thirteen degrees below zero. . . .

The sound of my own voice announcing that ridiculous temperature across the country made me feel even colder. I finished giving the starting lineups and we paused for a commercial break.

I looked over at the Dallas side and I saw all the players gathered around coach Tom Landry, another of my old teammates with the New York Giants. It was a weird scene. Landry was giving last-minute instructions but none of his players seemed to be listening. They were too busy jumping up and down to keep the blood moving in their legs, pulling the gloves on their hands even tighter, bending crazily as if making themselves a smaller target for the cold would make them warmer. At that moment, the instant before a championship game, a thousand thoughts go through your head. I knew the Dallas Cowboys had only one thought. What in the world were they doing out in that terrible cold?

I looked over at the Packers. They had to be as cold as the Cowboys but they wouldn't show it. Green Bay players might be more used to playing in colder weather than the Dallas players but nobody could be used to playing in a temperature of 13 degrees below zero. I wondered if it had warmed up any. It had not. One of the engineers said it had been 16 below at 4:00 o'clock in the morning and had warmed to 13. Now it just stayed there as the game was about to begin.

I turned it over to Jack Buck for the start of the game and motioned for one of the young runners in the press box to get me a cup of coffee. He ran to the big pot, poured me a cup, came back, placed it in front of me and watched the kickoff.

Green Bay kicked to Dallas. The Cowboys tried a couple of running plays to get a feel of the game, a feel of the field and a sense of just what the weather would do to their game plan. I made my comments about their offense and reached out for my coffee as Jack described the kick to Green Bay.

I couldn't drink my coffee. I needed an ice pick. In the few minutes it sat on the ledge of the booth it had frozen solid.

Green Bay's offense hardly seemed to notice the cold. They moved quickly down field, got a couple of breaks when penalties helped them and moved to the Dallas 8. Green Bay didn't know it was cold. There was evidence of Lombardi's power of positive thinking. Dallas might think it was a cold day. The television broadcasters might think it was a cold day. The fans might think it was a cold day. The Packers? They wouldn't have the slightest idea it was cold. Old Vince just wouldn't let them.

Vince might have the Packers convinced but he couldn't convince any of the rest of us. We switched to a shot of the stands and there were some dandy outfits. Most everybody wore a stocking cap with small slits of eyes peeking out of the top and a little hole for the nose and another little hole for the mouth. Some of them were real comical. I shouldn't have laughed. I figured they were a lot warmer than I was.

Now Bart Starr was back to pass for Green Bay. It was the first time the Packers had put the ball into the air. Boyd Dowler was cutting toward the left side of the end zone. Starr let go of the ball as Dowler cut away from his man and led him perfectly with the pass. Dowler caught the ball easily and Green Bay had a score.

Babe Chandler kicked the point and Green Bay led Dallas, 7-0, in the middle of the first quarter.

Starr had made another magnificent call. The Cowboys were not expecting the pass and were bunched tightly. It seemed too cold for defenders to have much luck catching a ball and too cold for receivers. It didn't seem like a day for passing, especially on the hard ground. But Starr had figured that Dowler would make a quick cut and that would be enough to get free. The receiver always has the edge on a bad field. He knows where he is supposed to go. The defender only hopes he finds out in time.

Babe Chandler was another of my ex-Giant teammates and I was glad to see him still kicking well. He had done so much for us.

As cold as I was, I didn't want to trade places with him. I wasn't about to take off my fur-lined coat for those thin silk pants of the players.

We took another shot of the Green Bay bench, all bouncy and jubilant over the first touchdown and I realized how you forget about the weather when you are winning and how miserably cold you get when you are losing. Lombardi had allowed a small warmer on the bench and the Packers gathered around it as the offense came off the field with the first score. Starr, naturally, was entitled to most of the time with the warmer. While Starr warmed his hands on the heater, Donny Anderson drifted over to the CBS sidelines microphone. The field microphone, covered with a sponge to keep out the sounds of wind, but still necessary to allow the sounds of the blocking and tackling to increase the drama of the game, looked like some kind of new heating equipment. Anderson clapped his hands a couple of times on the microphone and got a little heat out of it.

There was no more scoring in the first period and when the teams changed sides the Packers led, 7-0. The cold hardly seemed a factor in the game. It was just there and by now everybody had accepted it. We all had our jobs to do. I just wish I could have been able to do mine with hot coffee instead of frozen coffee.

With a couple of minutes gone in the second quarter, the Packers had the ball on a third-and-one situation on the Dallas 46. The book play was to go for the first down, especially on this kind of day. But Bart Starr hadn't become the master technician of the Lombardi Packer machine by always following the book play. He reached into his bag of tricks for a great call. He sent Dowler deep into the left side of the field and hit him all alone on the 10-yard line. Dowler trotted the last 10 into the end zone and the Packers led, 14-0, after Babe Chandler kicked his second straight extra point of the championship game.

We took a shot of the Packer fans in the stands and even they felt warmer as Green Bay went out to a commanding lead. On this kind of a day, in this town, it hardly seemed likely that the Cowboys could get back in the game. But Tom Landry was a great coach and he would rally the Cowboys to a great effort.

Dallas quarterback Don Meredith knew now that he would have to go to the air to cut into Green Bay's lead. It obviously was going to be as hard to move on the hard ground as it was in the air. Starr showed it could be done and now Meredith tried it. The play immediately backfired. Herb Adderley picked off Meredith's pass and moved it back to the Dallas 30-yard line. Another score by Green Bay now and it would be all over.

But the Cowboys wouldn't quit. Starr went back to pass and the hard-driving Dallas line landed on him for a huge loss. A couple of more unsuccessful plays and now the Packers kicked. Dallas wasn't able to move past midfield so they kicked back to Green Bay. The Packers were going for the touchdown that would lock the game up for them and Starr went back to pass.

Starr fades . . . he's being rushed . . . and hit by Willie Townes . . . the ball is loose . . . George Andrie has it on the nine . . . he's in for a Dallas touchdown.

Suddenly the momentum had switched. Just as quickly as that. Andrie had swooped up the loose football, carried it into the end zone in front of the charging Forrest Gregg and Jerry Kramer and raced in for a Dallas score. Now the Packers led only 14-7 instead of 21-0, and it was going to be a tough ball game.

Dallas had the ball again after Green Bay failed to move it, and, with the crowd urging the Green Bay defense to toughen, the Cowboys settled for three points when Danny Villanueva kicked a field goal from the 21.

The half was over now and Green Bay led, 14-10. As we broke for a commercial I tried to wrap my hands around another cup of coffee but it was no use. The stop in the action was just enough to remind me how cold it really was.

We described the scores on instant replay from the studio beneath the stands. It hardly seemed much warmer than being out in the open.

Green Bay, 14 and Dallas, 10, and here's the kickoff for the second half . . . deep into the end zone and out of it . . . Green Bay ball on their own 20. . . .

Now the crowd was yelling for another Green Bay score. They could no longer feel secure with only a four-point lead and urged Starr and the Packers on as they huddled on their own 10. My body had become almost totally numb to the cold. My fingers were nearly stiff and my throat felt raw every time I opened my mouth to say something. I wasn't sure whether it was easier to talk or play on a day like this.

Neither team scored in the third quarter. On the first play of the fourth quarter, Meredith came up with his great call. He sent flanker Lance Rentzel deep downfield on the right side and called for a pitchout to running back Dan Reeves. On the halfback option play, one of my favorites as a player, Reeves let go a perfect pass downfield to the flashy Rentzel. He caught it all alone behind the shocked Green Bay secondary and charged in for the touchdown.

Villanueva kicked the extra point before an almost silenced Green Bay crowd and the Dallas Cowboys led the Packers, 17-14. They were less than fourteen minutes away from the championship of the National Football League.

Dallas held the Packers again and got the ball back with a little more than seven minutes to play. They moved the ball on a couple of plays but had to kick. Green Bay had another scoring chance but Chandler was unable to kick it against the wind from the 46. Green Bay held again and took over the football on its own 32.

Green Bay ball again, less than five minutes to play, Starr calling the play in the huddle, the Packers trail 17-14.

Now the Packers, like true champions, went to work as Starr used the clock, the sidelines and the experience he had gathered in 12 seasons in the NFL. He hit Donny Anderson over the middle for five yards. Chuck Mercein, who had failed as a Giant, drove off tackle for five more and a first down. Starr passed 12 yards to Dowler for another first down. The Packers were on the move and the crowd was going wild. All of the factors of weather and wind and cold had been forgotten in the excitement of the Green Bay drive. Starr handed off to Anderson but defensive end Willie Townes smashed Anderson to the ground for a ten-yard loss. But Anderson caught a pass on the next play to make up the ten yards. The Packers were playing like the champions they were, always able to make the big play, always able to keep the drive going, always able to sustain the momentum. Starr came right back to Anderson again over the middle for another 10 yards and the Packers had a first down on the 30 with 90 seconds to play.

Here Mercein, the Yale man, was called on for another key play. Confidence is so much of the game and Starr was expressing his confidence in Mercein. The young fullback carried the ball to the Dallas eleven. Green Bay had two timeouts to go. It could try to score, and failing that, could kick the tying field goal from in close and try to win in overtime.

It was getting much darker and the lights were on. The crowd was standing and yelling for the Packers. Many people had pulled off their scarves and were waving them and more faces could be seen without stocking caps. Cold weather? What cold weather?

Starr went to Mercein again and he drove the ball through a huge hole in the middle of the Dallas line to the three.

Frank Gifford

Fifty-eight seconds left on the clock, and the Packers are trying for the winning score. They still have two timeouts left if they want to go for the field goal.

Anderson drove up the middle to the one. Forty seconds to play. Anderson drove up the same place again and got piled up. Time out for Green Bay.

The crowd is going crazy. Starr is standing on the sidelines now with Coach Lombardi. Now he's coming back. Here's the play . . .

Starr handed off to Anderson and he slipped as he hit the line of scrimmage and was piled up. The play took only four seconds and Green Bay called its final timeout. Sixteen seconds left with Dallas leading 17-14. The ball was a half yard away from a touchdown.

They are going for the win. Chandler isn't moving. Lombardi and Starr are talking on the sidelines. Now Starr trots back on the field.

Everybody's blood was boiling. Nobody remembered being cold. Bart Starr, bending in the huddle, calling a play, seemed the only calm man in the stadium in that riotous scene. Now he moved over the ball, looked at his backs and bent down. Center Ken Bowman snapped the ball and Bart Starr took it himself. Bowman and guard Jerry Kramer drove Jethro Pugh out of the play and Starr landed in the end zone. Touchdown. The Packers win the Championship, 21-17.

The fans swarmed on the field, patting the players, grabbing for souvenirs, beating on everyone's backs.

In a happy Green Bay clubhouse Bart Starr and Donny Anderson and Chuck Mercein and Boyd Dowler were all sharing the joy of the moment. Jerry Kramer, who had made the key block on Pugh for Starr's touchdown, stood on a platform with me and spoke about the victory and about Coach Lombardi.

"There's a great deal of love for one another on this club," said Kramer. "Perhaps we are living in Camelot. Many things have been said about Coach and he is not always understood by those who quote him. The players understand. This is one beautiful man."

I will always remember those warm words of Jerry Kramer on the coldest day I have ever known.

Bart Starr (15) burrows across for the winning touchdown.

Ernie Harwell

8

The Miracle of Coogan's Bluff

ERNIE HARWELL

CTEW-CUT, grey-haired Ernie Harwell, who covers the Detroit Tigers the way the dew covers his native Dixie, began his distinguished broadcasting career in his hometown of Atlanta, Georgia, on station WSB.

Harwell, known for his sweet-sounding voice and accurate, controlled reporting of baseball, football and golf, started his career at 15 as a correspondent for the Atlanta *Constitution* and *The Sporting News*.

He continued working for them throughout his high school and college days at Emory University.

In 1940 he went into broadcasting full time and quickly became a well-known sports broadcasting figure in Georgia, equally at home in all of the major sports.

Harwell went off to war in 1942 and served four years in the United States Marine Corps with service in the Pacific.

He returned home and obtained a job broadcasting the Atlanta Crackers' baseball games. Atlanta was one of the best franchises in minor league baseball. This enormous baseball interest was later proven when the Milwaukee Braves moved to Atlanta.

Harwell's work in Atlanta became well known to the Dodgers and in 1948 he was called to Ebbets Field to work Brooklyn games with Red Barber and Connie Desmond.

The Dodgers won a pennant in 1949 and the following season Harwell moved crosstown to broadcast the New York Giants games with Russ Hodges.

In 1954 Baltimore joined the American League after an absence of more than half a century when the St. Louis Browns moved east to Maryland and became the Baltimore Orioles.

Harwell was hired away from New York to do the Orioles' games and also broadcast the football games of the Baltimore Colts.

During his baseball career, Harwell fit in some professional football and at one time or another called the football games of the New York Giants, the Brooklyn Dodgers and the Colts. He has also broadcast college football, including the games of his favorite team, Georgia Tech, in his hometown, as well as many other college games.

In 1960 Harwell moved to Detroit to do the games of the Detroit Tigers as they became one of the power teams of the American League. They have been a contender almost every year Harwell has been in Detroit and won the pennant in 1968 after losing out on the last day of the 1967 season.

Some of the highlights of his career include covering Norm Cash's march to the batting title in 1961, the brilliant years of Al Kaline, Denny McLain's 31-game season in 1968 and the Tigers' World Series victory that year over the St. Louis Cardinals after being down three games to one.

Here Harwell describes a game people will always remember. The date was October 3, 1951.

Ernie Harwell

KEEP your eye on the monitor. Keep your eye on the red light. Don't talk too much.

These were the things I thought about as I awoke that day in my home in Larchmont, N.Y. I was about to broadcast the final game of the first nationally televised baseball series and after all those years on radio, it seemed a major adjustment.

As I dressed, my wife Lulu prepared a big breakfast and got the boys, Bill and Gray, ready for school. All seemed normal except for that red light that was about to stare me in the face for the next few hours.

I was working with Russ Hodges and he was going to start on radio while I started the description of the third playoff game between the Brooklyn Dodgers and New York Giants on television. It had been an exciting summer. Now, at last, it would be over one way or another.

I read the paper after breakfast trying to see if I could find any useful information for that afternoon's game. Sal Maglie was scheduled to pitch for the Giants and Don Newcombe for the Dodgers. The playoff was tied at one game each.

The Giants had beaten Ralph Branca in the first game on Monday but Clem Labine had come back on Tuesday to shut the Giants out to even things. Now it would be settled.

The Giants had come from thirteen and a half games back to tie the Dodgers for the pennant. Actually, the Dodgers had tied us. We had won our last game on Sunday while the Dodgers were still tied in Philadelphia. We all listened on the radio as Jackie Robinson saved the game for Brooklyn with a diving catch of a line drive and then won it for them with a home run off Robin Roberts.

The boys were off to school and Lulu was finishing with the breakfast dishes. I looked at the clock. It said 10:00 o'clock. I put on my jacket, slipped a couple of newly sharpened pencils into my pocket, picked a light topcoat out of the closet, checked to see that I had my car keys, kissed Lulu goodbye and walked out of the door toward the car.

"One way or another," I said to Lulu, "we'll soon know."

There was very little traffic at that hour as I drove carefully down the Henry Hudson Parkway toward the Polo Grounds. I wanted to make sure I didn't get stuck by a flat tire or pulled in by a cop for speeding. It was a crazy thought. The whole world was waiting for the game and I would miss it because I was fixing a flat.

The thought left me quickly and the ride was easy and comfortable. I listened to some pleasant music on the car radio and noticed that it was a fine, crisp fall day in New York.

I waved to the parking lot attendant as I pulled my car into my assigned spot next to the right field fence in the Polo Grounds. I got out of the car and looked up on the hill beyond the ball park, the place they called Coogan's Bluff. A few kids had already gathered to claim their locations for a free view of the baseball game.

The Giants were almost all dressed as I walked up the stairs in centerfield to their clubhouse. It didn't seem like a special game. The Giants had been playing crucial games for a month now and this seemed like just another one in the long season. Leo Durocher was in his office talking to some of the sportswriters. His voice was loud and clear and he showed no signs of emotion. He was telling funny stories and the writers were writing down his words.

Sal Maglie was talking to Whitey Lockman in the middle of the clubhouse floor and I walked over to say hello. Maglie looked as he always did on a day he was pitching—all business. He had a full day's growth of beard, his face seemed sharp and thin and his eyes were alert and clear.

"Well, Ernie, one thing is sure," said Maglie, "in a few more hours it will be settled one way or another."

"I think we'll be glad of that," I said.

That seemed to be the prevailing atmosphere in the Giant clubhouse. This team had been under so much pressure for a month that it was almost pleasant that it was all down to one game. The Dodgers had played well for the last month keeping their record for that time over .500. The Giants had won 31 of 41, cutting steadily into the Dodger lead each day but never being able to relax. Each time they played Brooklyn it meant two games in the standings and the Giants had won the last five out of six to close the gap in the final week to two games.

The Giants went on the field for batting practice. Durocher posted the lineup card in the edge of the dugout. It was the same lineup that had brought about the tie. Nobody was getting fancy today. Eddie Stanky was at second, Alvin Dark at shortstop, Don Mueller in right, Monte Irvin in left, Whitey Lockman at first base, Bobby Thomson at third, Willie Mays in center, Wes Westrum catching and Maglie pitching.

The Dodgers were just beginning to filter on to the field as the Giants took batting practice. Most of them sat in the dugout watching the Giants hit.

Shortly after noon I walked back to the press room for a quick lunch, a few words with the sportswriters and a final check with Jack Murphy, our director for the television production.

About a half hour before the game I walked to the broadcasting booth. It was located in the far right end of the press box, high above home plate, with a fine view of the action. I had to climb past a dozen photographers to get to the booth. There wasn't much room to move around.

Art Susskind, the assistant director, stood in the middle of the booth looking onto the field. He was shuffling through some papers.

"Do we have the statistics?" I asked.

"No," said Susskind. "I haven't seen Felker."

Clay Felker was our statistician but he wasn't in the booth with the statistics. At that instant he was talking to some people from *Life* Magazine. He had gotten hold of some secret scouting reports on the Dodgers and had sold it to the magazine. Now all the world knew that Jackie Robinson was a good curve-ball hitter, especially with two strikes on him.

Without Felker in the booth, I began writing down the lineups on my card, hoping he would arrive with the material before game time. It isn't easy doing a game without being able to refer to what a man has hit all season.

It was less than ten minutes to game time now and I began thinking how glad I was that it was a nice day. I hated doing a game in cold weather. This would be pleasant. The sun was warm and the air was clear and blue.

How could I know then that every aspect of this day would make history?

Hi, everybody, welcome to the Polo Grounds. It's a beautiful day for the third game of the playoff between the Dodgers and the Giants for the National League pennant. Sal Maglie is warming up underneath us for the Giants and Don Newcombe is finishing up his warmups for the Dodgers. We'll have the lineups and batting orders . . . but first this word from Chesterfield.

I was glad the first commercial was from the studio. I was still a little nervous and I hated to do the commercials until I was completely comfortable with the game. I tried to convince myself this was just another baseball game but I just couldn't make myself believe it.

Maglie gets his sign from Westrum, here comes the first pitch to Reese . . . strike one . . . and we're underway. . . .

Now I took a deep breath and relaxed. I was a professional and I was doing what I had trained all these years to do. The game was on and I was describing it for millions of television viewers.

Keep your eye on the monitor. Keep your eye on the red light. Don't talk too much.

I settled quickly into the routine of the game. Maglie and New-combe, who was now pitching his fourth game in eight days, were both excellent. It was the kind of game we had come to expect from both of them.

It was 1-1 into the eighth inning. The Dodgers broke through Maglie in the eighth for three runs. Now it was 4-1 as Newcombe took the mound for the Dodgers and the Giants batted in the bottom of the eighth.

Two out, nobody on for the Giants. Larry Jansen warming up in the bullpen. He'll come on to pitch to the Dodgers in the ninth. Stanky swings and hits a ground ball to Robinson. He has it, over to first, the Giants are down in the eighth. At the end of eight innings it's Brooklyn 4 and the Giants 1.

Newcombe, big and strong and fierce-looking, was throwing as hard as he ever had. The Giants seemed tired and spent. One inning to go for the Dodgers. Three outs left for the Giants.

Jansen got the Dodgers out in order in the top of the ninth. The next three batters would be Dark, Mueller and Irvin. If anybody got on, it would be Lockman, always a home run threat with the 255-foot right field wall in the Polo Grounds.

The clapping began in the bleachers as Dark walked to the plate. He swung a couple of bats, dropped one, tugged at his cap, dug his feet into the dirt and looked out at big Newcombe. The first pitch was in for a strike.

"He was still throwing hard," Dark remembers. "I knew I couldn't pull him. I just wanted an outside pitch I could punch into right field."

The next pitch was a ball. Then came a fastball, on the outside part of the plate.

Dark swings and there's a ground ball toward the right side, Hodges dives for it, it's off his glove into right field for a hit. The Giants have the leadoff runner on base.

"I knew I hit it good," Dark recalls. "The only thing that worried me was Gil's long reach. He had made some fabulous plays around the bag and seemed capable of reaching anything."

Now Dark was on first base and the batter was Mueller. Mandrake the Magician. He choked up on the bat and would punch balls in every direction. He could hit the inside pitch over the wall in right or the outside pitch just over the wall in left. He could drive a ball just past a fielder or bloop one into an open spot. His hits had eyes. They could find the open spot on the field.

Newcombe, who was not as fast from the stretch position as from the windup, seemed to lose a little steam with Dark's hit. He studied Rube Walker's sign more intently, finally went into his stretch and pitched.

Mueller hits a ground ball . . . through into centerfield for a base hit . . . Snider quickly up with it, Dark stops at second and the Giants have the tying run at the plate in the person of Irvin.

Charlie Dressen was on the top step of the Dodgers' dugout. Now he was walking to the mound and looking down at the bullpen.

Assistant director Susskind said, "Bullpen," and I watched the monitor.

That's Carl Erskine on the outside and Ralph Branca, Monday's starter and loser, on the inside.

Dressen reached the mound, looked into Newcombe's eyes and asked, "How are you?"

"I'm okay," said Newcombe, "I'll get this guy."

Dressen patted him on the backside, turned, walked away, peeked over his shoulder toward the Dodger bullpen and sat down in the Dodger dugout. The Giant crowd booed him as he disappeared from the field.

Now the hitter was Irvin, a tough right-handed batter, a definite home run threat in any ball park, a certain home run threat in the Polo Grounds. The crowd began to sense the game wasn't over after all. The Giants seemed to be performing miracles all season. Would this be another one? Did the Giants still have a chance to win the pennant despite being down, 4-1, with three outs to go in the final game of the season?

Newcombe took a deep breath on the mound, Irvin dug in and the pitch came in for a strike.

Here's Newcombe's next pitch. Irvin swings and pops it up. Hodges moving over from first base, he's under it, he's got it. One out.

Now the Dodger fans in the crowd began cheering. They still had the big lead and they eliminated a big threat in Irvin. Reese moved over a little from shortstop on the left-hand hitting Lockman and Robinson moved toward first a step. The Dodgers were in double play depth. Lockman, who had broken his leg in a spring training game several years earlier, was not the runner he once had been.

Newcombe threw a fastball and Lockman drilled it on a line to left center field. It hit the wall on two bounces and Snider raced over to cut it off.

Here comes Dark into score, Mueller slides into third and Lock-

man is on second with a double. Wait a minute. Mueller is hurt at third base.

Mueller had hit the bag hard on the slide and now he was lying on the ground in great pain. The Giant players were all around him and Leo Durocher stood there, with his hands crossed on his chest.

Clint Hartung, who had once been thought of as the second coming of Babe Ruth, was called in from the Giant bullpen to run for Mueller. He took over at third base as Mueller was helped off the field.

Dressen stood at the mound. Newcombe, his head down, his body sagging from a brilliant effort, stared at the ground. Branca was five feet away from the mound and Newcombe flipped him the ball. "Go get 'em," Newcombe said. Branca said nothing. Dressen said, "Thomson's the hitter. Get him out."

As Lockman had doubled, Dressen had placed a call to the bullpen. Coach Clyde Sukeforth had picked up the phone and Dressen asked, "Who's ready?" Sukeforth had answered, "Erskine just bounced a curve ball."

"All right," said Dressen, "give me Branca."

With those words the 25-year-old Dodger righthander from Mount Vernon, N.Y., was to step into baseball history.

Catcher Rube Walker said to Branca, "Let's keep the ball in on him."

Thomson liked the ball well out over the plate. Known as the Staten Island Scot, he had hit a home run off Branca in the opening game and had been one of the clutch hitters for the Giants down the torrid stretch.

All right. Branca's ready. Runners on second and third for the Giants, one out, the Dodgers lead 4-2, Branca throws . . . right down the middle. Strike one on Bobby Thomson.

Thomson never moved for the pitch. He never expected a fast ball down the middle in that spot. Branca had fooled him and gone ahead on the count.

Branca stretches, now he's ready for the 1-0 pitch . . .

"It was an inside pitch," remembers Rube Walker, "a bad pitch to swing on. I was surprised he didn't take it."

Thomson swings . . . it's gone.

The words were out of my mouth and I couldn't take them back. Now I saw Andy Pafko leaning back against the wall and I had this horrible thought that I had reacted too soon, that the ball wasn't that hard hit, that it would fade and hit the wall, that it might even be caught, that I had called a home run on a ball that would be an out, that fifty million people were watching the game and they would all be saying this guy Harwell doesn't know a fly ball from a home run.

It sailed into the stands and Thomson leaped into the air around first base.

On the radio side Russ Hodges was shouting, "The Giants win the pennant, the Giants win the pennant. . . ."

Thomson was nearing third now. Branca stood on the mound with his head down. Reese and Hodges had already turned toward the clubhouse. Robinson stared at Thomson as he went into third, touched the bag, leaped into the air, clapped his hands and headed home as all the Giants were pushing and shoving each other just back of the plate. Robinson was still in the game, hoping and praying that Thomson somehow might forget to touch home or some final miracle would call it all back.

But this was to be the Giants' miracle. Stanky was wrestling Durocher to the ground at third base. The fans were mauling Thomson as he leaped on home plate with his two feet. Now they all turned and raced toward the centerfield clubhouse, past the crowds, and over the infield, and into the grass and racing harder, holding their hats, leaping and laughing as they finally reached the steps of the clubhouse.

The crowd noise was deafening. It continued to grow and ring in my ears as if all the world had suddenly heard that Bobby Thomson had homered, that the Giants had won the 1951 pennant, that there had been a Miracle of Coogan's Bluff.

"Let the crowd break," Susskind said.

The television picture showed the field and the mass of humanity swarming toward the Giant clubhouse and the left field stands where the ball had landed.

Now I started talking again as the noise grew less.

The Giants win the 1951 pennant by defeating the Dodgers here today at the Polo Grounds, 5-4, on Bobby Thomson's three-run home run off Ralph Branca.

At home Lulu watched me describe the momentous event.

"You had a stunned look on your face," she said later. "Just like the look you had on your face the day our kids were born."

We signed off the air, broke for a commercial and raced down into the Giants' clubhouse. Russ was already there and we began interviewing the players as to their reactions to this miracle. There seemed to be as much noise in the Giants' clubhouse as there was outside with thousands of fans.

Ernie Harwell

Later on that evening I went on the Fred Robbins show and described the game and the day and the excitement all over again.

I think about that day often. And I think about the only regret I have concerning the most exciting sports event in my life, maybe in anybody's life. I remember that I did it on television. Nothing was taped on television in 1951.

I'm unhappy sometimes because I can't sit back in my living room and hear myself over and over again describing Bobby Thomson's home run and the dramatic winning of the 1951 pennant. But as I think about it, I realize that what really matters to me is that I was there for that one great moment.

*Rookies Ernie Harwell
and Ted Williams
in Atlanta, 1940.*

Curt Gowdy

9

A Wild Fish Story

CURT GOWDY

On April 21, 1970, at the annual luncheon held by the Broadcast Pioneers in New York City, Curt Gowdy became the first individual from the field of sports to receive a Peabody Award—for highest achievement in radio and television.

His citation read: "With sports occupying an increasing significance in broadcasting, Curt Gowdy merits recognition as television's most versatile broadcaster. Over the years, Mr. Gowdy has achieved top stature with a winning blend of reportorial accuracy, a vast fund of knowledge in many areas, intelligence, good humor and an infectiously honest enthusiasm for his subject. Curt Gowdy stands today at the top of his profession."

Also in 1970 Gowdy was selected as the top sportscaster in the country for the fifth time by his peers, the sports broadcasters and writers of America.

Gowdy, whose busy schedule includes NBC's Baseball Game of the Week plus the World Series, professional football for NBC and host for ABC's "The American Sportsman," is

93

Curt Gowdy

really a basketball man. He went from a career at the University of Wyoming into a broadcasting career only because a serious back problem ended his playing days.

Gowdy was born in Green River, Wyoming, in the southwestern part of the state but grew up in Cheyenne, where his father, a railroad man, became chief dispatcher for the Union Pacific Railroad.

Fishing and hunting were big sports in young Curt's life but he soon gravitated to basketball, despite his small size and slight build. He went on to basketball fame with the University of Wyoming, playing forward with Kenny Sailors, who became one of the outstanding players in the country.

A back condition cut short Gowdy's basketball career and ended his Army career almost as soon as he entered service. He went back to Cheyenne, took a part-time job on the Wyoming *Eagle* as a high school reporter and then began broadcasting made-up games in his room.

It was wartime and able bodied men were scarce. Gowdy applied for a job on the local radio station after his mother heard him broadcasting in his room.

After a year of local broadcasting of all sports around Cheyenne, Gowdy was tapped to do the University of Oklahoma football games over station KOMA in Oklahoma City. He began broadcasting Oklahoma A&M basketball at the same time and did the broadcast featuring Bob Kurland of A&M against George Mikan of DePaul in one of the early battles of these giants.

While at Oklahoma, Gowdy struck up a friendship with a young man named Bud Wilkinson, who as coach of Oklahoma was to become one of the most successful football coaches in the country.

Gowdy was doing the Oklahoma football games when the phone rang one day at his home.

"Curt, this is Red Barber in New York."

Barber was sports director of CBS and at the peak of his career as a sports announcer. Barber wanted Gowdy to handle the Oklahoma-Texas Christian game the following Saturday for CBS on national television. It was Gowdy's first national exposure.

That exposure led to Gowdy's next big break. Russ Hodges had just left the Yankee broadcasts as No. 2 man to Mel Allen to become No. 1 with the Giants across the river. George Weiss, general manager of the Yankees, decided to hire Gowdy for the job.

In 1949 there were two important rookies in the Yankee spring training camp. One was Gowdy. The other was Casey Stengel, who had just been hired by Weiss as manager after the Yankees had failed to win the pennant in 1948.

Gowdy stayed with the Yankees through 1950, did some college basketball from Madison Square Garden, track and boxing, and established himself as a major figure in sports broadcasting.

In 1951 the Braves and the Red Sox, who had been sharing a broadcasting team, decided to split the Boston broadcasts.

Gowdy gambled that it would be better to be No. 1 in Boston than No. 2 behind Mel Allen in New York and applied for the job.

It paid off. He began an association with the Red Sox that lasted fifteen pleasant years and he made friends with such well-known outdoorsmen as Boston owner Tom Yawkey and Ted Williams.

Gowdy left the Red Sox to become the baseball Game of the Week announcer and continues his work in football with the American Conference of the newly merged National Football League.

As a man of the West, Gowdy has always maintained his interest in hunting and fishing, and he is host of "The American Sportsman" on ABC Television. He tells now a tale about an amazing fishing trip.

It is February, 1962, and Gowdy is in a trout fishing contest in Lago General Paz, Argentina, along the Chilean border.

Curt Gowdy

THERE is something so personal, so exhilarating, about the sport of fishing. I have covered all of the great sports and yet, to me, there is an element of excitement and competition in fishing that there is in no other sport. The competition is really against yourself with the fish almost lost in the background. It is the excitement of doing the right thing at the right time with the forces of nature against you at times as well as the fish.

One of broadcasting's successful programs on sports for many years has been the American Broadcasting Company's "Wide World of Sports." The program spans the world to film every sort of sports event imaginable.

Why not fishing?

"I'd love to do a fishing show," said Roone Arledge, executive producer of the program, "but we have to have an element of competition in it. That's an integral part of the show."

I had about given up on the idea when Roone called one day

and said that Mort Neff, producer of an outdoor sports show in Detroit, had suggested a world's championship trout fishing contest. The idea intrigued me.

Not only did Arledge want to do the show but he was going along on the trip to Argentina where we would hold the contest. Five of us—including Roone, Jo Brooks, the writer, Bob Wood, director and cameraman, and Lenny Lencina, who would handle the sound—left for Argentina via Miami. There we were met by Mort Neff and two of his friends and fishing enthusiasts, Bebe Anchorina and Jorge Donovan, both wealthy Argentine ranch owners.

We got to Buenos Aires the next day and subsequently took off for the town of Bariloche, some 840 miles to the southwest. The prop plane made five stops, each scheduled for 15 minutes, but true to Latin custom each took more than an hour.

After our first delayed stop I asked an attendant when we would take off.

"We're waiting for a passenger," he said.

"One passenger?"

"We can't disappoint him, senor. He depends on us to get where he is going."

"Why not insist he be here on time?"

"He'll be here," said the man. "We phoned and he told us he'd be a little late."

It was a pretty significant lesson about Latin American customs.

The "Wide World of Sports" fishing contest was to be held on Lago General Paz, a big lake 400 miles north of Tierra del Fuego at the southern tip of the continent. The only way to get there was by car over terrain like our own West. Being from Wyoming, this type country would be familiar to me. The only difference was the roads. There weren't any. There were dusty paths of bumpy, rut-filled gravel. This wasn't the best thing for my bad back but I had brought along enough pain-killing pills for just such an emergency. I must have swallowed half of them on this 12-hour trip.

We skirted a forest fire and about 2:30 in the morning arrived at a lumber camp barred by locked gates. Joe Brooks and I ended up in an old shed with one bed. Joe got the bed and I got the floor. I was just as happy. My back still hurt and a bad bed wouldn't have done it much good.

To get to the lake we had to walk about a mile. We were about 500 feet away when we caught our first glimpse of it, the bluest blue water I've ever seen, nestled in a framework of snowcapped peaks.

After admiring its beauty I thought of a practical consideration for our fishing.

"The water looks cold," I said.

Then came the bad news. I was told the mean temperature was 48 degrees and it probably wasn't that warm now.

The lake wasn't quite as pretty to fish as it was to look at. The winds came howling down from the mountains, bouncing our skiffs around like corks as we moved to set up a base camp. We spent a couple of freezing nights in sleeping bags before we really got organized. As I tossed in my bag all night I wondered whether this had been such a good idea after all.

With our television equipment, cameras and sound equipment to be set up in this wilderness, it was more than a week after our arrival at Lago General Paz before the contest could really get started.

The ground rules called for one day of fishing with spinning rods, the second day with fly rods and the third day open. We would get one point per pound for every trout we caught, with a bonus to the man who reeled in the biggest fish of the day. The championship would be won by the team with the highest combined total after three days of fishing.

Roone Arledge was referee and timekeeper as well as producer of the show. Our opponents were to be Tito Hosman, a wealthy lawyer from Buenos Aires, and Erick Gornik, an outfitter and guide. When we first met them I knew we would have a good time, win, lose or draw, after they greeted us with big Argentinian bear hugs.

The fishing was going to be slowed by the demands of the show. The cameramen had to do a lot of running around and splashing in the water and each time they did that they scattered the fish. Which didn't help matters.

The sound men also had their problems. We couldn't fish far apart from each other since the noise of the lake and the fishing had to be caught on one battery-run tape recorder. All the sounds and conversation had to be caught when anybody caught a fish.

Joe Brooks had brought along a small scale designed to weigh the fish. Since points depended on the size of the fish, we had to weigh them but we couldn't weigh them without killing them. That we refused to do. We didn't want to kill every fish we caught. We wanted to show the viewing public that fishing was a sport and to be true sportsmen we would throw back every fish we weren't going to eat.

We decided we would estimate the weight except when somebody caught a real whopper. Then we would weigh it. On the last day, with the contest close, we weighed everything.

The water was so cold we almost lost our sound man. Arledge was a bear for getting live sound and he wanted the sound man, Lenny Lencina, to be in the water with us. Lencina had no waders and wasn't about to attempt the 48-degree water without them. Lencina just about congealed every time he attempted to step into the water to catch what we were saying. We finally solved the problem by patching up an old pair of waders Gornik had in his luggage.

Lencina did a good job in catching the natural sounds of the environment. We fished near the shore so he put mikes in bushes, under logs, on the ground near rocks—anywhere they would be protected from the wind that howled down the mountains and over the lake.

He could capture the sounds of the struggling fish splashing in the water, the whip of the rods, the click of the reels.

We solved the problem of our own voices by wearing small mikes under our shirts.

We weren't able to fish on successive days because of the changing weather so we had to load and unload all that equipment on the skiffs each day that we went back and forth. This was especially hazardous on the return trip when the whitecapped waves tossed us around as if we were in the middle of the ocean. I was always afraid something would fall overboard or the entire boat would tip. Fortunately, it never happened, but I wasn't really certain it wouldn't until we finally left the camp.

The actual fishing contest was interesting but not the heart of the story. The important thing was to bring to American audiences a magnificent segment of South American outdoor sports life. The central image was the beauty of nature in strange surroundings which few Americans would see except for television.

I got off to a bad start in the contest because I've always been a better fly than a spinning fisherman. After a while I realized I was working my lures too quickly. The others were pulling brook trout in with slow-moving wobbly lures and I was working my wobbler too fast. Joe and the Argentines began hauling in fish before I did, and they got some beauties. The fish ran four to six pounds and had the loveliest coloring I've ever seen on brook trout.

The trout fishing in that lake was the finest I had ever seen anywhere. I finally began pulling in my share of fish, with my change in strategy, but it was Joe Brooks who kept us from being murdered by the two Argentines. At the end of the first day they led us 54-44.

Four days of heavy weather kept us in our camp. We played chess, read, checked over our gear and told fish stories to each other.

We switched to fly rods, my specialty, on the second day of fishing. I did much better but the Argentines continued to move ahead. Despite a seven-pounder that I caught that gave us the bonus points for biggest fish, we lost by nine points on the day. With only one day to go we trailed the Argentines by 19 points.

Now we needed some dramatics to snatch victory from the jaws of defeat. Joe provided it. He got me in a corner at our camp, looked me in the eye, and like Knute Rockne before him, said, "Curt, remember this is going to be on nationwide television. Won't we look great if we get our brains beaten out again."

I agreed with Joe that we would have to bear down on this final day if we were to make a big catch and make up those points.

"I didn't come these six thousand miles to lose and neither did you. Tomorrow let's fish every cast out, take our time and not panic."

Pat O'Brien could not have said it any more dramatically.

Joe insisted we use spinning rods. The water was very deep so flies took too long to reach the fish. Spinning lures made it much faster and with the score 104-85 against us, we couldn't afford to lose a minute. When we started out the last morning I left my fly equipment behind. We would use all the time we had left in any attempt to score a come-from-behind win. Johnny Unitas couldn't have handled it any better using the clock against the Giants.

Maybe there is something to an ex-athlete's nature or just being around athletes all my life, but I had a hot morning that final round. I pulled in four five-pounders in a row while my opposite number from Argentina could catch only one fish.

Now it was a fishing contest again.

The clock was to run out at four that afternoon and the contest would be over. We needed one more big catch.

At ten minutes to four I looked over at Joe as he was fighting a big beauty. I knew if he landed this one we would win the contest. "C'mon, Joe," I yelled. Then he started to reel it home. It was the biggest, most beautiful trout I had ever seen.

They put him on the official scale, Joe posed for pictures with him and we got the winning points on Joe's six-pounder. We won the contest, 136-130.

Now it was over. We had spent the most marvelous fishing days of my life in this beautiful country. All that was left was the trip home.

We almost didn't make it.

On the way back to Bariloche from Lago General Paz our jeep suddenly went out of control. We were going fifty miles an hour when our driver felt the steering wheel come off in his hands. We careened along the dusty highway as the driver frantically tried to jam the wheel back while throttling down our speed. We went off the road but the drop at that point was only 40 feet. I thought we were about to turn over but the jeep, miraculously, kept its wheels and we finally came to rest without anyone suffering a scratch. A truck came by half an hour later and we were able to put our steering wheel back on.

As I wrote in my book, *Cowboy at the Mike*, with Al Hirshberg, "We were nearly drowned, nearly frozen to death in ice-cold water and nearly killed in an accident but it was one of the most thrilling experiences of my life."

The trip led to the creation of one of television's most exciting programs, "The American Sportsman," where hunting and fishing trips in the wildest locations are seen regularly.

It was the live sounds that made the show. It was not to be just another travelog with a voice narration from some New York City studio. It was this sound technique that led to "The American Sportsman" becoming the first TV show to later use sound wave remote mikes which added an extra dimension of excitement to fishing and hunting around the world.

I have seen most of the big baseball games and football games and basketball games of recent years, but nothing matches fishing in such conditions.

Maybe I would have thought differently if my back had held up and I had become Bob Cousy instead of Curt Gowdy.

Curt Gowdy with his seven-pound brook trout
at Lago General Paz, Argentina.

Ken Coleman and Carl Yastrzemski in the year that was.

10

The Impossible Dream

KEN COLEMAN

IF a man ever hitched his wagon to a star it was cherubic Ken Coleman, who spent 14 exciting seasons with the Cleveland Browns of the National Football League.

The star was Jimmy Brown, the bone-crushing fullback of the Browns, who dominated the NFL with his exciting running exploits for nearly a decade.

"I saw every game Jimmy played for the Browns, exhibition and regular season," said Coleman. "I don't believe any other man can make that statement."

There was much turnover of coaching staff and players in Brown's time with Cleveland but Coleman went on year after year describing the marvelous performances of the great running back. It was after Brown retired to become Jim Brown, movie star, that Coleman left Cleveland to move back to his native New England as the voice of the Boston Red Sox.

Coleman was born in Quincy, Mass., just outside Boston, and played baseball at North Quincy High. He later attended Curry College and began his broadcasting career in the ski country of Rutland, Vermont.

The affable, low-key Coleman then moved on to Quincy and Worcester, Mass., where he began play-by-play of the Boston University games.

In 1952 he moved to Cleveland to take over the broadcasting of the Browns' games on their extensive network as the team moved from the old All-America Conference to the NFL and dominated the older league as it had dominated the newer one.

His 14-season tour of duty with the Browns covered the Paul Brown era with Otto Graham and Marion Motley and the great Cleveland teams, through the Jimmy Brown era and their exciting battles with the New York Giants and a tough defense led by Sam Huff.

Four years after he began broadcasting the Browns' games each Sunday, he was selected to do the games of the Cleveland Indians. He is one of the few broadcasters in the country equally skilled and equally comfortable with major league baseball and professional football.

Coleman was summoned back home by the Red Sox in 1966 just in time to see the team fall on bad times with a dreadful ninth-place finish.

"I guess it helped me appreciate what was to happen later," said Coleman. "I guess if I came in on top the 1967 season would not have been as exciting."

Coleman now does the Red Sox games with Ned Martin and former shortstop Johnny Pesky, conducts a daily sports show on WHDH in Boston and describes the Harvard football games each fall Saturday.

Coleman lives in Cohasset, Mass., with his wife Ellen and their five children.

Here he recalls the highlight of his career. It is October 1, 1967, the day all New England dreamed The Impossible Dream.

Ken Coleman

I⊤ all began, really, on that July day when the Boston Red Sox returned from Cleveland after a winning streak and walked off their team plane into the waiting hands of 10,000 madly excited fans.

The scene was riotous. The kids waved banners and screamed at Yaz and Lonnie and all the Red Sox who suddenly were beginning to jell as a solid baseball team. Carl Yastrzemski seemed finally to be becoming the kind of all-around baseball player everybody had predicted some day he would be. And Jim Lonborg, tall, thin, handsome, had almost overnight become as good a pitcher as there was in the American League.

In 1966 the Red Sox almost fell out of the bottom of the American League. Only a worse fall by the once-mighty Yankees prevented them from finishing last and they had to beat the Yankees in the final weekend of the season to stay ninth.

Now there had been a dramatic turn-around under the new manager Dick Williams. He had put sparks into the team and Yaz and Lonnie led the way but the contributions came from a new star almost every day, from shortstop Rico Petrocelli, from big George Scott at first base, from Joe Foy at third, from rookie centerfielder Reggie Smith, from rightfielder Tony Conigliaro, from pitcher Jose Santiago, from almost everybody who got into a Red Sox uniform that summer.

The airport crowd sensed something big. They saw the Red Sox in contention again for the American League pennant. These fans had waited 21 years for another flag. The Red Sox had last won in 1946 and only Washington had gone any longer without a pennant in the American League.

The July streak had stamped them as a contender. The Red Sox would battle the Twins and the Tigers and the White Sox all summer long for a chance at the St. Louis Cardinals, who were busting up the National League race very early, in the World Series.

Excitement is contagious and I could see it spreading through the airport as we came off that airplane into the waiting rooms. The players wanted to go home after a long road trip but they realized the fans had waited a long time and they signed autographs and chatted with the kids and waved at the adults. It was all like a big open-air party and the smiles on the faces of the players showed the people how much they appreciated the affection.

The season moved into its final weeks. Tony Conigliaro had been hit in the eye with a pitched ball by Jack Hamilton of the Angels. He survived the serious accident but his career seemed over. It was a great loss to the club.

Then Ken Harrelson, the long-nosed flashy outfielder known round the world as The Hawk, who had had a spirited dispute with A's owner Charlie Finley, picked up the slack after being signed by Boston owner Tom Yawkey as a free agent.

The team drove down to its final destiny, bouncing in and out of first place, as first Minnesota, then Detroit, then Chicago seemed to be taking charge. The league was so well balanced that it was impossible for anybody to move out and take command. The schedule began to be the single significant factor in the final week. The Red Sox were to finish home Saturday and Sunday in friendly Fenway Park, with the Green Monster, the 315-foot left field wall, encouraging their hitters and frustrating the opposition's. That always seemed to be the way it worked.

With a week to go, Chicago won in California and went into first place by a game and a half. They were two up on the loss side. They were finishing with two in Kansas City and three in Washington. It didn't seem possible to catch them. The Red Sox had to play Cleveland in Cleveland and then the Twins at home over the weekend. Was it possible?

The White Sox were rained out in Kansas City on Tuesday and scheduled a doubleheader for Wednesday. It was a miracle rain for the Red Sox.

"It's not as easy to win two games in one night as it is to win two games in two nights," said Chicago manager Eddie Stanky.

The Red Sox lost to Cleveland but the White Sox lost two in Kansas City. It was a crazy horse race again. Detroit was slipping now and Minnesota was gaining.

On Friday night the White Sox, who looked like a sure thing on Tuesday, lost their third game in a row to Washington. They were eliminated from the race.

On Saturday Detroit played two games against the California Angels after they had been rained out Friday night in Detroit.

"It's not as easy to win two games in one day as it is to win two games in two days," said Detroit manager Mayo Smith.

The Tigers split Saturday and now had to win two games on Sunday to tie for the pennant.

On Saturday the Red Sox had beaten Minnesota, 6-4. Yastrzemski had homered, knocked in four runs, gone three for four and made a terrific catch. What else could he do?

Now it would all be wrapped up in one day, Sunday, in Boston. Al Hirshberg, a Boston writer, had called them The Cardiac Kids for the thrill a minute they had provided all summer long. Would it end without the fulfillment of The Impossible Dream?

We had been in and out of the pennant race so many times in the last few weeks that when I awoke Sunday morning I didn't feel especially nervous. We had to beat Minnesota today while Detroit lost at least one game to win the pennant. If we won, we would tie the Tigers if they won two games. If we lost, it would be a pretty exciting year anyway.

It was shortly after 10:00 o'clock that I finished breakfast with Ellen and the kids and prepared to drive to Fenway Park some 21 miles door-to-door from my house in Cohasset.

At that instant Carl Yastrzemski was sitting in front of his locker at Fenway Park pounding his right fist into his glove. He had already been awake for five hours. He and his wife had a house full of company. They left the house to the relatives and spent the evening before the Sunday game at George Page's Colonial Inn in Lynnfield. As the sun came up over the beautiful eighteen-hole course, Yastrzemski walked to the first tee. He carried no golf clubs. He just walked. He climbed the rolling hills and let his feet feel the smooth grass. He breathed the clean air of the pleasant fall day. He tried not to think of the game. He could only think of Dean Chance, the Minnesota pitcher. He saw him whirl and pivot his body and send that fastball in on him, trying to force him to pull the ball to the deepest stretches of right field in Fenway. Fenway was a right-handed hitter's park but in 1967 every park in the American League had been Carl Yastrzemski's park. Shortly after 9:00 o'clock Yastrzemski finished walking the eighteen holes, walked back into the clubhouse, exchanged a few words with the club pro, and started out for Fenway Park.

At 10:45 I walked out of the house, got into the car, turned the motor on, switched the radio on, pulled out of the driveway and headed for Fenway Park.

"Well," said the disc jockey, Alan Dary, "do you think we can win it?"

Why didn't he just play a song? I was nervous enough as it was.

It took a little more than half an hour to drive to the park and all the time I kept hearing the same question on the air, "Can we win it? Can we win it?"

I walked through the service gate at Fenway, waved to the gatemen, signed a few autographs for some early-arriving fans, noticed that the crowd was building early and went into the Red Sox clubhouse. I walked straight to manager Dick Williams' office.

"Good morning and good luck."

"Thanks," said Williams. "We've gone this far. We can't stop now."

The lineup card sat on Williams' desk and I checked it out of habit. I knew it by heart and didn't expect any surprises. There were none. Lonborg was the pitcher, Yastrzemski was batting third and all the others were in their accustomed spots.

I walked around the clubhouse shaking hands with the players and wishing them well. They seemed no more tense than usual. They had been in so many big games for so many days now that it seemed perfectly normal that the season would go down to this very last day. I wanted the Red Sox to win, of course, but I certainly didn't want a tie with Detroit. Another playoff would be impossible to take in Boston after what Cleveland had done to the Red Sox in 1948 when Lou Boudreau hit two homers in Fenway to give the Indians the pennant behind Gene Bearden.

The field was cluttered with reporters and photographers from most of the larger papers in the country. They were everywhere. With the normally large Boston press corps, I couldn't imagine a World Series game being any better attended. I checked the Minnesota lineup in their dugout. No surprises there, either. The name that frightened me, of course, was Harmon Killebrew. He was so strong he could hit any pitch, good or bad, off the screen for a homer. I knew Lonnie would have to work hard on him. He would have to work hard on everybody. There wasn't a soft hitter in the Twins' lineup.

I walked up the stairs to the rooftop boxes and entered the press room. There were many strange faces in the room as the out-of-town writers crowded in for a quick lunch before the game began. At 1:15 I walked over to our broadcasting booth with my partner Ned Martin to join Mel Parnell, the former Red Sox pitcher who was our color man, to go over final details for the game.

I was to do the first three innings on television, move to the radio side for the middle three and finish up on television again. I knew that if the Red Sox won we would have an interview show from the clubhouse and I would have to be down there for the final outs. My heart was beginning to pound a little quicker as I began the broadcast.

. . . and now ladies and gentlemen, our national anthem.

Jim Lonborg was ready to make his first pitch. He looked ready and rested. He had spent the night in Ken Harrelson's hotel room in downtown Boston as Harrelson moved out to spend it with his family. Lonborg, a bachelor, had a superstition that he pitched better on the road after getting a good night's sleep in a hotel room. Instead of staying at his own Boston apartment he psychologically prepared himself, as if this was a road game, by staying in Harrelson's room.

Now he threw the first pitch down the middle, I took a deep

breath, and was ready for whatever was to be.

The Twins quickly jumped to a 2-0 lead against Lonberg. It stayed that way until the Red Sox sixth. The first hitter was Lonborg. Would Williams hit for him?

Here comes Lonborg out of the dugout swinging a couple of bats to hit for himself. The Red Sox trail, 2-0, but Williams is sticking with the big right-hander.

It didn't seem a strange move. Lonborg had been the best pitcher on the team and a 2-0 lead in Fenway wasn't that much. Even if Lonborg went out the Red Sox would have the top of the order up against Chance.

Lonborg pumped the bat back and forth at home plate. Any man can hit a home run who swings a bat in Fenway and it appeared that Lonborg might have had that in his mind. That was the appearance he was trying to give.

Lonborg bunts to the left of the mound. Chance and Tovar go for the ball, the third baseman has it, throws, not in time. Lonnie is safe at first with a hit.

The Red Sox had been doing the unusual all year. When they got a break they were able to take advantage of it. Now with Lonborg on first and nobody out they had a good chance to catch the Twins. The crowd of 35,770, the largest of the year at Fenway, was on its feet going wild. The Red Sox quickly loaded the bases and Yastrzemski was at bat.

Yaz is the hitter. He holds the bat high over his head as he studies Chance. The Minnesota right-hander looks in for his sign, now he's ready, throws . . . Yaz swings and lines a ball into centerfield for a base hit . . . one run is in, two runs are in . . .

Yastrzemski had done it again. Another dramatic hit. For a month now he seemed to hit a home run when the Red Sox needed a home run or single when they needed a single or make a fantastic catch when that was called for. Now it was the final day of the regular season and he was still performing miracles.

The Red Sox got five runs in the sixth and when Yastrzemski went out to left field and Lonborg walked to the mound the crowd stood to cheer their heroes. There was nothing we could add to the scene. All we could do was listen to the crowd.

In the eighth inning I moved downstairs to the Red Sox clubhouse. The TV equipment was ready. All we needed was a Red Sox win. There were two outs to go. Now one. Rich Rollins was the batter.

A pop fly to shortstop . . . Petrocelli is under it . . . The Red

Sox win, 5-3 . . . the Red Sox have clinched at least a tie for the pennant.

The players came racing through the clubhouse doors laughing and shouting and crying and patting each other on the back. All but Lonborg. He was being held aloft at that instant by delirious fans who wouldn't let him go. They wanted to hold him and touch him and share this moment with him. Finally he came into the clubhouse, without a cap, his blond hair disheveled, his face filled with sweat, his body looking limp and burned out.

"Lonnie, Lonnie . . ."

I stuck out my hand and congratulated him and asked him what it had been like out there riding on the shoulders of the fans.

"Scary," he said, "I could only think of them dropping me in their enthusiasm and being trampled under the crowd."

There was much shouting and laughing and pushing in the Boston clubhouse. Finally, we were able to get Tom Yawkey over to the cameras. The popular Boston owner, who had waited so long for this day, was almost speechless.

"Wonderful, wonderful," he said, "now let's go upstairs and root for the Angels."

Detroit led California at that instant, 3-1, with Denny McLain pitching for the Tigers. If they won, it would be tied. If they lost, the Red Sox had the pennant.

In a few minutes our broadcast was over and the station switched to Detroit for a play-by-play of the Detroit game. The Angels had scored seven more runs and had taken the lead, 8-3.

The players were still in uniform and gathered around the radio in the clubhouse. The merriment was restrained as everybody awaited the outcome.

Lee Stange sipped a beer and Williams came over to him and said, "You have to take it easy. You're our pitcher if we have to have a playoff with them."

Stange put down the beer and moved closer to the radio. The Tigers were batting in the home half of the ninth inning trailing, 8-5.

The Angels were one out away from beating the Tigers. Al Kaline was Detroit's on-deck hitter. He was the tying run.

"Don't let that guy get up," Stange said.

Then the players let out a scream. The Angels had won the ball game and the Red Sox had won the pennant. There was applause for Mr. Yawkey and champagne glasses clicking all around. It had happened.

Twelve hours after I had left home I pulled the car into the driveway. Ellen and the kids had all calmed down by then and we finished a quiet dinner. I went to bed happy and exhausted.

A few days later a record came out with all the highlights of the season. It was called "The Impossible Dream," the marvelous song from the stirring play *Man of La Mancha.*

It was a couple of weeks later before I had a chance to sit down quietly in my den, put the record on the record player and listen to "The Impossible Dream."

I just sat there all alone in the dark room and cried.

Chuck Thompson

11

Sudden Death

CHUCK THOMPSON

A friendly, smooth delivery and a cocked Alpine hat on his head are the trademarks of Chuck Thompson, the bouncy voice of the Baltimore Orioles.

Tall, thin and distinguished looking, Thompson grew up in Reading, Pa. He was born in Palmer, Mass. He began his career as a vocalist.

"I knew in a hurry that I wasn't going to make it as a singer," said Thompson, "so I began moving toward announcing." He began broadcasting while still in high school on WRAW, a 250-watt station in Reading. He had played all sports in high school and drifted into the coverage of college sports, including his first games at Albright College and Carnegie Tech, then a national football power.

In the fall of 1941, Thompson was hired by station WIBG as a staff announcer in Philadelphia. He covered all local sports, including Temple football games, until he entered the service in World War II. He got into the tag end of the Battle of the Bulge, serving with the Recon Troop of the 30th Infantry in Europe.

Chuck Thompson

"After the war," he said, "I knew I definitely wanted to stay in sports broadcasting. That was one of the good things about the Army. It gave you plenty of time to think."

Thompson came back to Philadelphia, did high school basketball games and got his big break when John B. Kelly, father of movie actress Grace Kelly—Princess Grace of Monaco—liked his work and wanted him to do horse racing broadcasts.

"He wanted me to go to Florida to learn to do racing," said Thompson. "I had never done any race broadcasting before. My first chance to do baseball came at the same time. I broke in with Byrum Saam and Claude Haring in 1947."

Thompson did the Philadelphia Phillies and Athletics baseball, college football and high school basketball games in the Philadelphia area.

In 1949, Thompson moved to Baltimore where he did the football games of the Baltimore Colts in the old All-America Conference and the baseball games of the minor league Baltimore Orioles.

In 1950, the Colts became part of the National Football League and in 1954 the St. Louis Browns moved to Baltimore in the American League. Thompson became one of the few broadcasters of both major league baseball and professional football. It was also in 1954 that Thompson did the first weekly national telecast of NFL football—on Saturday nights with the Dumont Network. This was in the pioneer days with no analysts, no "color" men, no instant replay and no stop-action.

When sponsorship of the Oriole games was changed, he began doing the baseball games of the Washington Senators and spent fall Saturdays broadcasting Navy football games. Thompson resumed broadcasting of Baltimore baseball in 1961 and has done professional football as part of CBS's national staff.

A grandfather of four, he spent some memorable days with the Baltimore Orioles in 1966 and again in 1969 and 1970 when they won American League pennants. Here he describes a football game on December 28, 1958, regarded by many as "the greatest football game ever played."

Chuck Thompson

On Thursday night, three days before the National Football League championship game between the New York Giants and the Baltimore Colts, I sat in my room at the Roosevelt Hotel and printed my game plan for myself.

I did the same kind of scouting on both teams.

In my small note book, I wrote down the number and name of every player on both teams. Then next to his name I wrote down a few pieces of information about each player. This was to help me bring some color to the broadcast of the championship game. Most of the information on the Colts I had acquired from working with them. Most of the information on the Giants I had gotten from various sources, newspapers, magazines, personal interviews, press brochures and my own observations.

I tried to know as much about each player as I could. I remember the notations I had about the two most important members of the Baltimore Colts.

In my Baltimore page it read: number 19, Johnny Unitas, hometown, Pittsburgh, Pa., college, Louisville . . . acquired by the Colts as a free agent for an 80-cent phone call.

There could be no greater bargain in the history of football. Unitas hadn't been good enough to make a pro team when he graduated from college so he had spent his time playing semi-pro football. Then a phone call from Don Kellett of the Colts to Unitas at his Pittsburgh home resulted in the signing of Unitas.

"I would have to say that he represented the best 80 cents we ever spent," Kellett said. "It might be the best 80 cents anybody ever spent."

The Unitas story was familiar in Baltimore. I didn't think it was that familiar yet across the country. I knew it wasn't because the Colts weren't that familiar yet.

The entry on Alan Ameche, the big, bruising fullback from the University of Wisconsin, mentioned his uncle, Don Ameche, who did not really invent the telephone, and also Alan's deep love for opera and classical music. Here was this big, tough, hard-running fullback spending much of his off-time listening to opera either on record, on radio or actually in opera houses. We don't often think of professional football players as deeply sensitive human beings. Ameche was certainly the exception.

I went down my list and filled out my notes. I included some material on the coaches, Weeb Ewbank of the Colts and Jim Lee Howell of the Giants. Weeb had taken over the Colts in 1954 after they were 3-9 for the season and moved them up to first place in five years with a 9-3 record. His master stroke was, of course, recognizing the brilliance of Johnny Unitas when most others had passed him over. Jim Lee Howell's career was quite similar to Weeb's. He had also taken over a 3-9 club after the 1953 season and had moved the Giants into the world championship in 1956, the Eastern Conference title again in this year of 1958, and now a shot at the championship.

Friday afternoon I took a taxi from the hotel uptown to Yankee Stadium. I watched both clubs work out on the field, checked for any last-minute injuries and then went back downtown to the office of Commissioner Bert Bell.

At the commissioner's office, I received the usual briefing about the game and witnessed the coin-tossing so that the play-by-play schedule could be worked out. The commissioner tossed the coin, I called heads, it came up tails, and I was assigned the first half of the football game.

I sat in the hotel room Friday night, called home to inquire how excited my wife, Rose, and our three children were before the big game, watched some television and drifted off to sleep.

On Saturday morning the weather seemed perfect for a football game. It was clear and cold with the temperatures just slightly below freezing. I took a cab back up to Yankee Stadium and watched the two teams work out before they were secluded for the final hours before the game.

Saturday night I bought the evening papers and went to bed early. I knew I wasn't going to be able to sleep very late Sunday morning. I told the hotel operator to call me at 7:00 o'clock.

At 6:30 I awoke without a call, checked the watch, and saw that it was almost time to get up anyway. Now I began to realize this was a championship game and millions of people would be watching me. I was a little more nervous as I dressed than I would have been for a regular-season game but I was still under control. It was a lot like show business. You are supposed to be a little nervous and excited but you aren't supposed to forget your lines. I had a lot of my lines in that little notebook with all the names and numbers and I made sure it was in good order before I went down for breakfast.

I read the Sunday *Times* over breakfast and noted that there had been no lineup changes and both coaches were confident of victory. The Giants seemed to have the edge only because they were a veteran team with championship experience. They had won the title in 1956 and most of that experienced team was back in this game, led by Charlie Conerly, Frank Gifford, Alex Webster, Kyle Rote, Sam Huff and Andy Robustelli.

I finished breakfast, went back up to my room, packed my notebook and took off for Yankee Stadium. I got into a cab outside the hotel and told the driver where I was going.

"You gonna see the game?" he asked.

"Yes, I am," I said.

"Who do you like?"

"Baltimore."

"Geez," he said, "I don't think they got much of a chance. That kid quarterback, what's his name?"

"Unitas."

"Yeh, Unitas, that's him, he don't seem ready for such a big game."

"Well, that's what we will find out today."

"Yeh, I guess so."

Unitas was the main point of interest for both teams as well as for cab drivers. He had joined the Colts in 1956, and now, with less than three full seasons as the quarterback of the Colts, he had them in a championship game. Nobody could be sure how he would hold up.

The cab pulled up in front of the press gate at Yankee Stadium. I walked inside the big ball park.

I followed the ritual I had followed all season. I first went to the officials' room and chatted with them for a while. They were a little tense. A championship game does that to people. You try and tell yourself it's just another game but you never believe it. Everybody from the players to the peanut vendors know there is something special about a championship game.

The players were, of course, the most tense. There was little conversation in the dressing room of the Giants as I said hello to Jim Lee Howell and wished him well. You could hear the tugs and grunts in the locker room as the players pulled on their heavy equipment. The Colt locker room was about the same. I looked over at Unitas, waved a greeting and kept moving around the locker room to Weeb. Football players just don't have time for much sociability before a championship game.

"Good luck, Weeb," I said.

"Thank you, Chuck. I hope we give you a good game to broadcast."

There was no doubt about that. A championship game has drama built in. No matter what the score, there really can't be a dull championship game. This one was certainly not going to have any problems like that.

I left the locker room, walked over to the press room, had a sandwich, chatted with the Baltimore and New York writers and walked to the elevator in the Stadium Club. I rode to the press level and walked across the press box to the NBC broadcasting location.

I checked the program for any number changes, put my notebook in front of me, prepared the information on my spotting board and looked at the clock. We had twenty minutes before air time. I asked the press box runner to get me a cup of coffee.

The day was perfect for football. The sky was clear and the temperature was 28 degrees. There was very little wind as I checked the flags atop the Stadium. I looked out across the field to where the baseball monuments sat in centerfield. This was a historic ball park, maybe the most historic in all sports, with its grand baseball tradition and its years of excellent football.

Good afternoon, ladies and gentlemen and welcome to Yankee Stadium in New York City for the National Football League championship game between the Baltimore Colts and the New York Giants.

I had covered the Colts all season and I was closely identified with them but I made a point of not showing any difference in my voice when I described the Baltimore players or the New York players. This was a national telecast and fairness and objective reporting were the main objects of the broadcast.

. . . and at quarterback for the Baltimore Colts, out of Louisville University, number 19 . . . Johnny Unitts.

There were 64,185 people in the stands that afternoon, most of them home fans rooting for a New York victory, but they stood and cheered and whistled as Unitas ran on the field. He was a dramatic figure, a reject, who had by his own determination and courage, forced his way into a first-string job with the Colts. He had thrown a touchdown pass in every one of the games he had played for the Colts since taking over the number one job from

George Shaw in October of 1956. People were beginning to recognize his great skills.

The crowd let out a huge roar as Steve Myhra approached the ball, kicked it, and the 1958 championship of the National Football League was about to be settled.

The Giants, playing conservatively, carefully, feeling out the Colts, stayed on the ground. They alternated ground plays with first Alex Webster carrying, then Frank Gifford, then Mel Triplett coming off the bench for a key carry.

New York moved to the Baltimore 36 in the middle of the first quarter where they stalled. On fourth down Pat Summerall, their great kicker, came in off the bench for a field-goal try.

There's the snap . . . Conerly puts the ball down . . . the kick is . . . good. The Giants lead, 3-0.

The home crowd cheered Summerall's kick and settled back to watch the Giants kick off to Baltimore. The score had come with a tough ground attack and a field goal and the Giants had drawn first blood. That was supposed to be the way to win football games. Make the other guy play catch-up football and force him to put the ball into the air.

In the second period it was Baltimore's turn to move. With Unitas dropping quick passes to Ameche over the middle and to his ends, Raymond Berry and Jim Mutscheller, the Colts drove to the Giant two-yard line. There Unitas called on Ameche to drive it in and the opera-loving fullback drove across the goal for the first Baltimore score. It was 7-3 for Baltimore as Steve Myhra kicked the extra point.

The Giants failed to move on the tough Baltimore defense and Unitas, brilliant in his play selections, drove them downfield again. Now the ball was on the Giant 15.

Unitas back to pass, he looks downfield, he's got Berry all alone . . . touchdown Baltimore.

Berry, who wasn't that fast, but was very sharp with his moves, had cut in front of two Giant defenders, moved quickly to the outside and had caught the ball over his right shoulder without a defender within three steps of him. Now the Colts led the Giants, 14-3, with less than five minutes to play in the half.

New York again failed to move and punted to the Colts with two minutes to go in the half. Coolly, quickly, methodically, Unitas moved them back downfield again. A score now might break the game wide open and that was what Unitas was trying to do. He hit Berry again for a first down on the Giant 47.

The Colts huddled again, taking so much time that it was obvious Unitas was outlining a pass pattern. They broke the huddle and quickly came to the line.

Unitas back to pass, looks downfield, he throws long to Mutscheller . . . incomplete.

Unitas couldn't keep them moving and the half ended with the Colts ahead 14-3.

When the second half began, the Colts came on the field with the knowledge that they just had to hold the Giants for 30 more minutes and they would be champions of the world—the first championship in the team's history.

The Giants weren't about to give up that easily. In the middle of the third quarter they began a drive that carried them down to the Baltimore one-yard line. Charlie Conerly gave the ball to his husky fullback, Mel Triplett, who charged in over right tackle and scored standing up. Now the Colt lead was down to 14-10.

Unitas couldn't move the Colts and the Giants took over early in the fourth quarter. Conerly passed to Rote for seven. Gifford hit the middle for three. Conerly hit Gifford with a pass over the middle. Webster gained five.

Conerly back to pass, he's got Gifford in the right side of the end zone . . . touchdown . . . the Giants lead, 17-14.

Yankee Stadium was going crazy. The Giant fans had a strange feeling about Conerly. He had been with the team for ten years and had some brilliant days and some not-so-brilliant days. When he was good they loved him. When he was bad they booed him. Now he was being cheered madly as he jogged off the field and all the Giants bounced off the bench to congratulate him. Charlie Conerly was the man of the hour.

But the hour of football wasn't quite over.

Babe Chandler boomed his punt to Baltimore and with 90 seconds left in the game, Johnny Unitas put a football helmet on over his crew cut, said something to Weeb Ewbank, pulled the chin strap tight and trotted on to the field.

The greatest drama of the day was about to begin.

The Colts had the ball on their own 14-yard line, and Unitas went to work. He passed to midfield to Raymond Berry, who made a brilliant catch between two Giant defenders at the sideline. He passed again to Berry for 12 yards. He tried a couple of running plays. He hit Berry again with 48 seconds to go. Now there were 13 seconds left in the game and the Giants led, 17-14. Steve Myhra was running in from the Baltimore bench. The Colts had no time-outs left and the clock was running.

Twelve seconds . . . 11 . . . 10 . . . 9 . . . the ball is snapped . . . seven . . . Myrha's kick is up . . . good. The Colts have tied the score 17-17.

The fans were confused, shocked, upset, surprised. They thought the game was over, they thought the Giants had won, and now the referees were gathered in midfield and there was a new toss of the coin.

The Giants have won the toss and will receive . . .

Now they had all the momentum. This was sudden death. One score and the game would be over. Pat Summerall, the brilliant field-goal kicker for the Giants, stood on the sidelines watching the Colts kick off. If the Giants could move the ball some 60 yards downfield Summerall had a chance to win it for them. He was a deadly accurate kicker from anywhere inside the 40-yard line.

Third down for the Giants from their own 27. The biggest play of the game for them. Conerly over the ball. Back to pass. He's trapped, he charges forward, is hit . . . is piled up . . . it's very close, and they are bringing out the chains . . . the chains are down . . .

The sounds of frustration and agony filled Yankee Stadium. The Giants had missed the first down by six inches and now had to kick the ball to Baltimore.

Unitas was ready on the sidelines. Don Chandler punted for New York and Baltimore had the ball on its own 20 as Unitas called his first play. He hit Berry with a pass for 10. He sent Ameche over the middle for three. He passed to Berry again for 12 along the right sideline stripe. Now the Colts were moving again. They had the ball on the 44. Now Unitas hit Berry for a long gain into Giant territory. It was another first down.

The ball was on the 38-yard line. Baltimore could have kicked a field goal from here. Steve Myhra was ready. He had kicked the tying field goal from the 20. Unitas wanted the ball a little closer.

As the Colts huddled, Harry Coyle, who was directing the show for NBC, told me we had lost our picture. The game didn't stop. Unitas broke the huddle and the Colts came to the line. Now I was on television with no picture. I quickly switched to radio-type coverage, describing just about everything I saw. The red light staring at me with no picture in the monitor was a disturbing sight.

The Colts continued to grind the ball toward the goal—I had to tell everyone how they were doing it. When the ball came to rest on the Giant 18, we broke for a studio commercial.

"Are we all right, Harry?"

"I think we have the picture back okay now. We'll know after the next exchange," was Coyle's reply.

The studio commercial ended and the picture of Yankee Stadium came back clean and clear. It took a lot of pressure off me. Considering the happenings on the field, it's a good thing we did get that picture back.

We had used up all commercial time-outs so the game went on without a break as Unitas gathered the team in the huddle. They were still not going to try a field goal. A pass to Berry on the sideline at the 11. Now to Ameche over the middle to the four yard line. The Colts huddled again. The crowd was on its feet. Unitas' head peeked out from the top of the huddle to look at the Giants' defense.

"We didn't want to go for a field goal," Weeb Ewbank explained years later. "We just didn't want to take a chance of something going wrong with the snap or of Myhra missing the kick. We felt we were that close and the easiest way to get it into the end zone was to carry it in."

Here come the Colts to the line of scrimmage . . . Unitas over the center . . . the ball is snapped . . . given to Ameche . . . he is over . . . for a touchdown . . . the Colts are the world champions. Alan Ameche has scored from the one-yard line . . . the Colts win, 23-17.

The clock showed eight minutes and 35 seconds gone in the first overtime period in the history of the professional football championship and the fans were racing on the field to get near Ameche, to get near Unitas, to get near any of the Colts and just touch them before they disappeared into the locker room.

It was dusk as I got back into a cab and rode back downtown to the Roosevelt Hotel. The cab driver, this time, was quiet and I had time to think about the game. It was such a marvelous contest and I was so glad to have been part of it. I thought of the brilliance of Unitas and the drive of Ameche and the toughness of all the Colts. I was glad I knew them. I was glad I was part of all this.

After all, as sports writers were to write later, "This was the greatest game ever played, this was football's finest hour."

Baltimore's Alan Ameche wins it with his score in sudden-death overtime.

Don Dunphy

12

Knockout

DON
DUNPHY

In the golden era of boxing some 25 years ago, when the Friday night fights were as much a part of the New York sports scene as Toots Shor, one voice brought the sport to all America.

It belonged to Don Dunphy, whose controlled eloquence captured the drama and excitement of the great bouts of the 1940s and 1950s.

Dunphy, who is now a free-lance broadcaster and still specializes in boxing with the Fight of the Month Series, has broadcast almost every sport including baseball's World Series, football bowl games, track meets, bowling and wrestling. He has also done some marvelous word pictures of such varied events as the St. Patrick's Day Parade and the Easter Parade in New York City.

Dunphy began his career after graduation from Manhattan College in New York. He worked as a part-time journalist on the *New York Journal-American* and the *New York World-Telegram* and then became the public relations director of the New York Coliseum in the Bronx where he became interested in boxing and began his on-the-air career with the sport.

"I got a job doing fights for station WINS," says Dunphy, "and that was my first break. WINS broadcast the Diamond Belt Bouts and I did 24 three-round bouts in the same night wearing a stiff tuxedo. If you think that didn't test a man, you are wrong."

Most of the big fights of the day were network broadcasts. The old Red and Blue networks of the National Broadcasting Company, Mutual Broadcasting and the Columbia Broadcasting System controlled the bigger events. WINS had a Saturday boxing show before big fights. Dunphy interviewed fight people on that show.

"I still couldn't get a chance to do a big bout because the networks would use Sam Taub, Bill Stern or Ted Husing for championship fights. It wasn't easy to break through," he says.

Because of a network conflict, there was an opening to do the heavyweight championship fight on June 18, 1941, from New York's Polo Grounds, between Joe Louis and Billy Conn.

"About six weeks before the fight," Dunphy says, "I heard Husing couldn't do it. There was going to be an audition for the job."

The audition would be held live the night of the Gus Lesnevich-Anton Christoforidis light heavyweight championship fight.

Some of the people auditioning for the job included Paul Douglas, who later went on to fame as an actor, Jimmy Powers, the sports editor of the New York *Daily News*, Bert Lee, a local sportscaster, and Dunphy.

"We each did two rounds of the fight," says Dunphy. "I won it easy."

Dunphy's skill was evident. His cleverness was just as evident.

"While the others were doing the fight and struggling over the names of Gus Lesnevich and Anton Christoforidis I decided to call the fighters Gus and Anton," Dunphy says.

While the other auditioners were falling over the names, Dunphy was giving a clear, complete, concise description of the fight.

Dunphy embarked on his fight broadcasting career which lasted 24 years until 1964. When the fight business declined, Dunphy confined his broadcasting to other sports.

Dunphy, who has two sons in the broadcasting business, enjoys continuing in the fight game again now with the revised Fight of the Month Series.

But it will be a long time before an audience will sit as spellbound alongside their radios (or TV sets) to hear a fight as they did one hot night in New York.

It is June 18, 1941, and Don Dunphy is at the ring apron in the Polo Grounds.

Don Dunphy

On the morning of June 18, 1941, the first edition of the New York newspapers were filled with the latest news from the fight camps of Billy Conn and Joe Louis.

The handsome tough Irishman from Pittsburgh and the Brown Bomber from Detroit were scheduled to meet that night in the Polo Grounds for the heavyweight championship of the world. The drama had been building for weeks.

Louis, the first black heavyweight champion since Jack Johnson, was the heavy favorite for the fight. Louis had been eliminating all his opponents and Conn just seemed to be the most available man around for a fight.

Conn, cocky and brash, had told anybody who would listen that he was going to beat the heavyweight champion. It certainly seemed like an idle boast. Conn wasn't big enough, strong enough or skilled enough to withstand the pounding Louis was expected to give him. Conn had one thing going for him. He was quick. He could box and hit and move.

"Nobody," wrote one sports writer, "can keep moving long enough to stay away from Joe Louis all night."

Louis, 27 years old, was at the physical peak of his brilliant career. He had come out of the black ghetto of Detroit, Joseph Louis Barrow, with fists flailing to win the Golden Gloves and launch a brilliant career. It was marred only by an upset knockout at the hands of Germany's Max Schmeling, and Louis avenged that loss with a devastating knockout of the German the next time they met.

Conn, 24, was handsome and dimpled, a flashy dresser, a quick talker, a guy who liked the attention of the public and the affection of the girls. In interviews he left little doubt that, despite what sportswriters were saying, he would knock Louis out and prove he was the best fighter in the world.

"I'm going to knock Louis out and be the champion for the next 20 years," Conn said.

The preliminary bouts were almost over. Now it was almost time for the main event, the heavyweight championship of the world between Billy Conn and Joe Louis.

I sat in my seat against the apron of the ring and looked up at the preliminary fighters finishing their eight-rounder. Louis and Conn were in their dressing rooms under the stands at the Polo Grounds getting ready for their appearance.

The electricity began building as the clock moved toward fight time. I could see several famous people in the audience as I looked over my shoulder at the mass of humanity gathered behind me. Ace Parker, the great football player of the Brooklyn Dodgers, was a couple of rows behind me. James Farley, President Roosevelt's Postmaster-General, was a few rows to my left. James Cox, who had been defeated by Warren Harding for the Presidency of the United States in 1920, was off to my right.

From the Polo Grounds in New York City . . . the heavyweight championship of the world. Joe Louis, the champion versus Billy Conn, the challenger . . .

Now the noise from the crowd told me that one of the fighters was making his entrance from under the stands. More than 55,000 people were on their feet screaming and whistling and yelling.

Billy Conn, all smiles, his head covered with a towel, his arm raised high in the air, was marching down the aisle to the ring. He appeared confident and sure of himself. The reputation of Louis had done nothing to damage the self-confidence of Conn.

Conn approaches the ring, climbs over the ropes, dances to his corner and begins loosening up.

From the other side of the ball park, from approximately where Mel Ott used to hit his home runs, they applauded as Joe Louis made his way to the ring. He moved slowly, carefully, his head almost buried under a towel, his face bent down, his eyes on his shoes, his huge hands hanging loose at his sides. He reached the ring, climbed up slowly, and quietly made his move toward his corner. He took off his towel and began throwing quick punches into the air.

The crowd was almost all on its feet now as ring announcer Harry Balough began introducing the celebrities in the crowd. "The light heavyweight champion of the world, Gus Lesnevich." The crowd cheered Gus and I felt like getting up in the ring and shaking his hand myself. I knew that Gus and my friend Anton were responsible for me being in this seat as I broadcast the championship fight to all America.

Now Balough was preparing for his introductions and the timekeeper rang the bell several times as Harry readied for the announcement.

"In this corner . . . from Pittsburgh, Pennsylvania . . . weighing 174 pounds . . ."

There was a gasp from the crowd. They couldn't believe Conn's weight. He had actually come in under the heavyweight limit and seemed so much smaller than Louis that people were actually afraid for him.

Conn is wearing purple trunks with a white stripe. He pulls his towel down over his neck now and his curly brown hair seems to shine under the ring lights.

". . . the challenger, Billy Conn."

The noise was deafening. It seemed as if twice the crowd that was in the Polo Grounds was cheering Conn.

Now Louis was introduced and before Harry could get out too many words the cheering drowned out his introductions. We could hear them up front and on our broadcast but I was certain nobody heard them in the bleachers.

". . . from Detroit . . . weighing 199, the Brown Bomber . . . Joe Louis."

The noise filled the air and rose like a tidal wave across the ball park and out beyond the streets. All New York had to hear it. Now the two fighters were in the center of the ring.

Referee Eddie Joseph is talking to the fighters, giving them their instructions, Louis, his head bent, Conn, smiling, looking at the champion, Joseph, holding onto the microphone . . .

"Let's have a good, clean fight, now touch gloves and come out fighting," Joseph said.

The air was filled with tension. I felt my voice and my throat going dry for an instant. I took a deep breath and I was fine. I knew I would be ready as soon as the bell rang. Bill Corum, the columnist for the *Journal-American*, was my color man and he was sizing the fighters up as they went back to their corners.

There was a clang of the bell, another huge roar, and the fight was on. Joe Louis and Billy Conn for the heavyweight championship of the world.

Conn dances out quickly to the center of the ring, flicks a left to Louis's nose. The champion moves around it. Now Louis moves toward Conn, throws a light left, looks for an opening, stays away from a short right by the challenger . . .

It was not long before the pattern of the fight was set. Conn would not slug with Louis. No man in his right mind would. He would box and move with him. He would throw long left-hand leads and try to catch Louis off balance. The champion would stalk

129

Don Dunphy

Conn, moving relentlessly after him, trying to get inside, trying to slow the challenger down.

Louis hits Conn with a hard left to the face, a short right on the side of the head as Conn moves away . . . ten seconds to the end of round one. . . . Louis a long left. . . . There's the bell. . . . Bill.

Corum gave the first round to Louis. He said the champion had caught Conn with a couple of lefts even though the challenger had moved quickly. It was obviously Conn's hope to box and run all fifteen rounds and tire Louis out. Joe had been knocking out most of his opponents so early nobody knew if he could last the full fifteen rounds if he had to.

There's the bell for the second round. Conn quickly reaches out with a long left . . . Louis, a sharp right to the chest of Billy Conn . . . Louis another left to Conn's jaw . . . Conn, backing up, moving away from the champion, flicks out a right, misses with a left . . . Louis after him, throws a short right-handed burst to the head, grazes Conn, who keeps moving, dancing, feinting . . .

Conn was quick. There was little question of that. He knew that he had to keep away from Louis to win. He would make the champion chase him all over the ring, flick at him, and hope to wear the heavier man down.

Ten seconds until the end of round two . . . Louis a left hand, Conn blocks it, Louis a soft right hand. . . . There's the bell.

Round three. The pattern continues. Conn, moving back, away, ducking the champion's punches. Louis moving in, looking for his opening, throwing punches, waiting for that one spot where he can land the killing blow.

Louis reaches out just above us, lands a hard right and a left on Conn's nose . . . Billy is down . . . it's a slip, not a knockdown . . . referee Eddie Joseph rubs off Billy's gloves and motions for the fighters to continue . . . Joe after the challenger, throws another left . . . Conn, backing up toward the ropes . . . there's blood coming from the bridge of Conn's nose . . . Louis is after him . . . throws another left . . . Billy slips away, ties Louis up and Eddie Joseph breaks the fighters apart in the middle of the ring . . . thirty seconds until the end of round three . . . thirty seconds . . . Conn dances away from the champion . . . Louis looks for his opening, throws a short left . . . ten seconds to go . . . there's the bell. Bill.

"That was the best round for the champion," said Corum. "He has opened up a cut on Billy's nose and the challenger is being worked over in his corner. Louis sits quietly in his corner waiting for the bell for the fourth round, Manny Seeman rubbing the back of his neck. There's the bell, here's Don."

Round four for the heavyweight championship of the world, fifteen rounds, Billy Conn in purple trunks, the challenger, and Joe Louis, in white trunks, the champion . . .

The blow to the nose seemed to wake the challenger up. Billy came out quicker that round and threw punches faster. Now he seemed to be moving better and throwing more punches. Louis wasn't able to throw as many punches as Conn continued to hit him on the the shoulders, on the neck and on the chest. Conn hit Louis with a hard left to the stomach and the champion winced. It seemed to take some of the steam out of him. This was Conn's first good round. Now Louis was moving slower. This was what Conn had been trying to accomplish all night.

In the fifth round, Conn came out with more confidence. He had obviously won the fourth round and now he was moving faster around the champion, poking him with lefts and rights, flicking at his face and shoulders, not doing much damage, but tiring Louis a little and annoying the champion, who just couldn't seem to get his fight going.

In the sixth and seventh rounds, Conn worked around Louis with great speed. The champion would almost corner him and he would slip away and reach out to smack Louis on the nose. Then a quick right hand over the heart and another combination to the champion's stomach.

Conn flicking his punches at Louis, moving, moving, moving . . . Louis looking a little annoyed . . . moves after Conn, reaches out with a left hand, misses . . . Conn hits Louis with a hard left hand to the ribs and Joe is forced back a little.

Conn was starting to gain confidence now as he was hitting Joe as he moved away. He hit Louis a hard left hand, smiled at the champion and said, "How did you like that one, Joe?" The champion never answered. He just kept moving after Conn, working for his opening, hoping to push the challenger into a mistake.

Conn continued to poke away at Louis in the eighth, ninth and tenth rounds. There was still some blood coming from Conn's nose but he seemed to be gaining the upper hand in the fight.

Conn, a hard left to the champion's head. Louis winces but moves back in. Ten seconds to go in round ten, ten seconds. Conn a left hand to the jaw misses, Louis a short left, Conn moves away from it. There's the bell for round ten. Bill.

"Don, the fight is even on my card. I have Conn taking four of the last five rounds and the champion is getting tired. He has been chasing Billy all night. If Conn can keep this up for five more rounds I believe the world will see a new heavyweight champion crowned here tonight. But remember that Louis hasn't uncorked that killing right hand yet tonight. If he gets that loose, it could change things."

Now the noise was increasing with every blow and it was impossible to determine if they were rooting for a comeback by Joe or if they were rooting for Conn to continue with his hit and run attack on the champion. With each blow the crowd got louder and louder as they were carried away with the action. I just concentrated on the fight. I have always believed that I would continue broadcasting a fight if the fighters stayed there even if a building fell down beside me.

Round eleven. Both fighters move to the center of the ring. Louis is short with a left. Conn, a left to the head of Louis. A right by Joe is short. Conn, a left to the head moves Joe back. . . . There's the bell.

Round twelve. Louis looking awfully tired. Conn, bouncy and fresh, flicks a left at the champion's head. He moves away from Louis, throws a right, misses with another right, ties Joe up . . . Conn staggers Louis . . . There's the bell for round twelve.

"Those were Conn's rounds," said Corum. "I have Billy ahead 7-5 on my card. It's unofficial, of course, but the champion is in trouble."

"Round thirteen. Here's Don."

Conn came out from his corner with a wide smile on his face. He knew he had the fight if he could keep away from Louis for three more rounds. Joe was tiring and the lighter man still had some steam left. They boxed in the middle of the ring, Conn flicking out his punches, Louis short most of the time, moving after Conn, trying for that one opening, that one move that would change the complexion of the fight.

Conn hits Louis with a short left. Now the challenger moves in, pursues Louis, throws a left and a right . . . Conn looks like he is trying for a knockout, he throws a long left, misses, Louis, a hard right to the mouth of the challenger . . . Billy is staggered . . . that hurt him . . . Louis moves in . . . a hard right hand uppercut to Conn's jaw . . . Conn is reeling back . . . the crowd is going wild . . . Louis crashes a left hook to the side of Conn's face . . Conn is trying to get away . . . Louis hits him with a vicious right to the head . . . Conn is down . . . Billy Conn is down . . . Louis going to a neutral corner . . . referee Eddie Joseph picks up the count . . . Conn is on his back trying to roll over . . . seven . . . eight . . . Conn is getting to one knee . . .

Now Conn was struggling to get up on that one knee. He was brave. He just couldn't make it.

. . . nine . . . ten . . . it's over, it's all over . . . Joe Louis has knocked out Billy Conn to retain his heavyweight championship of the world. Conn is being led to his corner. He doesn't believe the fight is over. He is pleading with referee Eddie Joseph to let the fight go on.

Harry Balough moves to the microphone as the crowd screams and people push their way forward for a glimpse of the fighters. Hundreds of people are trying to get into the ring and the fighters are surrounded by police, by photographers and by the crowd. Now Balough moves to the microphone.

"The time . . . two minutes and 58 seconds of the thirteenth round . . . the winner and still heavyweight champion of the world . . . Joe Louis."

Balough lifted the right arm of Louis high in the air and the champion made a small wave to the crowd. His face was as clean, and unmarked, as when the fight started. He was impassive in victory as he had been throughout the entire night.

Louis is standing in the center of the ring surrounded by photographers now. Manny Seeman is hugging the champion and looking for Conn. Now he goes over to the other side of the ring, shakes Billy's hand and pats him on the back. The challenger is shaking his head. He still seems bewildered. Billy Conn was within three rounds of becoming the heavyweight champion of the world.

In the dressing room later, Conn sat on a table, his face still handsome and his eyes still clear, despite a cut on his nose and a slight cut on his lip. He had avoided being hit most of the fight but in the space of a few seconds in the 13th round he had felt the power in the fists of Joe Louis. Reporters wanted to know if he thought he had won the fight. Most reporters agreed he was ahead in the bout until the fateful minutes.

"Yeah, I knew I was ahead," said Conn. "I just thought I could knock him out. I wanted to be the heavyweight champion of the world. I wanted to win it for my mom and my family and for myself. I wanted to do it clean. I wanted to knock him out."

"What happened, Billy," one reporter shouted. "Why did you change your style?"

"I guess I got too much Irish in me," he said. "I lost my head and a million bucks."

Louis was to make $154,404 as his share from the fight and Conn was to receive $77,200 for his share.

I have broadcast thousands of fights but I will never forget that one, for drama, for excitement, for a sudden change in fortune. Billy Conn never got to be the heavyweight champion of the world but he made it a memorable evening for everyone of us who sat in the Polo Grounds that night.

And to this day I always have to be thankful for Lesnevich and Christoforidis having easy first names like Gus and Anton.

*Don Dunphy is at the microphone
as Joe Louis's hand is held aloft,
following his knockout of Billy Conn.*

Marty Glickman

13

The Case of the Missing Miler

MARTY GLICKMAN

MORE than two decades ago, when college basketball was at its peak of interest in New York City, kids would hit on a two-handed set shot in any playground in town and shout, "Good—like Nedick's."

The man who made the phrase and the college basketball games popular from Madison Square Garden was Marty Glickman, the first of the athletes turned sports announcers.

Glickman stepped from the playing fields of Syracuse University right into the broadcasting booth. He moved as easily on the air through baseball, basketball, football, tennis and track as he had as an athlete at Syracuse and as an Olympian on the United States track team in the Berlin games of 1936.

Glickman was born in Brooklyn, played football, basketball and ran track at James Madison High School. At Syracuse University he starred in football as a running halfback and was an outstanding dash man.

"A big day on the football field against Cornell started my broadcasting career," Glickman remembers. "We had beaten Cornell,

Marty Glickman

14-6, and I had scored both touchdowns. A local haberdasher wanted to put me on the air to take advantage of my big game and all the publicity I had received."

Glickman's reaction was hesitant. He had never thought about broadcasting and didn't feel qualified to go on the air.

"You don't want me," he told his prospective employer. "I stammer, I'm nervous and I've never been near a microphone."

"I'll pay you $15 a week," the man said.

"You've got yourself a broadcaster," said Glickman.

Glickman combined his undergraduate career at Syracuse with his sports broadcasting. He was graduated in 1939, took a job with radio station WHN in New York and played pro football on the side with the Jersey City Giants, the farm club of the New York Giants.

In 1942 Glickman teamed with Dick Fishel and Bert Lee on a pre-game and post-game show before and after the Brooklyn Dodger games. Ward Wilson later joined the show as did tennis player Gorgeous Gussie Moran, who made lace panties famous. The shows, called Warm-Up Time and Sports Extra, used the successful format of fans just arguing sports, something all listeners could identify with.

Glickman served as a lieutenant in the Marine Corps with service in the Central Pacific during World War II and returned in 1945 to his broadcasting duties at WHN.

Glickman became the station's sports director and broadcast college basketball games, track meets and most other sports. In 1948 he started doing the play-by-play of the New York Giants football games, an association that continues until the present time.

In basketball his call of "swish" for long, successful shots and "Good —like Nedick's" (a restaurant chain called Nedick's sponsored the games) became part of the lingo for most young basketball players growing up and playing basketball in New York City.

In addition to his play-by-play with the football Giants and basketball announcing, Glickman is president of his own company, Marty Glickman Enterprises, handles high school football games Saturdays on WPIX in New York, is vice president of Manhattan Cable TV, which telecasts all Garden events to subscribers' homes, and is in the camp business.

Glickman, who has two married children and is a youthful-looking grandfather, lives with his wife and two younger children in New Rochelle, New York.

Here he tells the story behind the most unusual track event he ever announced.

Marty Glickman

It was the summer of 1936 in Berlin, Germany, that I first got to know Lou Zamperini.

He was a black-haired boy, wiry, always smiling, with light eyes and wavy hair. He had been born in Olean, New York, but had moved at an early age with his family to Torrance, California, where he had grown up.

Too small and too slight for most other sports, Lou had become a track man in high school and at one time held the interscholastic record for the mile run. He entered the University of Southern California the same year I had entered Syracuse University. I was a dash man and I never thought our paths would cross.

All track men had their minds and their hearts set on one thing in that summer of 1936 and that was making the United States Olympic team. The Games were to be held in Berlin, Germany, some three years before Hitler's legions were to march across Europe and plunge the world into the holocaust of World War II.

Lou Zamperini and I made the team and after the long boat ride across the Atlantic Ocean, we arrived in Germany full of high hopes. Zamperini, Bobby Brown and myself, the three youngest members of the team, became friends. We spent most of our time together in training and seeing the sights of Berlin.

There was one time I wasn't with Zamperini and was glad of it. He had been wandering around downtown Berlin when he had spotted the Nazi swastika flying from the top of the Chancellory Building. Lou decided that he would like to have that flag as a souvenir.

Several afternoons later, wearing his Olympic uniform with the shield of the United States, he went back to the Chancellory Building. He climbed to the top floor and then started up the flag pole that held the flag. He got to the top, captured the flag and slid down the pole. He climbed down right into the hands of a German soldier. I can't remember where I was at the instant the Germans put their hands on Zamperini but I was sure glad I wasn't with him. It just wasn't a healthy time for someone of my faith to be caught stealing Nazi flags in Germany.

The German soldier took Zamperini to the office of the commanding officer. He was interrogated by the officer and asked why he had stolen the Nazi flag.

"I wanted to have a memento of my stay here," he said. "It was just for fun. I didn't mean any harm by it."

The Nazi officer continued to question him, demanding the real reason he had climbed the pole, wanting to know what his political leanings were and if he intended any slight on the Third Reich.

"No, no," said Zamperini. "Nothing like that. I just wanted the flag as a souvenir."

The questioning continued for some time. Finally, the Nazi officer was willing to accept Zamperini's explanation. To show his goodwill he even allowed Zamperini to keep the flag. It was a triumphant Zamperini who returned to Olympic headquarters and showed off his flag.

In a few days the Games began. Zamperini got to run in the 5000-meter race and finished seventh against the best in the world, a highly successful finish for an 18-year-old sophomore in college.

The Olympics ended and Zamperini returned to USC and I went back to Syracuse. I followed his career closely after that and we were together again at a few meets in Madison Square Garden and in the national championships.

In 1938 Zamperini won the National Collegiate Athletic Association mile run in Minneapolis in four minutes, eighteen and three-fifth seconds, an impressive time in those days.

As a result of his good showings in the nationals and in USC meets, Zamperini was invited to run the mile the following season in Madison Square Garden.

A press conference was held before the meet to introduce Zamperini to the New York sports writers. The flag incident in Germany had made him a newsworthy person apart from his exploits on the track. One writer asked if he thought he was lucky being here after being caught by the Nazis.

"I have had a lot of close calls," he said. "I guess it's just my nature to escape from them."

Zamperini then went on to tell the track writers about injuries and illnesses he had survived during his time. It was amazing he could still compete.

"I guess it all started when I was three and a half," he said. "I almost had a toe cut off by a buzz saw. When I was ten I was fooling with some piping, slipped and fell. The pipe went an inch and a half into my right thigh. I was in the hospital for six weeks.

When I was 16 I slipped in a schoolboy track meet, fell on my leg and tore my kneecap loose."

Zamperini said that as soon as he recovered from that injury he was into another. One day he was riding a horse near his home.

"I got off the horse," he said, "the horse reared up and kicked me in the ankle. I was back in the hospital. This time they thought they would have to amputate my leg. But I recovered and here I am."

It was obvious Zamperini was a lucky young man. How lucky he really was would be proven some years later.

Zamperini continued to run for the next couple of years and lowered his time in the mile to four minutes and three seconds. He had a good shot at achieving the national record or perhaps even the world record in the mile when World War II intervened.

By 1942, most healthy young men, including myself and Lou Zamperini, had been called to service. I was in the Marines in the Marshall Islands and Zamperini was in the Army Air Corps in the same area. We didn't get to see each other. Both of us were busy with our separate duties and we lost contact with one another. One day I read the news in Stars and Stripes.

LT. ZAMPERINI REPORTED MISSING; OLYMPIC RUNNER SHOT DOWN

Zamperini had been on a bombing mission over one of the islands in the South Pacific. His plane had been hit by enemy fire, was seen smoking and going down. That was all the Air Corps knew about the incident.

In Torrance, California, Zamperini's parents received the news early in 1944. "We regret to inform you," the telegram said, "that your son, Lt. Louis Zamperini . . . has been reported missing in action."

Mrs. Zamperini told newsmen, "I am sure he will be found. I will not give up. He has gotten into a lot of danger and always come out of it."

The Army Air Corps sent out search parties for the plane but couldn't find any trace of it. On May 28, 1944, the Air Corps declared Zamperini dead.

Mrs. Zamperini was firm. "I will not believe it. I don't care how long he is missing," she said. "I know he will be found some day."

I returned home in 1945 and resumed my broadcasting duties with WHN. The war ended and Lou Zamperini was still listed as killed in action.

The 1946 track and field season was being planned. This would be the first season since the end of the war and it was decided that a special mile run would be held at the Garden during the meet of the Intercollegiate Association of Amateur Athletes of America. One of the events would be called the "Lou Zamperini Memorial Mile." A call was placed to Torrance, California, to invite Lou's parents to witness the meet.

Mrs. Zamperini hadn't changed. She still clung to the hope that her son was alive even though the war had just ended and no trace of him had been found.

"I know he's alive," she said, "and I don't want any event to be called the 'Lou Zamperini Memorial Mile.' "

The Garden agreed to call the event the "Lou Zamperini Invitational Mile" and Mr. and Mrs. Zamperini agreed to come to New York.

It was a few days later that I picked up the newspaper and almost fell over. Mrs. Zamperini's faith had been rewarded. Lou Zamperini was alive!

Zamperini had been discovered with a group of American prisoners of war in the northern part of Japan. He had been there nearly two years.

Soon the papers were filled with his amazing story. Lou had been shot down in the South Pacific. His plane had crashed into the water but several crew members had managed to get out a lifeboat before the plane went under. The lifeboat had drifted 47 days in open sea, covering more than 1600 miles, through intense heat and tropical rains, before being discovered and picked up by a Japanese fishing boat. The fishing boat had taken the survivors back to Japan, where Zamperini had been imprisoned. On the open sea he had survived on nothing but raw fish and in captivity he lived on more raw fish, some rice and a few garden vegetables grown by the prisoners in their camp. His weight went from a high of 155 pounds just before his capture to a low of 87 pounds. He was suffering from malnutrition, malaria and other diseases but was alive.

He was brought back to the United States, placed in a hospital and soon was on the road to recovery. He got back to 147 pounds after an American diet of fresh meat, potatoes, vegetables and gallons of milk and ice cream.

When he was discharged early in 1946 he was asked by reporters if he might actually run again.

"Oh, I think my career is over," he said. "I just will never have the strength again to run competitively." Lou accepted an invita-

The Case of the Missing Miler

tion to come to New York for the start of the "Lou Zamperini Invitational Mile." Mrs. Zamperini had been right in her objections. There certainly would be no memorial mile for Zamperini.

The 1946 season was an exciting one for track and field. All of the athletes were back from service now and competing with the young men who had matured during World War II. Interest was at a high pitch and the Olympics were being planned again for 1948 after a 12-year gap during the war.

The 25th annual IC4A games were scheduled in the Garden for the night of March 2. It was announced that Lou Zamperini would take the starter's gun from Jack Lavelle for one race and give the signal for the start of the mile run. Mrs. Zamperini and the program would call the run the Zamperini "invitational" mile but the press insisted on referring to it as the Zamperini "memorial" mile. There had been few races in track history that had so much drama built in, even before the running, than this one had.

A few days before the race Zamperini came to town and we met for lunch. I hadn't seen him since 1940, but I had read about his exploits in the Pacific, the hardships and the long recuperation period. I didn't know quite what to expect. His appearance surprised me. He looked just marvelous.

"Marty, how are you?"

"I'm fine. How are you? You look great. I can hardly believe it."

"They really fattened me up since I got back," he said.

He seemed a little older, as we both were, but not much else was different. The same smile, the same quick laugh, the same lean, lanky body. He looked as if he could get into a pair of short pants and start running a mile right that minute.

"I don't know what I'll do," he said. "I haven't decided. I guess I'll just rest for a while until I know what I want."

On March 2, 1946, I took a cab from the station to Madison Square Garden. The early crowd was already pouring through the front doors at Eighth Avenue and 50th Street to watch the meet. The two service schools, Army and Navy, were still strong after cornering the market on athletes for the war years and were favored in the meet. Still, the appearance of Zamperini was the highlight attraction.

I climbed into the mezzanine broadcasting booth on the 49th Street side of the Garden to start the broadcast. We did a few of the events and waited for the start of the "Zamperini Invitational Mile" scheduled to be run at 10:00 o'clock.

The story had been in all the papers and was quite familiar to

143

most of the fans in the Garden. Shortly before 10:00 o'clock the milers were called to the officials for registration. Les MacMitchell, who had returned from the Navy and was a student at NYU again, was the favorite in the race.

I could feel my heart pounding a little faster as Zamperini moved on to the track. He was wearing a dark business suit and looked fit and healthy as he stood near the starter, Jack Lavelle. I guess I couldn't help having a lump in my throat when I started describing the scene just before the race.

It is with a great deal of feeling and joy that I am about to broadcast this race. It's certainly wonderful to see him down there. He looks fine and I am happy to report that Lou Zamperini is in good health again.

Now the runners were peeling off their warm-up jackets and loosening up on the 50th Street side of the Garden. The mile would soon start. But first there would be the introductions of the runners.

". . . From New York University . . . Leslie MacMitchell. . . . Representing France . . . Marcel Hansenne. . . . From the New York Athletic Club . . . Tommy Quinn. . . ."

The runners bounced up and down the track, waving upon the announcement of their names, looking at the crowd, waiting for the starter's gun. It was obvious on the track that this time, for the first time in the experience of any of them, the starter seemed more important than the start.

Now we will have the introduction of Zamperini and the start of the race. Listen to the crowd . . .

The noise crashed through the Garden. We could hardly hear Lou's name as the Garden announcer told the crowd what they already knew, that Lou Zamperini had come back from a brush with death to be here this night.

". . . ladies and gentlemen, Captain Lou Zamperini. . . ."

Zamperini waved and more than 18,000 people stood almost as one to applaud the dark-haired young man. He smiled and laughed that hearty laugh of his and said a few words to the officials on the track. Then he turned to the athletes and asked them to get on their marks. This was his night but this was still their race. He didn't want to take any of it away from them.

Lou has called them to their marks. The Garden is still noisy with excitement. Jack Lavelle stands off to one side watching Lou start his race. There's the gun. . . .

Again the fans cheered the start of the race. They were caught up in the emotion of the moment and the noise of the starter's gun was a release for them. They had cheered and yelled and applauded. Now they could settle back and watch the mile run. They had expressed their warmth and affection for Lou Zamperini.

It would be nice to say that the race was historic and that Les MacMitchell or the Frenchman or Tommy Quinn had raced off to a dramatic win and had set a record or had, miraculously, on this emotional night, crashed through the then unreachable barrier of four minutes for a mile.

But none of that was to be.

MacMitchell stepped out quickly. He opened up a long lead on Quinn and Hansenne and by the time the first quarter was run it was evident this would not be a memorable mile. MacMitchell ran a tactical race, keeping enough space between himself and his opposition to coast most of the way. He glided across the finish line in four minutes and sixteen seconds.

MacMitchell is the winner, Hansenne is second and Tommy Quinn is third. There's Lou congratulating Les, smiling, and posing for pictures with him.

It was over now. Lou Zamperini had come back to the Garden, had been accorded a hero's welcome as was fitting and now he would return home to California.

Zamperini decided later that his life would have more meaning if he became a minister. He traveled extensively around the world, telling of his incredible experiences and trying to help people where-ever he went.

In 1952 Lou Zamperini preached in an open-air stadium before the largest crowd he had ever seen at one time. There were close to 75,000 people in the stadium as he addressed a revival meeting. The location of the stadium was in Tokyo, Japan. I could only wonder what might have been in his heart and his mind that day as he addressed the Japanese.

I have never seen Lou Zamperini since that March day in Madison Square Garden when he started his own "memorial" mile. If I ever do, I will tell him how I have always remembered that emotional day.

Russ Hodges

14

All the Way with Willie

RUSS HODGES

Russ Hodges, born in the famous Monkey Trial town of Dayton, Tennessee, where famed lawyer Clarence Darrow defended the teaching of evolution, grew up in Covington, Kentucky.

He suffered a fractured leg as an athlete at the University of Kentucky and switched from playing in games to talking about them. He got involved in campus broadcasting, did some sports, described campus events and broadcast band nights.

"I moved around pretty good in my Stutz Bearcat," says Hodges, "and was able to do several events a night for the lordly salary of $7.50 a week."

Hodges then landed a job in Cincinnati as a straight radio announcer.

"I was the only guy on our station who knew anything about sports so I got involved in doing football games and broadcasting an occasional wrestling match. Wrestling was the same then as it is today, pure entertainment."

Hodges made a discovery about his broadcasting abilities about that time that turned his career around completely.

"I found out I was a lousy commercial announcer," he says, "so I started concentrating on sports."

He has been one of the very best in the business for more than 35 years now.

His first full-time sports job was with station WIND in Chicago, where he did the home games of the Cubs and the White Sox.

"I did baseball for 154 games, did Big Ten basketball, football, wrestling, horse racing, just about every sport there is," he says. "It was a very educational way to learn the sports broadcasting business."

Hodges was then hired to be the number two man in Washington behind Arch McDonald, one of the early kings of sports broadcasting.

Larry MacPhail brought Hodges to New York where he worked with Mel Allen on Yankee games. In 1949 he switched across the Harlem River to the Polo Grounds where he became the number one announcer for the New York Giants. It's now nearly a quarter of a century later and he's still doing the Giant games.

Hodges says the "creme de la creme" of his career was Bobby Thomson's memorable home run against the Dodgers in the last of the ninth inning in the Polo Grounds on October 3, 1951. "The Giants win the pennant . . . the Giants with the pennant . . . the Giants win the pennant."

But many of the memories of his career with the Giants are tied to one man, Willie Mays. Here, Hodges describes highlights of 19 years with Willie, keynoted by Willie's historic shot on September 22, 1969.

Russ Hodges

I'VE got the greatest job in the world. I get paid to see Willie Mays play.

I will never forget that May day in Philadelphia when he joined us after hitting .477 in 35 games at Minneapolis in 1951. We all gathered around the batting cage at Shibe Park to see him hit baseballs in batting practice out of every part of that field.

"That's nothing," said manager Leo Durocher, "just wait until you see him field and run and throw."

It didn't take an expert to see that Mays had qualities not seen by any of us before. He did everything well and he did it with incredible grace and style and excitement.

He was nervous, as any young kid would be in that spot, and the Philadelphia pitchers took advantage of him with hard-to-reach curve balls. He was 0 for 12 when we left Philadelphia and was a very discouraged young man when the Giants reported at the Polo Grounds to play the Boston Braves. He was so upset he went to Durocher and asked him to take him out of the lineup and send him back to the minors.

"I can't do it, Mr. Leo," Mays said. "You better bench me."

"You are my centerfielder no matter what you do, so just go out there tonight and relax," said Durocher.

In the first inning Warren Spahn, already on his way to his fourth 20-game season, tried to sneak a fastball on the outside past Willie. Whack! I can still see the ball today racing over the roof in left field and heading for the street beyond. Willie Mays had hit his first home run and we knew there would be many, many more to come. I don't think we had the slightest idea that May day in 1951 just how many more there would be.

Mays had a fine season, winning the Rookie of the Year Award, finishing with a .274 average and showing the baseball world how centerfield was supposed to be played.

I recall my next memory of Willie was on the day Thomson homered. Just before I called the homer I mentioned that Mays was the on-deck hitter. There was only one out as Thomson came up and I remember thinking that would be a heck of a spot for a rookie, with the pennant riding on every pitch.

Mays played 34 games for the Giants the following season. Then he was drafted into the army, missing the rest of the 1952 season and all of the 1953 season.

He left the Giants a boy. He came back a man. He was filled out to his full size, 187 pounds spread on a solid 5-11 frame with huge biceps and thick shoulders. As wide as his shoulders and chest were, his waist always stayed thin and supple. You didn't have to know who he was when you saw Mays. You were sure he was an athlete.

In 1954 Mays came back from service to lead the Giants to another pennant. He won the batting title with a .345 mark, hit 41 homers, had 110 runs batted in and continued to amaze everybody who saw him with his fantastic fielding.

I remember the play he made on Billy Cox against Brooklyn when he raced to the centerfield wall, leaped up to spear a line drive, whirled and threw out Carl Furillo who was trying to go to third base.

Charlie Dressen, the Dodger manager, couldn't believe his eyes. He uttered one of his great lines:

"Yeh, it was a pretty good play," said Dressen, "but let's see him do it again."

Mays might not have performed such an impossible feat again but his spectacular fielding plays, his legs whirling, his hat flying, his glove reaching out for the baseball became his trademark almost as much as his crashing bat.

One of his more spectacular catches came in the first game of the 1954 World Series against the Cleveland Indians. The Giants and Indians were tied, 2-2, in the eighth inning. Cleveland had two men on and two out and the hitter was Vic Wertz, a dangerous left-handed pull hitter. Wertz caught a pitch thrown by Don Liddle, who had just replaced Sal Maglie, on the fat of the bat and drove it toward the centerfield wall. Mays, racing back, losing his cap, gloved the baseball with his back to home plate some 460 feet away.

Mays had three more marvelous years in New York and then the club moved to San Francisco in 1958 where he showed off his skill to the Californians with a .347 year. Orlando Cepeda, who had never played with the Giants in New York, became a San Francisco favorite after a .312 rookie season. It took the local folks some time before they fully appreciated the greatness of Willie Mays.

In 1965 Mays had his greatest home run year with 52, batted .317 and knocked in 112 runs. There was no longer any question as to the greatness of Willie Mays.

The figure filberts had gone to work and soon it was discovered that Mays was closing in on Mel Ott's all-time National League home run record of 511 and had an outside chance of getting past Babe Ruth's mark of 714 if he could continue playing until he was past 40.

"I keep myself in good shape," said Mays. "I don't know how long I can play. I'll play as long as I can help the Giants."

In late April of 1966 Mays hit his 511th homer to tie Ott for the all time National League lead.

Then he failed to hit a home run the next day. And the pressure built. And then another day without a homer. And the writers started wondering in print when he would get it. Another day and another and another.

"I hope I hit it soon," said Mays, "so we can get on with the season."

The pressure built as Willie tried for the home run to pass Ott. Now it was into May and the Dodgers were coming into San Francisco for a tough series. Willie was hitless in the first game of the series against Sandy Koufax.

Claude Osteen was the pitcher in the second game of the set. On a 1-1 pitch he threw a curve ball to Mays.

"I tried to get it inside on him," said Osteen. "I wanted him to go for a bad ball. I guess there is no such thing as a bad ball when Willie Mays is batting."

The crack was heard through the park. There was no doubt about it.

Bye, bye baby, number 512 for Willie Mays, deep into the left field stands.

Then Willie relaxed, hit 29 homers that season and finished the year in the airline terminal in Cincinnati as the Giants waited the outcome of the second game of a doubleheader between the Dodgers and the Phillies. If the Dodgers lost, the Giants would be in another playoff. The Giants were two for two in playoffs with Willie Mays, winning the 1951 playoff and the 1962 playoff, both against the Dodgers. Sandy Koufax beat the Phillies in the last regular season game he ever pitched and the Dodgers won the pennant.

Mays continued for the next three seasons, hitting home runs, leading the Giants each year, playing most every day in the gruelling expansion schedule, working his way higher in the all-time home run list. After catching Ott, he passed Ted Williams at 522, passed Jimmy Foxx at 534 and moved after the only one ahead of him in all baseball history, Babe Ruth and his 714.

With night games and extra travel, with more demanded of him all the time, Willie's home run total slipped from his high of 52 in 1965 to his low of 13 in 1969.

But one of those 13 can never be forgotten.

In mid-September it was obvious Mays had a chance at reaching the 600-homer mark, only the second man in history to get that many.

Back in New York, Frank Torre, the former first baseman of the Milwaukee Braves, decided it was time to move. Torre worked for Adirondack Bat Company and Mays had a job with the company. They agreed to commemorate the 600th homer, award Mays some prizes and mark it for all time in the baseball annals. Torre was assigned to stay with Mays until Willie hit it.

"He had 598 when I left," said Frank. "I expected to be out a few days and that would be it. Once Willie made up his mind to hit a couple of homers everybody knew he would get them."

Torre was with the club a week when Mays finally connected off Pat Jarvis of Atlanta on September 15 in Candlestick Park.

Willie ready, Jarvis throws . . . Mays swings . . . there's a high drive out toward left field . . . that one's gone, number 599 for Willie Mays. . . ."

"I sure felt relieved," said Frank Torre. "Now I knew the next one would come and I could go home to my wife and my kids."

The Giants, who had always seemed to be in pressure pennant races all through Willie's career, were in another one. It was the first year of expansion into Montreal and San Diego and a two-division 12-team league. Mays had grown weary as the season went on and now, with less than two weeks to go, he wasn't as strong as he had been earlier. Four teams—the Giants, Dodgers, Reds and Braves—were all battling for the Western Division title as the Mets were wrapping it up in the East.

The following night, after he had homered off Jarvis, Mays was out of the lineup.

"Well," said Frank Torre, "I guess my wife will have to wait for me for a few more days."

Then a couple of days without a home run. Then another day with a couple of base hits but still no home runs.

The Dodgers beat the Giants on Sunday, September 21, and Mays failed to hit a home run.

"I hope he does it before the season's over," kidded Frank Torre. "I'd hate to have to follow him all winter."

On the night of September 22, 1969, the Giants were playing the San Diego Padres in San Diego. The Padres had become a nuisance team, knocking off all the contenders in turn as the Western race went down to the final days with a new leader almost every day.

Willie was tired and injured. I went downstairs to check the lineup cards and Mays wasn't starting against a 23-year-old hard-throwing righthander from Riverside, California, named Mike Corkins.

Frank Torre also checked the lineup card. He was discouraged.

"Willie wasn't in there and I had visions of going back to New York without the 600th homer and feeling pretty embarrassed for Willie, for my company and for myself."

Torre decided to just relax and enjoy the game and hope that Willie would feel better tomorrow and start. Maybe, just maybe, he was ready to hit one. A week had passed without a home run and without anything looking like a home run.

The pressure was beginning to tell on all of us around the club. We were in a tough pennant race and we were suffering the extra burdens of waiting out Willie's every at-bat. Now, at least tonight with Willie on the bench, we could just concentrate on the game.

The whole world seemed to be tuned in to our broadcast as we announced that Willie wasn't starting the game. I wasn't happy because our sponsor was holding a fan contest to pick the time and date of Willie's 600th homer and even our listeners were getting restless.

"I figured if Willie didn't hit one in the next couple of games I would start giving him batting lessons," said Torre. "I was ready to try anything to get a home run out of Willie. I love baseball and I love Willie but I just wanted to go home."

The starting pitcher for San Diego, Mike Corkins, had been in Elmira most of the year and I noticed that he seemed like a pretty hard thrower as he warmed up under us.

Mays sat with a jacket on the bench, Torre sat quietly in the stands, Corkins went to the mound, and Lon Simmons, my broadcast partner, and I, were trying to root the Giants in for another win.

Like all bottom baseball teams in the history of the game, the Padres were loose and relaxed, playing another tough game against a contender. It was 2-2 as Bobby Bonds, the Giants' young outfielder, who looked like he might be another Willie Mays some day, came to bat. The count went to 1-2.

Corkins gets the sign, now he's ready, throws, strike three swinging. Bonds is out of there.

"I'm glad," Torre said, "we aren't advertising that Bonds uses our bat."

Now the game went into the seventh inning. The score was still 2-2. Corkins was pitching a fine game and the Giants had a runner on at first base. The pitcher was the scheduled hitter.

Lon Simmons was on the air at the time and he saw Mays take off his warm-up jacket in the Giant dugout and move to the bat rack.

"Here comes Willie as a pinch hitter," said Simmons.

I moved to the edge of my seat and studied Mays as he swung a couple of bats near home plate to get loose. I thought of the young man I had known in New York, and the stickball games in the streets of Harlem they used to talk about, and the glory years in San Francisco.

Frank Torre thought of only one thing.

"Why not now?" Torre asked out loud.

Why not, indeed?

A young, hard thrower in a tough spot. He might make a mistake and if he does Willie can still drive it long and far. This could be a perfect spot. Then I thought a little more realistically. Mays had been on the bench all night. He was cold. Playing regularly all his life, he had never been an especially good pinch-hitter since he had relatively few chances to practice the art. All we needed was a single to keep the rally going. If Willie could do that . . .

"I got so I almost knew every pitch they would throw him," said Torre. "They knew Willie was getting along in years and they liked to keep him from pulling the ball with hard stuff outside. This kid was throwing a little smoke. I really couldn't expect very much on this at-bat."

Mays took one last swing of the extra bat and dropped it in the hands of the bat boy. Now he moved to home plate and studied young Corkins. Willie hadn't ever faced the young right-hander and I thought back to the first time he faced another hard-throwing righthander named Gary Nolan in Cincinnati. Nolan had embarrassed Willie and struck him out four times in a single game. The next time they met Nolan was the one to be embarrassed. Willie hit a 400-foot homer off him.

Now Mays studied the young righthander. He bent in his familiar stance, his feet spread, his bat held high, his eyes staring at the pitcher. He dug his shoes into the dirt a little deeper, pumped the bat a few more times and waited. Now Corkins was ready. He stretched, looked over at first base and thought about the pitch. He wanted good, hard stuff low and away. That's how they all were pitching Willie these days.

The pitch came in and Willie cracked it on a line to the deepest part of left center field. I knew that was it. Forget it right now. I heard Lonnie say, ". . . a home run . . . number 600 . . . for Willie Mays. . . Russ . . ."

There was a frog in my throat and my eyes filled with tears. For once in my life I was almost speechless. I watched Mays jogging around the bases and all I could think of was how amazing this man is.

"Lon, I've seen them all," I said, "this is one of the greatest."

Now Mays was rounding third base and jogging toward home plate. He was met with a sight that I had remembered only once before in my career, when Willie Mays was on deck that October day in 1951, and all the Giants poured out of the dugout to greet Bobby Thomson, and Eddie Stanky wrestled Leo Durocher down at third base. Now they were swarming over Mays, pounding him on the back, rubbing his head, touching his uniform shirt. All these professional players, in a tough pennant race, sharing the joy and the triumph of the moment, as Willie Mays had hit his 600th career homer.

Mays came across home plate and got into the dugout finally as his teammates let him up. The Giants won the game, 4-2, and now as Mays was surrounded by the press in the clubhouse after the game he seemed terribly moved.

"A lot of great things have happened to me in this game," Mays said, "but I have to tell you it was a thrill to see all my teammates standing there at home plate waiting for me."

Frank Torre had rushed down into the clubhouse to share the moment with Mays. Now he stood, all smiles, congratulating Mays on the historic blow.

"Frank," said Willie, "I think I'm as happy for you as I am for myself. Now you can go home to your family."

"It was worth it," said Torre, "every second of it."

Mays admitted that he was glad it was all over. He admitted now that the pressure had started to get to him.

"I remember when I was chasing the Mel Ott record," he said, "and each day I didn't hit a home run I felt exhausted. This was the same thing."

Mays sat in front of his locker, that marvelous body, those strong, muscled arms, those thick shoulders and thin waist, still looking like a much younger man. But Willie admitted he was tired. He seemed to feel he could no longer catch Ruth who remained some 114 home runs ahead of him.

"That's 40 homers for three more years," he said. "I'm not capable of that anymore. Maybe Hank Aaron can do it."

Aaron was closing fast on Willie and Ruth and might even catch them both in a few more years but for now 600 homers seemed like an impossible total. Ruth had played 22 seasons but the first six of them were as a pitcher. Mays was now in his 17th full season and had missed most of the 1952 season and all of the 1953 season. It is not inconceivable that he would have had another 75 homers had he played those two years.

Mays had earned the plaudits of the small crowd, the adulation of his teammates and the thanks of Frank Torre with the homer. That was not all. He also earned a $12,500 sports car from the bat company and 390 shares of their stock.

"We decided to give him one share of company stock for each foot of his home run," said Torre. "That way he would never forget how far that home run went and neither would we."

Mays didn't hit another home run that year and went into the 1970 season with 600. He had a fine spring training and proved there was some life left in him yet when he hit number 601 off Fred Gladding of Houston in the early days of his 19th season.

Perhaps, Mays proved just how great a ball player he still was in the first week of the season, when he chased a fly ball off the bat of Bobby Tolan of the Reds, raced to the wall in right field, leaped in the air, collided with Bobby Bonds and still caught the baseball. It was a tangle of arms and legs on the ground as both players went down. Nobody could tell if the ball was caught and, if so, who made the catch. Then Bonds got up and reached down into Willie's glove to pull out the baseball.

Another memorable Mays moment occurred on a cloudless Saturday afternoon, July 18, 1970, in San Francisco. The Giants were playing the Montreal Expos. Mays was at bat against young right-hander Mike Wegener.

Willie swings . . . ground ball . . . base hit . . . hit number 3000 for Willie Mays. A single to left field. They are stopping the game and the ball is being flipped over to Willie. Now here come National League President Chub Feeney, Willie's former boss, and Stan Musial, the other member of the 3000-hit club here today to congratulate Willie.

Hank Aaron, the only other living member of the exclusive 3000-hit club, was in St. Louis that night with the Braves.

I've been in the broadcasting business for a long time and I've seen a lot of great players and experienced a lot of great games. For thrills, there can never be anything to match Bobby Thomson's pennant-winning homer in one game, but for excitement for some 20 years now, there can be no one to match Willie Mays.

I remember that day he hit his 600th homer in San Diego and someone went over to the young pitcher, Mike Corkins, and asked him about the blast. Like all young pitchers in a spot like that, he was angry. He was actually quite upset at giving up the homer to Willie, even though it was so historic and would be remembered as a significant blow in Willie's marvelous career. Corkins' name would last forever in the baseball record books since Willie Mays will go marching into the Hall of Fame five years after he quits playing.

None of this drama could console Corkins. "Why me," he asked. "Why did it have to be me?"

For my part, all I could think of was the fact that I was sure glad it was me.

I was pretty happy I hitched my career to Willie Mays instead of staying a band announcer for $7.50 a week.

Russ Hodges and Willie Mays
have been communicating
for two decades.

157

Jack Brickhouse

15

The Giants Ice It

JACK
BRICKHOUSE

THIRTY years ago Jack Brickhouse lost a contest. It was the beginning of his marvelous broadcasting career.

"The guys who judged the contest weren't the guys who owned the radio station," he said, "so I got the job anyway."

Brickhouse, who does the Chicago Cubs games with a fan's enthusiasm, was born in Peoria, Illinois, and attended Bradley University in his home town.

"I majored in speech and dramatics," he said, "and I always thought I might want to be an announcer. One day the local radio station sponsored an audition. There were six finalists and four prizes. I finished fifth. The guy I beat out was sixty years old."

Despite losing the contest Brickhouse was hired by the station as an announcer and allowed to work two weeks for free.

"They liked my work so they raised my salary to seventeen dollars a week," said Brickhouse, "but for that I also had to double as a switchboard operator."

Brickhouse got some sound advice from an

159

old timer around station WNBD who told the young announcer, "Be yourself on the air. The public detests an imitation."

Brickhouse, like all young announcers, was trying to pattern his work after the giants of the industry.

"One week I would sound like Ted Husing and the next week I would be Harry Von Zell. It got so, after a while, I really didn't know what my real air voice was like."

Taking the advice to heart, Brickhouse began to develop his own easy-going, warm style, which led to an opportunity to do the telecasting of the Chicago Cubs and Chicago White Sox games 21 years ago.

In addition to his full schedule of baseball broadcasting, Brickhouse has found time to do several World Series, professional football games, All-Star baseball and football games, the Rose Bowl, championship fights, including Louis-Charles, Charles-Walcott and many others. He now does the Cubs games exclusively on WGN in Chicago with radio and television coverage.

"Phil Wrigley believes in advertising," says Brickhouse, "so we are on the air with all the radio games and almost all of our games on television."

Brickhouse suffered through the 1969 baseball season as the Cubs lost the pennant to the Mets but he looks on it as one of his most exciting sports memories. He especially remembers the no-hitter turned in by young Cub lefthander Ken Holtzman against the Braves.

"Henry Aaron hit a ball into the stands for what looked like a homer," said Brickhouse, "but the wind carried it back out and Billy Williams caught it. That saved the no-hitter."

That is an example of why Chicago is called the Windy City.

Now, Brickhouse remembers another windy day in another city in another sport. It is December 30, 1956, and the scene is Yankee Stadium in New York.

Jack Brickhouse

THESE were the days before the weather bureau invented the wind-chill factor. I'm sure I was as cold as if the temperature was 30 degrees below zero. Maybe the real reading on the thermometer that day was seven degrees.

I awoke early Sunday morning, December 30, 1956, in my room at New York's Hampshire House. This was my first pro football championship game and I was really excited about it. Guys from Chicago don't get too many chances to do a network telecast of a championship game and I wanted to make sure I was ready for the big game.

For a week, I had been reading and studying everything I could get my hands on about the New York Giants and the Chicago Bears. I had covered the Bears all season so I wasn't too worried about them. The Giants had won the Eastern Conference championship and I researched all available information on them. I studied films by the hour. I had all this material typed out on three-by-five cards and I was sure, as I awoke that morning and quickly examined my cards to see that they were in order, that I knew more about the players on both those football teams than their own mothers.

The Bears hadn't been in a championship game since Sid Luckman's days in 1946. Luckman had passed for one touchdown in the 1946 championship game and scored another himself on a bootleg to give the Bears their last league title. They had beaten the New York Giants that day, 24-14, and this was the first time in ten years the two old rivals were meeting for the title.

My broadcasting partner that day was Red Grange, old number 77 of the Fighting Illini, and I felt certain we would make an excellent team and give the fans across the country a fine broadcast. Red would handle the color and analysis and I would do the play by play from Yankee Stadium to the millions of viewers across the country.

I dressed quickly, went down to the dining room for breakfast and prepared myself for any last-minute emergencies by reading the sports sections of all the New York papers for any late developments. There were none. There would be no surprises this day as far as the players were concerned.

After breakfast I went back up to my room to dress for the game. I had listened to the weather forecasts on radio and checked the temperature and wind conditions with the weather bureau. It was not encouraging. The temperature was seven degrees and the wind was reaching gusts up to 30 miles an hour. I wasn't thrilled by this but I was certain provisions would be made for us to stay warm.

I put on an extra sweater, scarf, gloves, warm stockings and my heaviest overcoat and took the elevator downstairs to the street. I was wearing just about everything I owned. I couldn't believe I didn't own enough.

The doorman at the hotel called a cab for me and in the few seconds I waited to get in I saw my breath before me. It seemed to freeze in the air. I tried to think of some colder and windier days I remembered in Chicago. I couldn't remember any. Chicago was the Windy City but New York, that day, seemed windier and colder.

The cab driver was a fan and we talked about the championship game and he was quick to offer his opinion, as New York cab drivers always are, about the outcome.

"You guys from Chicago don't have a chance," he said. "The Giants will kill youse."

I wanted the Bears to win, of course, but I wanted a good, exciting game to describe. Any time a broadcaster gets an opportunity to do a championship game, he forgets what team he roots for and just tries to give the best report of the game he possibly can.

The cab moved quickly through the light early morning traffic and we pulled in front of Yankee Stadium shortly after 11:00 o'clock. There were two hours left before game time, two hours to warm up, to get ready, to settle down to do the big game.

Then I stepped out of the cab.

The wind almost knocked me off my feet and the cold bit at the tips of my face and nose and seemed to chew right through my heavy clothing as if I were wearing a summer suit.

I walked through the press gate, waved to the attendants and made my way toward the press room for a cup of coffee. The cold seemed to collect in the concrete tunnels of Yankee Stadium. I was already hoping that the weather might change by game time, the sun might come out and the wind might die down. I was dreaming. It would get a lot colder before it would get any warmer that Sunday.

Several of the writers were beginning to gather in the press room and the topic of conversation was the same with everyone. We were all talking about the weather. Nobody could do anything about it. Endure it, maybe.

I drank a couple of cups of coffee, studied the program, checked the starting lineup and visited the dressing rooms. Jim Lee Howell, the big, friendly Giants coach, greeted me with a smile and said, "Nice day, isn't it?" I just smiled.

Bears coach Paddy Driscoll, who had taken over the on-field duties of the Papa Bear, George Halas, was moving around the locker room giving last-minute instructions to his team before they were to go on the field for their first warmups.

"Good luck, Paddy," I said.

"Thanks, Jack. I hope we are good as well as lucky."

The Bears moved out to the field and I waited until they were all out of the door before I followed them out. I didn't want to rush off into that cold. The wind struck me just as I lifted my head out of the baseball dugout. The stands were almost filled more than a half hour before game time. I could see the heavy fur coats and the parkas and the scarves and the gloves. This wasn't a day for the fans to be fashionable. This was a day for the fans to stay alive.

I checked the condition of the field. It was frozen. I wondered if the Bears or the Giants would switch to sneakers as the Giants had in the famous 1934 sneakers game when the Giants came out for the second half with basketball shoes on, got traction on the frozen ice at the Polo Grounds, scored 27 points in the last quarter and won, 30-13, over the Bears. That day was wet and cold and the ground was frozen from snow and ice. This day was just cold and windy.

Now it was time to move to our broadcasting booth and Red and I took the press elevator to the press level. We trudged through the press area to our broadcasting booth. For the first time, as we neared our booth, I realized we had been sabotaged. The booth was located in a far corner of Yankee Stadium, hung from under the stands and completely exposed to the wind and the cold and the noise of the fans. It wasn't really a booth; more like a basket hanging out over the upper deck.

"How in hell are we supposed to do a game from up here?" Red asked me.

"I don't know. Maybe they just planned this game for a warm day."

The wind whipped through the open booth as I tried to collect my three-by-five cards, with all my detailed information, for the broadcast. Red was going over the starting lineups. Our young spotter was dancing up and down behind us trying to stay alive.

"I think you can get warmed up playing on a day like this," said Red, "but I don't see how we can get warmed up sitting here."

I looked out on the field and tried to spot the players as they warmed up far away from me. All I could see was haze and fog and my own cold breath. Then I looked for the time clock. I couldn't find it. I felt the pangs of panic creeping all over my cold body. The clock must be here somewhere in the park but where?

I mentioned it to Red. He couldn't find it. Our young spotter, who had examined the seats long before we got there, was too cold to talk. He just pointed down under our vantage point.

We had been placed in a booth, in a corner of the park, away from the action, with the time clock directly under us.

With just a few minutes to go before air time we realized it was too late to change anything.

"We'll just have to call down to the press box every so often for the time. I think that will be the best way." Red agreed and we instructed our spotter to make calls during the commercial breaks to get the correct time from the press box.

The director said we had thirty seconds and I tried to hold down my program card in front of me but the wind was giving me a tough battle. Now the red light flashed on and we were on the air across the country.

Good afternoon, everybody, welcome to Yankee Stadium in New York City for the National Football League championship between the Chicago Bears and the New York Giants . . .

The words seemed to blow back into my face. The microphone was cold and I could feel the chill in my nose and eyes and mouth as I tried to talk.

The temperature is seven degrees and there is a stiff crosswind . . .

I tried to stay calm and objective. After all, I didn't want anybody feeling sorry for me sitting in that frozen booth with my feet tingling from the cold and the tears collecting in my eyes from the wind. People had tuned in to hear us describe the championship game and not to listen to us suffering on the air.

The lights were on in Yankee Stadium and the gloom and cold and wind gave an eerie appearance to the ball park. The sounds of the fans were muffled under their hoods and caps and scarves as we prepared for the kickoff.

Here's the kick . . . it's a good one, deep, taken on the eight-yard line by Gene Filipski . . . He's up to the ten, he's up to the 20, he cuts away from one Bear defender, he's free at midfield and he's knocked out of bounds finally at the 39-yard line of the Bears. Red.

Red Grange described how Filipski had broken two tackles near his own twenty and converted a short run back into a marvelous 53-yard runback with tough, aggressive running.

Now the Giants were coming out in their tight T formation with Don Heinrich at quarterback. Heinrich and Charlie Conerly had been sharing the Giant quarterbacking and for the opening series of downs it would be Heinrich on the field and Conerly on the phones. I wondered how the phones were working in this cold weather.

Heinrich went back to pass on first down, trying to catch the Bears bunched in for a line play. Frank Gifford slipped out of the backfield, cut to his left and caught Heinrich's pass over his shoulder at the 17. Now the Giants had a first down on the Chicago 17, the Bears were moving in to defend their own goal early in the game and the wind was screaming through our booth.

The Giants drove into the Bears' line for no gain and now Heinrich called a running play to the right side of the Bears' line. Mel Triplett, the hard-running back of the Giants, took the handoff, broke through the tackle spot, knocked over the linebacker with a head-on rush and cruised into the end zone.

Triplett is in for a Giant touchdown. The Giants lead, 6-0, and they have scored after only four plays of the game.

Automatically I looked for the clock to give the time. I realized that we couldn't see it. Our spotter hadn't been able to call and now I was giving a score without giving the time of game. I explained the situation to our viewers and hoped they would understand.

Ben Agajanian, the Giant place-kicker, trotted on to the field. The ball was snapped, didn't blow away in the wind, was placed down and booted between the uprights. The score was 7-0. The spotter had made his call. He gave me the time.

The Giants lead, 7-0, with only two minutes and 48 seconds gone in the first period. Now here's Red.

Grange analyzed the drive and I tried to take a sip out of a coffee cup. But my hands were too cold to hold the cup steadily in the wind and I gave that up as a lost cause and returned to the game.

Now the Bears had a chance to get back in the game as Agajanian boomed a long kick toward the Chicago end zone. It was wisely placed down by the Bears and they began the first drive from their own 20. The Bears moved well and were driving into Giant territory when the first break of the game occurred. No, the sun didn't come out, the Bears just fumbled.

Quarterback Ed Brown over the ball calling signals. He hands off to Casares, who is hit hard at the line of scrimmage, fumbles. Giants' ball.

Rick Casares had taken the icy football, run it straight into the Giant line and had been attacked by Roosevelt Grier, the massive defensive tackle, who tackled the Bear fullback and knocked the ball free. The wonder of the play wasn't that Casares had fumbled the frozen football but that all the ball-carriers didn't fumble every play.

Now the Giants, seemingly unaffected by the icy blasts off the Harlem River, drove back downfield. The drive was stalled on the 17 and Agajanian came back on the field.

The snap, the kick . . . good. . . . The Giants lead, 10-0.

My words seemed to fly back into my throat. Every time I opened my mouth to talk I found myself almost gasping to get the words out over the wind that was rushing into my system. Nothing helped. Red Grange, who had been such a great football star, sat huddled under his heavy coat as I described the plays. I had worked with him many times but this was the first time I had ever seen him almost disinterested in a football game. He kept blowing his breath into his gloved hands all afternoon.

The Bears failed to move again against the massive Giant line and had to kick. New York fought its way back up field and their drive stalled. Agajanian, who got to be a familiar sight all afternoon, trotted slowly onto the field again and the Giants went for another field goal. Agajanian kicked this one from the 43 just before the quarter ended.

There's the gun ending the first period. The Giants lead the Bears, 13-0.

We broke for a studio commercial and I got up and bounced around the broadcasting booth. My feet were numb and I was sure I was a victim of frostbite. My face felt raw and my nose twitched with needles from the vicious cold.

The Giants had the ball again and were driving on the Bears. Chicago seemed helpless against the Giants. They couldn't handle them on offense and they couldn't handle them on defense. The Giants were moving on the ground and in the air and the Bears seemed like a beaten ball club.

With two minutes gone in the second period the Giants had driven to the three-yard line. Conerly, in at quarterback now, handed off to his big, bruising fullback, Alex Webster, and Big Red charged into the end zone for a touchdown. The score was 20-0 and it no longer was the kind of game you wanted to stay out in the cold to watch.

The fans in the Polo Grounds, all 56,836, hardly cared. They were New York fans, having a grand time, and they cheered each Giant drive through their stocking caps as if each play was the most important of the game.

The Bears were deep in their own territory and were forced to punt. The ball floated lazily to Emlen Tunnell and somewhere in the haze and clouds and bad lights he lost the ball. It bounced off his cold hands and the Bears recovered. They were on the nine-yard line of the Giants.

The ball goes to Casares, he's over the right side, and in for a score. The Giants' lead is now 20-6. Rick Casares has scored for Chicago.

George Blanda came in to kick the extra point and suddenly it wasn't as cold anymore. The Bears had scored, they were still alive in the game and I was sure if they could score again, I could withstand the cold the rest of the afternoon.

It wasn't long before I realized it wasn't to be. With Gifford and Webster slashing the Bear line and Kyle Rote catching passes in front of two and three Bear defenders, the Giants drove downfield again. Webster smashed over from the one-yard line and the Giants led, 27-7. I could just see what was left of the fight in the Bears disappear that instant. They had been able to score on a break and now before they had a chance to enjoy it or close the gap a little, the Giants had come back again. This was not the afternoon to be for Chicago. Especially in the frozen broadcasting booth in Yankee Stadium.

Just before the end of the half, the Bears were in their own end zone. They tried to punt and Henry Moore, a rookie back, charged through the Bear line, blocked the kick and landed on it for a touchdown. Agajanian kicked the extra point again and the Giants led, 34-7.

We broke for a commercial at half-time and I looked up from my statistics sheet to see the kids from one of the local high schools parade on the field for their halftime show. I could not believe it. Some of those girls were in short skirts. I knew they had to be frozen solid but they did their strutting and formation as if it were a mild fall day in October. They had waited a lifetime for the opportunity to do this game so the cold didn't bother them. I had waited a lifetime too but the cold bothered me. I guess that was the difference between moving around and having to sit still.

The Giants got another touchdown in the third quarter when Charlie Conerly hit Kyle Rote for a nine-yard touchdown pass and scored again in the final quarter when Conerly connected with Gifford for a 14-yard touchdown pass play.

Mercifully, the gun sounded, and the Giants had beaten the Bears for the championship, 47-7.

The Giants were excited in their dressing room and talked of the great performance by their defensive line and the clutch passing of Conerly, the running of Webster and Triplett and the receiving of Gifford and Rote.

"We just kicked the hell out of them in every department," exclaimed Frank Gifford.

New York hadn't won a title since 1938 and they were allowed to glow a little in the heat of the win.

The Bears weren't glowing. They were just frozen. They sat almost still in their clubhouse as they tried to thaw out from the uncomfortable and rough afternoon. They didn't have much to say. They were too busy blowing their noses.

I waited in the press room as the crowd thinned out. I had a hot cup of coffee and checked to see if all my fingers and toes were still there.

Everything seemed in order and Red and I left to go back downtown to our hotel before leaving for our homes.

I sat in a warm bath in the Hampshire House and let the water wipe away the chill from my body. I couldn't help wondering if I would have felt any warmer that afternoon if the Bears had won.

At least NBC understood my problems. They even let me do another championship game on a much warmer day. It was only zero for that one.

Jack Brickhouse takes time out with Phil Rizzuto,
Yankee-turned-broadcaster.

Dan Kelly

16

Mr. Orr's Stanley Cup

DAN KELLY

ONE of the more difficult broadcasting coups has been pulled off with much aplomb by Dan Kelly.

Kelly, a Canadian from Ottawa, has brought the sport of hockey to mid-America with calm, clear descriptions of the fastest game in the world.

Kelly broadcasts the games of the St. Louis Blues of the National Hockey League over KMOX and does the weekly hockey game of the week over the Columbia Broadcasting System.

Kelly's hockey career dates back to his school days in Ottawa when he played the sport along with football and some baseball.

"I knew I was never going to be a professional hockey player," says Kelly, "so I did the next best thing and started broadcasting the game."

Kelly's older brother, Hal, was already one of Canada's top sports announcers and Dan spent much of his free time watching his brother at work.

After graduation from St. Patrick's College

in Ottawa, Kelly became a full-time broadcaster. He got his big break when he won an audition to do the games of the Canadian football league.

He spent four years covering Canadian football and became friendly with a number of players, including Joe Kapp, who was a star in Canada before leading the Minnesota Vikings to the championship of the National Football League.

Kelly also worked with Danny Gallivan on the English-speaking broadcasting crew of the Montreal Canadiens, the team that dominated the National Hockey League for so many years.

After the first year of expansion to St. Louis, Kelly was hired to do the games of the St. Louis Blues and educate the population of mid-America to the Canadian game.

"I probably did a little more explaining in the early days of the St. Louis Blues broadcasts than I did with the Canadiens," he says, "but by now most everybody around town knows the game."

Kelly still tries to define some of the more difficult rules of hockey when he does his weekly broadcasts on the Columbia Broadcasting System.

In addition to his hockey duties, Kelly also does a regular sports show on KMOX.

Here, it is May 10, 1970. The Boston Bruins and the St. Louis Blues are in Boston Garden for the fourth game of the Stanley Cup playoffs for the National Hockey League title.

Dan Kelly

FOR the third straight year, the St. Louis Blues were in the final of the Stanley Cup playoffs. They were the only expansion team in any sport to get that far that fast.

When hockey expanded they established a unique playoff system. The East Division, including all the established clubs, and the West Division, including the newer clubs, would play for the championship. This meant an expansion team would be in the championship round from its very first year.

St. Louis had made it in each of the three seasons in the league.

Now they were back for their try at the Cup against the Boston Bruins, who had come from nowhere to win the championship of the East.

Boston was being called the Gashouse Gang of hockey. They had some free-wheeling guys on that club led by Bobby Orr, Phil Esposito and long-haired, flamboyant Derek Sanderson, who had become the darling of the Boston crowd with his wide-open play and willingness to comment. He was as colorful a hockey player as had been in the league in a long time.

The Blues had played as good hockey as they were capable of playing. Still, the Bruins had taken the first three games in the playoffs and were on the threshold of winning the Cup for the first time in 29 years.

As I thought about the final game on Sunday I was hoping that if the Bruins did win, it would be an exciting game. Sunday was the big day for television and we wanted some drama to build the game. I thought, by chance, we might get something like the six goals scored in one game by Red Berenson in Philadelphia a couple of years before. It was the greatest single scoring show of my viewing career and excited the entire hockey population. Red never got a cheap shot that day and even had a chance at the seventh goal as the puck hit the post.

I remember that afternoon when Berenson came down from his hotel room. There had been a power failure and we all stood around the hotel lobby waiting for the repairs. We had trouble getting to the rink due to plane and bus delays. It all must have been an omen to plant the memory of the night in my mind. I was looking for another such omen today. I found none.

I checked both dressing rooms before I went up to the booth. Both teams were ready. The Blues had played well but still thought they could play better. They had had a long team meeting the day before and had vowed to make Boston work for every shot they got.

Scotty Bowman, the St. Louis coach, had devised a plan to stop the great Bobby Orr. Bowman felt if Orr was stopped, the Blues would have a chance to win.

Orr, the first defenseman to lead the league in scoring and considered by many the best hockey player of all time, had been a terror in the earlier rounds of the playoffs. Bowman assigned defenseman Jim Roberts to shadow Orr. This was an almost unheard-of compliment for the young defenseman, who had just turned 22. Now Bowman was about to change his strategy.

Dan Kelly

"We haven't won with Orr being shadowed," he said, "so we are going to return to our normal game and hope we can generate more offense ourselves."

I climbed to the booth in the Boston Garden and surveyed the scene. We had a good vantage point for the game and an even better one for the banners that dotted the old building. Banners proclaiming the fans' allegiance to their favorites could be seen everywhere. The Boston Celtics had a bad year in basketball but the Bruins had stepped in to replace them in the affections of all with their inspired hockey play.

Now they were a game away from their first title in 29 years and the Blues, battling hard, were still trying to win their first playoff game in the round.

I went over all the vital statistics and read over my notes on both teams. I had seen the Blues all year, of course, and knew them as well as I know my own brother. I had seen the Bruins many, many times and felt comfortable with them as well. Of course, the young man who had gotten all the publicity, Bobby Orr, was the one to watch closely for the national television audience.

Orr is a fantastic athlete with grace and speed and power. He seems to be able to do anything he wants at any time on the ice. He is an effortless skater, an incredible shooter and a determined defenseman. He has the knack of being in the right place at the right time, playing both ends of the rink as it has never been played before.

Good afternoon, ladies and gentlemen, and welcome to Boston Garden. It is the fourth game of the Stanley Cup playoffs between the Boston Bruins and the St. Louis Blues. Boston leads three games to none. If they win today, they win the Cup for the first time in 29 years. If they lose, the same two teams play again Tuesday night in St. Louis.

The Blues were on the ice ready to go, in their white uniforms, trimmed with blue and gold. The Bruins wore gold uniforms trimmed with black and white. Hockey was a good color television game.

There's the faceoff and we're underway . . . controlled by Boston at center ice . . . Phil Esposito has it . . .

The crowd exploded into a long, loud roar. They were letting loose, it seemed, after waiting all these years for the Bruins to get this close. Now they were just sixty minutes away, one game, from being champions of the hockey world. Esposito, who had been the first man in history to score over 100 points in a season, never got a shot away. That hardly mattered to the Boston fans. They

174

knew it was just going to be a matter of time. Just sixty minutes to a championship.

The Blues played aggressive hockey. They banged away at Boston goalie Gerry Cheevers and forced him to make several fine stops in the early going of the game. Boston was playing its normal offensive game, charging hard down the St. Louis end of the rink and firing the puck at Glenn Hall, the 38-year-old veteran, who had been guarding the goal for professional teams since 1951 when he broke in with the Indianapolis club in the American Hockey League.

For more than five minutes neither team could score. There were opportunities but both goalies were equal to the challenges. Now Boston had the puck behind its own net as it moved up the rink. The puck was in the St. Louis zone.

Then Sanderson came up with the puck on the right side. He flipped a pass to Rick Smith just in front of the cage.

Smith fires a hard shot at Cheevers . . . he scores . . . the Bruins lead, 1-0. Smith has scored the first goal of the game for the Boston Bruins.

The time was announced as 5:28 of the first period and the Boston fans applauded wildly. In their hearts, they knew they would win. Now they wanted to win big. They cheered Smith's goal and urged the Bruins on for more.

But there was no more for a while. The pace was furious but the Blues kept the pressure on the Bruins. They would not quit. They had not won a Stanley Cup game but they would not give up. They didn't want the lead to get any bigger.

One minute to play in the period . . . one minute . . . Tim Ecclestone has the puck on the right wing . . . he passes off to Bob Plager . . . Plager to Berenson . . . Red shoots . . . he scores . . . Red Berenson has scored for the St. Louis Blues. St. Louis has tied the game, 1-1.

The goal came at 19:17 of the first period and the crowd's reaction was as expected. There was a gasp of surprise and then a quick silence. The Boston fans had expected St. Louis to fold up after the first goal, accepting the inevitable, but it hadn't worked that way. The Blues had not folded up and now with the first period coming to a close they were tied 1-1.

The period ended and the teams left the ice for their dressing rooms. Now there would be 15 minutes before the action would resume. It gave us a chance to catch our breath from a furious first period. I had watched the Blues all year and I knew if the Bruins were to beat them they would have to play tough hockey. The

St. Louis Blues weren't about to give anything away, especially the Stanley Cup.

The crowd relaxed and watched the ice being swept in one of the necessary and amusing rituals in hockey. Despite all the cutting and stopping for 20 minutes by both teams, the ice was clean and glistening as the referees came back out minutes before the start of the second period. They glided along the ice, checked the smooth surface, inspected the nets in the goal and waited for the teams.

We're ready for the faceoff for the start of the second period. The Bruins 1 and the Blues 1. A scramble for the puck . . . controlled by St. Louis. . . .

The crowd was shouting at the Boston players. They expected more of them. They wanted a win and they wanted a big win. They weren't in any mood to sweat out a close game. They came to Boston Garden to share in the joy of the championship and instead of laughing all the way to the Stanley Cup they were struggling for the go-ahead goal.

St. Louis kept the pressure on Cheevers in the early minutes of the second period. They were checking hard. They were skating well. They were defensing the Bruins well whenever Boston had the puck. A check against the boards. St. Louis had the puck again. Cheevers bent low in the goal to await another attack.

St. Marseille has the puck in the Boston end . . . passes off to Sabourin . . . he shoots . . . scores . . . Gary Sabourin has scored for the Blues . . . they lead 2-1. Frank St. Marseille took the puck off the right boards, passed to Gary Sabourin in front of the net and Sabourin knocked it in right under Cheever's sliding form. The Blues lead 2-1.

"St. Louis goal by Sabourin . . ." intoned the public address announcer ". . . the time, three minutes and 22 seconds of the second period."

Now the rubber ducks came out on the ice and the brown paper bags and the orange peels and the paper cups and the spoons and newspapers and programs. The Boston fans were expressing their anger at the turn of events with all the garbage they could get their hands on. They felt cheated. They had fought their way into the Boston Garden and they weren't interested in seeing their team lose today.

St. Louis leads 2-1. If the Blues win, the next game in the series will be played Tuesday night in St. Louis . . .

There was a mixture of cheers and boos at the next faceoff. The fans wanted to cheer the Bruins on but they wanted to make sure they knew they were displeased. Even long-haired Derek Sanderson, the darling of the gallery, came in for his share of boos when he came on the ice. The fans had sort of a love-hate relationship with Sanderson. He wasn't the best player on the Bruins but he certainly got the most attention. He was also one of those players that was easy to spot from a booth. The fans look for the players on ice by their numbers. The broadcasters have other ways. I get to know a man by the shape of his haircut or the way he wears his uniform or the way he skates or how he just bends on the ice. Once in a while you know a player by the color of his hair. Then all of a sudden he starts wearing a protective helmet. Only a few of them do but it's enough to throw off your spotting system.

One of the players that has always been easy to spot is Phil Esposito of the Bruins. He is a big man, as hockey players go, some 200 pounds on a 6-1 frame, with black hair and a heavy beard. It's easy to find him. He's always around the cage. The press and the players kid Esposito sometimes by calling him the "garbage man." They say he sits around the cage and picks up other people's rebounds and puts them in. If he does do that once in a while, he still has to be good enough to be there. Defensemen just don't let you camp near the goal singing your college song while waiting for the puck to show up. However he did it, Esposito was a man who was always near the puck and the puck would more often than not wind up in the goal with a goalie sprawled forlornly on the ice.

St. Louis clung to its one-goal lead as Boston fought for the tie. They were in St. Louis ice now most of the time as the second period moved along. About six minutes remained in the second period of play. The crowd was anxious for a Boston goal. The boos had almost disappeared now. They just wanted that tying goal. Boston was about to get it. There was Esposito, dark and strong, forcing his way toward the goal. The puck was loose now in front of the cage and there was a scramble. A lot of sticks were moving at the slippery, black rubber.

Hodge has it in front of the goal, gets it to Esposito . . . he shoots . . . and Esposito scores. Boston has tied the game 2-2.

Now the crowd let go in all its frenzy. This was the goal they were waiting for. Boston had fought from behind to get even and the fans knew, they just knew, that the Blues were finished. They had battled hard, made the good try, and would now fold up nicely and forget about the cup. That's the way the Boston fans had it figured.

Esposito's goal had come at 14:23 of the second period. The score was tied. The Bruins were just 26 minutes away from the Stanley Cup if they could score again and keep the Blues away. Boston had waited 29 years for the Stanley Cup.

Both teams battled for control of the puck the rest of the period. Nobody could mount a scoring attack.

Two minutes to go in the second period . . . two minutes . . . the score is tied 2-2 . . . Boston has the puck in its own ice. Orr has it . . . comes up center ice . . . passes off to Johnny Bucyk . . .

The great Bobby Orr had been stilled all game. For the fourth game in a row Orr had not scored against the Blues. Jim Roberts had shadowed Orr in the first three games and now, in this fourth game, Orr had been held in check. The strategy had worked so far. Orr had been held without a goal and the Blues were still tied as the seconds ticked away in the second period.

Thirty seconds to play in the period . . . just thirty seconds . . . Boston has the puck behind its own goal . . . ten seconds left . . . three . . . two . . . there's the buzzer for the end of the second period of play. At the end of two periods, Boston 2 and St. Louis 2.

Twenty minutes remained in the game. If neither team scored in the next twenty minutes there would be a sudden-death playoff. We had explained the hockey scoring system of two points for a victory and one for a tie many times during the regular season. Now we reminded the viewers that there are no ties in the playoffs. A sudden-death overtime (first goal is winner) would be played if the score remained even.

The ice was cleared and resurfaced again and the third period was about to begin.

Here we go, final period, score tied 2-2 . . . the faceoff goes to . . . St. Louis . . . controlled by Roberts in his own end . . . St. Louis comes down ice . . . Roberts gets it to Goyette on the left side . . . Goyette over to Larry Keenan . . . Keenan shoots . . . scores . . . Larry Keenan has put St. Louis ahead 3-2.

There were shock waves traveling through Boston Garden. It had happened so fast the Boston fans hardly knew how to react. A lot of them hadn't even returned to their seats when the goal went in.

"The time . . ." said the public address announcer, "nineteen seconds of the third period."

The crowd gasped at that. A goal that quick in a Stanley Cup playoff game just takes your breath away. It happened so fast the fans hadn't even had the time to throw any rubber ducks on the ice. Jim Roberts had taken the puck in his own ice, gotten it over to Phil Goyette and the veteran center had placed it neatly on Larry Keenan's stick. Keenan had whipped it by Cheevers before he had even settled down to his goal-tending tasks. I had often wondered how many more goals would be scored in a game if there could be more shots that early in a period. I think it takes the goalie some time after the start of the period to relax and get the feel of the game.

The Bruins had to come back again. St. Louis led, 3-2, and that was enough to get the fans worked up to a fever pitch. They shouted and cheered and booed and heaved paper on the ice in an attempt to get their team moving. The Blues held on stubbornly, defending their own ice with a passion, trying to keep the Bruins away from any good shots. They had Orr in check and Esposito and all the rest of the Bruins as the minutes ticked away. There were eight minutes left to play in the game, eight minutes more and St. Louis would have its first Stanley Cup playoff win.

Now Rick Smith had the puck for Boston at center ice with a good move away from two St. Louis defenders. He got it over to John McKenzie.

McKenzie passes to Johnny Bucyk . . . shoots . . . he scores . . . Boston has tied the game, 3-3. Johnny Bucyk has scored for Boston and the game is all even.

The time was 13:28 of the third period. The score was all even at three goals each and the fans were hysterical. Boston had come from behind again and could win the game and settle things with a score in the remaining few minutes.

The action was furious. Neither side played defensively. Each wanted to win. Each worked hard at getting the puck away and getting that one shot that would turn the game around. Three minutes remained. Now two. Now just one minute.

Thirty seconds left in regulation time . . . Boston has the puck . . . it's being fought for . . . goes loose along the right side . . . ten seconds . . . five . . there's the buzzer . . . we'll play sudden death . . . the score is tied 3-3.

The Blues, who had never won a Stanley Cup game, were now in another sudden-death game. It had become their specialty. They weren't winning Cup games but they weren't losing very easily, either. The teams left the ice for a 20-minute break before play resumed.

The first team to score wins. If Boston scores, they win the Cup; if St. Louis scores, they play again on Tuesday night. Now, here's the faceoff . . . controlled by St. Louis . . . it goes to Larry Keenan . . . he has the puck behind his own goal . . . he's skating along the right side . . . tries to get away from Orr . . . loses the puck to Orr, who passes behind the St. Louis net to Sanderson . . .

Orr had gambled on the play. Instead of skating back to guard Boston territory, Orr had charged at Keenan and taken the puck away. Had Keenan been able to get past Orr with the puck he might have been able to get down ice all by himself for a shot at Cheevers. It could have been the shot that might have given St. Louis a win.

But Orr had taken the puck away and gotten it to Sanderson. Now Orr was skating toward the St. Louis goal and Sanderson was firing the puck back at him.

Orr in front of the goal . . . shoots . . . goes down . . . he scores . . . Bobby Orr has scored . . . The Boston Bruins have won the Stanley Cup.

Orr lay dazed on the ice. His teammates covered him with their bodies. The fans leaped on the ice, slipping and falling and sliding, in an attempt to get at their hero. The garbage and the paper cups and the rubber ducks came hurtling out from the seats. No one could hear the announcement. "Bobby Orr scores on an assist from Derek Sanderson, the time . . . 40 seconds of overtime."

Boston had won the Stanley Cup on Bobby Orr's magnificent shot, 4-3, with the puck slipping past Glenn Hall and the red light flashing and the crowd exploding at the same instant as Orr was taking a wild spill. Noel Picard, the bruising Blues defenseman, had landed on Orr just as he let the puck fly. The puck was going in the cage for Boston's first Cup in 29 years as Orr was flying through the air.

Let's look at it again on instant replay. Here's Orr getting the puck from Keenan, passing to Sanderson . . . getting the puck back and shooting. Now watch Orr . . . look at him flying through the air . . . he's down and the puck is in.

The wonders of television's instant replay had captured the moment on CBS video tape and I think they will be looking at that shot for years and years to come.

I looked at it myself several times and I've thought about it since. I can see Orr getting the puck from Sanderson. I can see the shot and Orr flying through the air. Of that I am sure.

I think I see something else as the puck goes in. I can't be sure. I may have to watch the instant replay a thousand more times. I think I see Bobby Orr smiling as he flies through the air.

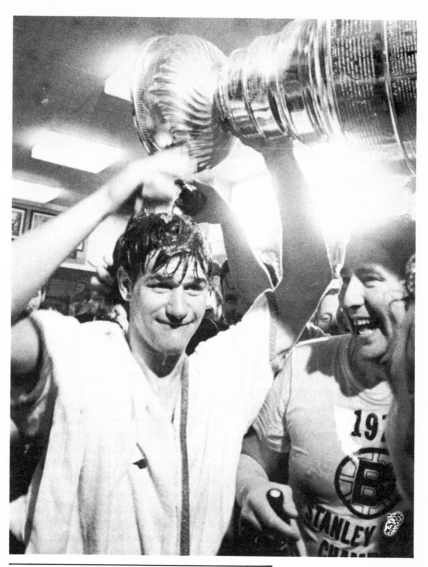

The Stanley Cup runneth over with champagne
on the head of Bobby Orr,
whose overtime goal did it.

Bill Currie

17

The Greatest of Groat

BILL CURRIE

BILL Currie, the universally proclaimed "Mouth of the South," was covering a football game at North Carolina State some years back when he became ill under the hot fall sun.

A stretcher was called in to remove The Mouth and he was carried off the field amid much buzzing from the stands and great consternation. Just then he waved his hands in front of his face.

"There's old Currie dying," said a fan, "but he has to wave goodbye before he goes."

"He wasn't dying," said a man who was there, "but the sun got in his eyes and he was shading his face. It was just that everybody expected him to go out in style and it looked like he was."

Currie is a rebel with a cause. He is the talkingest critter in the South and has turned on thousands to his combination of preachin', teachin', and entertainin' as he does sports broadcasting for WSOC in Charlotte, North Carolina. His assignments include Atlantic Coast Conference basketball, University of North Carolina football, most major events in the Tar Heel state and just about any public speaking event he can make.

Currie is one of the few big play-by-play broadcasters to work alone when he is doing a game.

"I don't need a color man," he says. "A color announcer is a guy who is paid to talk when everyone goes to the bathroom."

Currie has been making such brash, but honest statements, ever since he first sat behind a microphone at a small station, WHPE, in High Point, North Carolina.

Currie was born in High Point on December 6, 1924, and began talking almost immediately. In his biography, he announces he "died" March 12, 1950, which he explains was his wedding day.

After a few unsuccessful years in college, Currie turned to journalism. He was the sports editor of *The Enterprise* in High Point for seven years, moved to Winston-Salem, where he earned $2 a day for broadcasting the minor-league baseball games and expanded his voice across North Carolina with the Tar Heel network.

In Raleigh, North Carolina, Currie began making inroads on the establishment with his off-beat, highly entertaining way of calling a sports event. "Stay tuned folks," he would say, "I'll be coming up with a funny soon."

Currie talks straighter and entertains less in proportion to the excitement of the game. A good game doesn't need much help. A bad game —and most games are—receive aid from The Mouth from funny stories to poetry readings.

Currie hasn't been able to crack the national scene because, he says, "My voice is too damn southern." But he isn't afraid to offer some opinions about the state of broadcasting in the rest of the country.

"Sports announcers nowadays are about as colorless as a glass of gin," he says. "They are so immersed in themselves and so determined to pontificate about what really is nothing more than a game that they have forgotten that sports are supposed to be fun."

Despite all the words that pour from his tongue, Currie finds time to pour some more from his typewriter. He has written for *The Saturday Evening Post, Readers Digest, The New York Times* Magazine and *True Detective.* He is now working on a book, which he promises "will be banned in Boston."

Basketball is the biggest sport in North Carolina and Currie is the biggest thing in basketball. He has expanded his college duties to include the professional games of the Carolina Cougars of the ABA.

Here The Mouth goes back some 20 years to recall the greatest basketball game he ever saw or ever called. The Mouth is above the floor at the Reynolds Coliseum in Raleigh, North Carolina, on December 30, 1950.

Bill Currie

It was the kind of afternoon I knew I would enjoy. I could keep my mouth going most of the time. That's about the best thing I have going for me.

Duke and Tulane were meeting in a consolation game in the Dixie Classic in the afternoon before North Carolina State and Colgate met in the finals of the Classic at the Reynolds Coliseum in Raleigh. NC State was the host team in the tourney, took most of the money, had most of the good players, enjoyed most of the national publicity and was about to cap the whole darn thing with a championship.

Four North Carolina teams, NC State, North Carolina, Duke and Wake Forest, were regulars in the tournament, with four outsiders being invited down over the Christmas holidays for some Southern hospitality—usually in the form of defeats.

It was as much a social event as it was a sports event with kids and their dates filling the Coliseum every day and every night during the four days of the tournament and staying up partying most of the rest of the time.

You have to broadcast four basketball games a day from a hard, wooden chair and when you are finished with a tournament like this you are ready for an orthopedic specialist. Some of these consolation games get so dull you could read a newspaper and broadcast the basketball game at the same time and not miss a thing in each. That's what I thought this afternoon's game would be like. I was ready with a big, thick paper and a lot of tall stories for my day's work on WRAL in Raleigh.

There was one thing and one player that made the consolation game a little different and a little more worth watching.

There was a kid in the Duke lineup that everybody down South and everybody in the country was talking about. He was a thin, serious-looking, dark-haired lad by the name of Richard Morrow Groat. He was a junior at Duke, acclaimed as everybody's All-

185

America and one of those really exciting scorers from almost anywhere on the floor.

Dick Groat, who was to go on to baseball fame with the Pittsburgh Pirates and win a Most Valuable Player Award in 1960
along the way to his 14 major league seasons, was a jump shooter
when the two-handed set shot was still popular. He would drive
to the basket with force and knock anybody down in his way. They
were not so quick to call charging fouls in those days as they are
today and you could get away with a lot more.

Duke wasn't much of a ball club. Groat was the whole team.
If he had a hot day they might be able to handle Tulane. If he
didn't they could forget about it and I might read some poetry
on the air.

Just before the game was to start I went down to the locker
rooms of both schools to check the boys out. I knew most of them
without any trouble but once in a while those college teams have
a way of sneaking in a kid you have never seen before. I'm so blind
I'd never spot a number from upstairs so I had to check on how
they walked, how they bent over to tie their shoelaces, how they
reached for the water bucket so I could know them at a glance.
Groat was easy to spot. He was the one never smiling.

He had come down from someplace called Swissvale, Pennsylvania, near Pittsburgh, and looked like he had spent all his time
in the mines there. His face was drawn and his cheeks were sunken.
You could hardly see any color in them and before he went out to
play you wondered if he was going to live through the game.

But he could play the game. His coach, Hal Bradley, just about
loved him. Groat was an unusual star. He would listen to the coach.

"If you see that he is doing anything wrong in the game," Bradley said, "you just go up and tell him about it. He listens carefully, nods his head and you know he has it. The next day he is
on the floor practicing the thing you told him about and before
long he is so good at it, he has made a weakness into one of his
strengths."

When Groat first came to Duke he was little more than a
shooter. There was an assistant coach there at the time, a guy who
almost had as big a mouth as me, named Arnold Auerbach. Yeah,
that's the same Arnold (Red) Auerbach, who was to go on and
dominate the game with Bill Russell and the Boston Celtics for
several hundred years. Well, anyway, Arnold really knew the game
inside and out. He'd tell you that just as soon as looking at you.
Well, one day he gets a look at Groat and decides that the kid

from Pittsburgh is a good shooter and all that but he would be better if he knew how to move on the floor. Auerbach wanted to teach Groat how to fake and pivot and get away from his man instead of driving through him. So Red and Groat would get in these one-on-one games alone in the gymnasium down there at Duke until one or the other of them would collapse. It wasn't always Auerbach, either, even though he was about 15 years older than Groat.

With all this work, Groat had become a real faker on the court. You'd look at him there and he'd be here. You'd look at him here and he'd be laying the ball in. He was already averaging 25.2 points a game and would go on in this 1950-51 season to score 831 for the best average in the country. He was a sure All-America, so even though Duke and Tulane had already been beaten and were out of the tournament title game, everybody was interested.

Thre were 12,400 people in the Coliseum. And they were all ready to root against Groat and Duke. You have to understand that the North Carolina college basketball fans hate each other so cordially. This was NC State's big tournament, the Dixie Classic, and they were the dominant school. I'd say that students and fans of NC State made up 10,000 of the crowd. They were watching all the games of the other North Carolina schools to root against them. The whole afternoon was just a practice session for the final at night when they could yell at the Yankees from Colgate and root NC State home. They were just ready as could be to shout Duke off the floor.

And that Groat had the big reputation, All-America and all, leading scorer, all the rest, so he would be their particular target. They just might boo him out of the building if he even missed a free throw.

I didn't think much of this would really bother Groat. He had been through some tough tournaments already and never seemed to be slowed down. God knows he was competitive so I expected he would have a good game and Duke might win and we could get on with the serious business at hand, which was the night final between Colgate and NC State. NC State had all the money in the till. Now they just wanted to finish up right with the title game.

I finally got settled down in the chair in the broadcasting booth and hoped my back would make it. I had some seat. I had a choice of sitting back in my uncomfortable chair and missing the game or leaning forward, seeing the game and ruining my back for life. I leaned forward in my chair. What else could I do? People were skipping their naps that afternoon to hear me. I had to give them something besides the funny lines I stole from the papers.

Afternoon, everybody, and welcome to the Reynolds Coliseum here in Raleigh. This afternoon it's Duke and Tulane in a consolation game of the Dixie Classic. The boy to watch is All-America Dick Groat of Duke and we intend to watch him for you all afternoon.

The teams had finished their warmups and now they were both sitting along the sidelines on their benches as the public address announcer gave the starting lineups. Now they were almost all introduced with lots of rebel yells for Tulane and lots of hissing and booing for the Duke boys. And now they were about to introduce Groat. Well, that noise started somewhere up there in the top rows and it spread down to the bottom rows in a hurry and before you knew it that whole arena was one big boo palace for Dick Groat. You got the impression real quick-like that this crowd wasn't taking kindly to Dick Groat. They didn't like all the publicity he was getting and they didn't like his school and they just sure didn't like him. Dick Groat, whatever he did this day, was going to do it in front of an audience about as friendly as a roomful of starving tigers.

Coach Hal Bradley of Duke stood there talking to his players. They acted like they didn't even hear the crowd. All the attention was focused on Groat but he never showed that he noticed. His face was just that same, impassive, stoic look it had been all through his career. His cheeks looked a little more sunken to me but maybe I was just imagining it. The fans really were getting on him now but he never showed that he heard it. I always thought years later that it was a good thing he still had his hair. He didn't have any when he was a baseball player later in his career. If he didn't have any now they sure would have made some bad jokes about it. We all would have. That would have added something to the noise, too.

Groat had come to Duke because it was as good a baseball school as there was in the country. He had been a fine shortstop at Duke and one of the few players to ever be able to combine great baseball skills with great basketball skills.

Y'all ready? Here we go. The tap goes to Tulane. Well, right there we got an upset. The ball bounces around and now Duke has it. There's Groat at the key. They're looking for him, they find him, he shoots . . . he doesn't find the basket.

Now they really started to let him have it. Groat had gotten the first shot of the game and hadn't scored. Hell, anybody could have done that but when a big college player with that kind of reputation does that they really give him the business. I guess all Dick Groat could have done that afternoon to quiet them down was score 100 points or so. That would have gotten the crowd off his back, maybe, but nothing less. They wanted to see North Carolina State win the tournament and the rest of the North Carolina schools lose. But if they weren't going to lose, at least they could see a great show. It would give them something to talk about on their way back to class the next week after the holidays.

Before you knew it Tulane had jumped ahead by fifteen points and Groat just couldn't buy a basket. I don't know if it was the crowd or what but he wasn't doing a thing. Whenever he shot he missed, whenever he was fouled he missed the free throw. He just wasn't any kind of player. All-America? He didn't look like he was going to even be All-Duke.

I guess they started marching out in the middle of the first half. Duke trailed by 20 points and Groat had a total of two points. That's right, two points. One itty-bitty field goal and nothing else. He had missed three free throws besides and looked about as bad as a basketball player can look when he's doing just everything wrong. The fans were really giving him the business now.

Well, here we are with just one minute left in the first half. The score is Tulane 56, Duke 27, Groat four. He sure has smelled out the place. They can't leave fast enough. They're pouring out of the aisles as if they were train riders tryin' to escape from Jesse James.

Some of the NC State kids were going down the aisles booing at Groat as they walked out the doors. He was having as awful a time as he had ever had in his life.

There's the buzzer for the end of the first half and Tulane is just running away with this little old ball game, 56-27. If my arithmetic is correct that puts Duke's Blue Devils some 29 points behind the Green Wave. It isn't easy to figure out why. All-America Dick Groat has four whole points.

I'd guess more than half of the Coliseum had emptied out by this time. A lot of them just wanted to rest up for the championship game at night. Some of them probably had been put asleep by the game. Others needed a cool drink to take away the bad taste in their mouths.

A few hung on to watch the second half. A million of them

later said they did. I have to admit I might not have been one of them if I wasn't getting paid (not enough) to do both halves of the game.

Well, here comes Duke back out on the floor. Groat is with them. You could hardly blame the old boy if he had taken the day off but he'll try it again. Maybe he can keep the score a little respectable in the second half.

The second half started and a lot of people really didn't notice. The building had thinned out so much that people were standing around a lot just chatting and being friendly like. It was a social occasion like I said and there was just no better time to be social than in the second half of a lost game in the consolation round of a tournament with the championship coming up a few hours later.

I can't rightly tell when it happened.

Maybe I was reading the paper then or reciting some poetry or doing some sermonizing but all of a sudden Groat had ten points. When he came out for the second half, his face looked more serious and more determined than ever. The boy had been embarrassed in that first half and for an athlete being embarrassed is an awful lot worse than being beaten. They were laughing at Groat instead of booing him. Now they were just ignoring him when the second half started. I don't really think he noticed. He was just too busy performing a miracle.

Groat with the ball at the key, jumps up high, shoots . . . good . . . Groat has another . . . he's got 18 points now . . . Duke has closed the game to 12 . . .

All of a sudden Groat was everywhere. He was stealing the ball on defense, he was getting it back quickly on offense, he was shooting the eyes out of the basket when he got up court, he was passing the ball to the free man underneath. You really didn't think it was the same boy. He still wasn't cracking a smile but Duke was closing in on Tulane.

The crowd stopped talking and started watching about this time. The Duke fans had continued to encourage Groat and his teammates but there weren't very many of them. But now they were yelling so loud for him they sounded like five times as many. The NC State fans and all the rest of the people in the building just quit rooting and started admiring him. He was everywhere. I couldn't imagine how a ball player who looked so bad for one half could look so good for the next.

Soon I was so excited I even put down my newspaper. All I could think of was Dick Groat. I tried to tell the folks everything

I knew about him because that's all they were going to be talking about for a long time. So I told the listeners how he ran and how he looked and how he didn't talk very much and how that thin, skinny face of his seemed set in that expressionless way.

Now Groat had 28 points and Duke was two points away from tying the ball game. Tulane had scored 16 points for the whole second half and Groat by himself now had 24. I hate statistics in sports. I hate those announcers who give you all the numbers and forget to tell you what the band is playing or how the hot dogs taste or what color drawers the cheerleaders are wearing. But once in a while you run into a couple of numbers that tell a pretty good story.

Time out for Tulane. There's 90 seconds left in this game. Tulane has scored 16 points in this half and Groat has scored 24 for Duke. Now ain't that somethin'? Duke is just two points back and Dick Groat has made this one of the greatest one-man shows these eyes have ever seen.

Now the Blue Devils had the ball again. They came up court quickly and the ball went to Groat. He was on the right side, just off the key when he jumped and let another one fly.

Groat lets 'er go . . . good . . . Dick Groat has scored again for Duke. The score is now tied, 72-72. Dick Groat has scored 30 points. He has 26 points in this half. He had four at halftime and Tulane led, 56-27, when they went inside. I don't know what was said in between halves but whatever it was, Duke ought to try it every game.

Now the crowd was really going wild. There were less than 6,000 people in the Coliseum by now but they were basketball fans and they cared. A lot of them who had been rooting against Duke and against Groat seemed to switch. They were just interested in seeing if this skinny kid from Pensylvania could come all the way back.

Just 25 seconds to go . . . the score is tied . . . Duke has the ball . . . it goes to Groat . . .

I was leaning so far forward by now that I was almost on the floor. If they threw me the ball I probably would have thrown it in myself. My back was killing me from sitting in that hard seat all afternoon but I hardly minded it. You get a feeling you're floating when you get involved in a ball game like this. You don't even feel any pain, you don't even feel tired, and if your mouth is dry, you suddenly get extra juices and figure you can go on talking now for six or seven days without stopping for air.

Groat is guarded closely . . . he moves to the basket, stops, jumps

. . . in . . . Groat has scored again . . . Duke goes ahead, 74-72 . . . Groat has scored 32 points.

Then the buzzer came and they poured on the floor and mauled Groat. I could almost see the edges of a smile breaking through. He had a lot to be laughing about.

His shooting was a great contribution to basketball. But maybe there was a bigger one. I think Groat proved that if you play the game all-out, both halves, some amazing things can happen. It was the greatest comeback I ever saw a basketball player make.

I guess it was Groat years later, as a captain and shortstop of the Pittsburgh Pirates, who proved it again in baseball against the Yankees. He sure is one fellow you don't want to mess with if he is way behind in anything.

Dick Groat's comeback was like nothing ever seen by Bill Currie, the Mouth of the South.

Bob Wolff

18

The Perfect Game

BOB WOLFF

DUKE University gained a broadcaster and lost a ballplayer the day Bob Wolff broke his ankle.

"I was a sophomore and I had once batted .583 in high school. I thought I could be a big leaguer," Wolff said. "When I was injured I did some broadcasting on the local radio station. When I got well they offered me a full-time job."

Wolff still nursed ambitions about playing center field for the Yankees or the Giants so he asked his coach, Jack Coombs, for an opinion.

"I want an honest answer, coach," said Wolff. "Do you think I can make the major leagues or should I take the broadcasting job?"

"You better keep talking," said Coombs.

So the baseball career ended, except for some serious sandlot efforts, and the broadcasting career began in earnest.

Wolff, who was born in New York, was raised on Long Island and attended Woodmere Academy. He worked on station WDNC in Durham, North Carolina, while an undergraduate at Duke. After finishing school in

1942 with Phi Beta Kappa honors, he entered the Navy as a supply officer. He was assigned to Camp Peary, Virginia.

"I have always had some lucky breaks," he says. "That was one of my best. That's where I met a Navy nurse by the name of Jane Louise Hoy." Nurse Hoy is now Mrs. Wolff and the mother of their three children, Bob, a Princeton graduate, Rick, an underclassman at Harvard, and Margy, a high school senior.

While still in the Navy in the Solomon Islands, Wolff wrote a book explaining how the Navy's method of handling advanced base supply questions should be revised, and sent it on to the the the Navy Department in Washington.

"I could have been court-martialed or commended," he said. "When they called me to Washington I wasn't sure which it would be."

It turned out to be the latter and he was put in charge of revamping Navy supply regulations. The Navy position in Washington gave Wolff a chance to resume his broadcasting career at WINX in Washington.

After his discharge, Wolff became the first sports announcer on WTTG, a Dumont station operating in a new field called television.

Wolff teamed with Arch McDonald in broadcasting the games of the Washington Senators. He stayed in Washington from 1947 through 1960 covering Washington baseball and a variety of other assignments including the Redskins in football, a hockey team called the Washington Lions, the Washington Caps basketball team, tennis, boxing and golf.

He also handled college football in the Washington and Baltimore areas as well as bowl games before doing the pro games of the Baltimore Colts and the Cleveland Browns.

"Around that time I began commuting in the winters to New York to televise the New York Knickerbockers in basketball and the New York Rangers in hockey. I would leave Washington at 3:30 P.M. and get back to Washington about 1:00 A.M. the following morning. Most people never even knew I was gone," he says.

His commuting was discontinued in 1962 when he moved to New York to be a play-by-play telecaster on NBC-TV's Baseball Game of the Week. He teamed with Joe Garagiola in that capacity for three seasons while continuing his Garden assignments as well.

When the Chairman and President of the Madison Square Garden Corporation, Irving Mitchell Felt, was seeking a Director of Public Relations, Wolff was selected for the job. He left the broadcasting field to accept this new post. Shortly thereafter he was named a Garden Vice President. Three years later he assumed new responsibilities, leaving his public relations position to become Executive Assistant to the President.

"I welcomed the challenge of the administrative side of sports," Wolff said. "It was also an opportunity to spend more time at home with my growing family."

Now it is October 8, 1956, and Bob Wolff is in the broadcast booth at Yankee Stadium for the fifth game of the World Series between the Brooklyn Dodgers and the New York Yankees.

Wolff, and all the baseball world, will long remember this very perfect afternoon.

Bob Wolff

FOR ten seasons I had waited for the Washington Senators to do something exciting.

As the Senators' baseball broadcaster my opportunity for doing the World Series was slim. Gillette, sponsoring the games, had a policy of hiring broadcasters from the competing cities for the coverage of the classic plus a few others who had gradually become regulars on their events. The last time the Senators had been in the World Series was 1933 and a repeat performance still seemed many years away.

Every time I suggested that the selection system was not designed for broadcasters in cities like Washington I got the same answer from the Gillette people.

"Have patience," they would say, "your chance will come."

I kept hoping, and waiting.

Then came two breaks which combined to finally get me into the broadcasting booth just in time to describe a once-in-a-lifetime baseball game.

The All-Star game was scheduled for July 10, 1956. It was to be played in Washington's Griffith Stadium. Gillette decided they would add me to the broadcasting team to get some local color. The National League beat the American League, 7-3, in my home park. I must have done a good job on the game because in September I was told that I was being considered as a broadcaster on the World Series even though Washington had finished in seventh place.

There was only one hitch. Brooklyn had to win the pennant.

The Dodgers were in a three-way battle with Milwaukee and Cincinnati for the flag. It went down to the last day of the season.

I was doing the Washington games with one eye on the Dodger games. Cincinnati announcers and Milwaukee announcers had already been picked. Vin Scully, who did the Dodger games, and Mel Allen, who broadcast the Yankee games, had been selected to do the television of the Series. Gillette didn't want another Dodger announcer or a Yankee announcer for the radio side as well, so I was to get the job.

Finally, the waiting was over. The Dodgers clinched the pennant on the last day of the year and Gillette hired me to do the radio broadcast with Bob Neal over Mutual. I received a call from Ed Wilhelm, an executive with Gillette's advertising agency, confirming the assignment.

I flew up to New York two days before the Series was to open at Ebbets Field on October 3. I checked into the Warwick Hotel in Manhattan and bought every one of the New York newspapers. Herb Heft, the publicity man for the Washington Senators, joined me in my room and we began preparing for the Series opener. Herb's job was to aid me with notes, statistics and background information.

There is only one way to prepare for a big broadcasting event. Do your homework. I handle every big sports event as if it were an examination in college. My best assurance against nervousness is preparation.

Herb and I went over all the material on the Dodgers and the Yankees. We filled out three-by-five cards with all the information we could gather on the players. We had their basic statistics, their averages, an anecdote or two about each player, any fact or tidbit we could gather that would help me inform and entertain.

Brooklyn won the first two games in Ebbets Field. The Yankees came back to win the next two. The Series was now tied at two games each. Game five was scheduled the next afternoon, October 8, 1956, in Yankee Stadium.

The Dodgers had won their first World Series ever in 1955 and now were trying to prove that that triumph was no fluke. The Yankees, embarrassed by the defeat, were being driven by their crafty old manager, Casey Stengel, to prove that 1955 was an accident.

We ordered dinner in our room at the Warwick and Herb and I looked up from our small, white cards for a break when it arrived. Don Larsen and Sal Maglie were the pitchers for the next day. Larsen, 26 years old, had been 11-5 for the season. He had improved tremendously after a slow start when he switched from a full over-the-head windup to a no-windup motion. Casey Stengel had always liked Larsen as a pitcher and protected him when the freewheeling righthander had driven into a telephone pole in Florida early one spring training morning.

Maglie, 39 years old, a Dodger through a trade with Cleveland, was 13-5 for the season. He had been the tough Sal the Barber for the Giants, a Dodger-killer, before coming back to the National League with Brooklyn. He had been a marvelous pickup and had pitched a no-hit, no-run game against the Phillies on September 25, 1956, in a must-win game for the Dodgers. He was one of the oldest men in baseball history to ever record a no-hitter.

"Wouldn't it be something if Maglie pitched a no-hitter against the Yankees?" I said to Herb.

"Nobody pitches no-hitters in the World Series," said Herb.

Nobody had. In 53 years there had never been a no-hitter in a World Series game.

We finished our dinner, went over our cards, talked about the next day's game and felt confident we would have another good broadcast from Yankee Stadium. The Yankees and Dodgers had always played exciting Series games. All I had to do was describe the action. They would provide the drama.

I finished writing my 15-minute introduction, went over it thoroughly with Herb and felt confident and at ease going into this fifth game.

There was some nervousness in the morning as there always is. But I knew I was prepared.

At 10:00 o'clock I was outside the hotel waiting for the car sent over by the Gillette people. We got to Yankee Stadium about 10:30 and I spent most of the ride up there reading and editing my 15-minute preamble. I would set the scene for the fifth game, Bob Neal would do the first four and a half innings and I would do the last four and a half.

I spent some time in both clubhouses, wrote down whatever chit-chat I thought I might use on the air and left the benches when they became too crowded with sportswriters.

Herb and I walked into the crowded press room under the stands at the Stadium. We talked to some of the sportswriters, checked the starting lineups, drank a glass of milk (my stomach was too nervous for much more) and went up to the booth. The radio booth was in the mezzanine section of the Stadium, directly behind home plate, with a fine view of the action.

Besides Neal and myself, Herb Heft was in the booth, along with Giff Campbell and Ed King, our engineers; Frank Zuzulo of Mutual; and Joel Nixon, our producer. Paul Jonas, who had been Mutual's sports director for many years, and Art Gleeson, who was now in that position, came by to wish us well. We were minutes away from the start of the fifth game of the 1956 World Series. The drama was about to unfurl. What a drama it was to be.

. . . and now to carry you through the play-by-play of the first half of the game, here's Bob Neal.

The 15-minute introduction had gone well, the game was about to begin and the butterflies were gone. Once you start a game, even a World Series game, the description becomes routine. You don't have to build excitement into a World Series game. The crowd does that. You just have to describe what you see and make sure your concentration never wavers.

Jim Gilliam, Pee Wee Reese and Duke Snider went down easily. Reese had a 3-2 count before he went out as the Dodgers had nothing across in the first inning. Neal concentrated on describing Larsen's new no-windup pitching style.

Hank Bauer, Joe Collins and Mickey Mantle went down in the Yankee first inning against Sal Maglie. Neal mentioned Maglie's late-season no-hitter against the Phillies.

At the end of three innings neither team had come up with a base-runner. Nothing but outs. During the commercial break, I talked to Joel Nixon.

"Pretty clean score card," I said, beckoning to the unsullied hit columns. "If it's still that way when I take over, the way I'd like to handle it is to keep informing everyone of exactly what's happening—there are countless ways and synonyms to describe how a pitcher has not yielded a hit—without using the specific words 'no-hitter.' Is that all right with you?"

"Fine," said Nixon. "As long as you make it clear."

Only three innings had gone by. It all seemed very academic. Nobody pitches no-hitters in World Series games. But I always believed strongly in preparation.

During my years in Washington I had considered many times what my approach would be if the no-hit situation were ever to arise. Whether people should or should not be superstitious was hardly the question. The fact is that some were, and they were entitled to their rights as well as anyone else. If I could inform everyone without offending this group, I'd be fulfilling my broadcast role in the broadest possible manner.

But the key I knew was not just the choice of words—it was when they were used. A broadcaster, I felt, could make any reference he wanted to the no-hitter in progress, including the actual words "no-hitter" if he desired, as long as he avoided using them just before the pitch was made that could end it all. The pitching feat could be described as frequently as necessary, after each half inning or after each out if need be, but when the new batter stepped in, the play was what counted.

The Dodgers went down in order in the top of the fourth inning. The Yankees came up to bat. Bauer grounded out, Robinson to Hodges. Collins was out on a called strike three.

Mickey Mantle up. Two out. Bottom of the fourth inning. Here's Maglie's pitch to the Yankee centerfielder . . . there's a high drive out to right field . . . it's going . . . it's going . . . that one's gone . . . a home run by Mickey Mantle and the Yankees lead 1-0.

Mantle, a switch-hitter, batting left-handed against Maglie, had hit a long fly ball that landed half way up the first deck in right field for a Yankee lead. There was no question about the first hit of the game. It was tagged. Maglie got out of the rest of the inning without damage as the Dodgers came up to bat in the fifth. This was Neal's last half inning. I would begin broadcasting in the bottom of the fifth inning.

One out. Gil Hodges is up. Larsen ready, here's the pitch . . . a line drive to left center field . . . Mantle racing over . . . racing over . . . he makes a back-handed catch . . . Mickey Mantle has robbed Hodges of a double, maybe more, with a brilliant backhanded catch of a line drive deep into left centerfield.

Sandy Amoros went out and the Dodgers were down in the top of the fifth inning. Larsen still hadn't allowed a single base runner. He had retired 15 straight with the help of Mantle's fantastic catch. I was about to take over at the microphone.

Nine years before, in 1947, Red Barber had been broadcasting a World Series game between these same two teams. Bill Bevens hadn't allowed a hit through eight and two-third innings. The Yankee right-hander then gave up a double off the wall to pinch-hitter Cookie Lavagetto. The Dodgers not only broke up the no-hitter but won the fourth game of the Series with that blow. Barber had used the words "no-hitter" as the game went along. He had mentioned it just before Lavagetto doubled. Superstitious people blamed

Barber—a most able and honest reporter. These cries might have been muted had there been a different word cushion between the no-hit reminder and Lavagetto's hit.

. . . and now to carry you through the rest of the game, here's Bob Wolff.

Hi, everybody. It's not only a great game—but what pitching performances! Larsen has retired all fifteen men he's faced; Maglie has given up the game's only hit and only run, the homer by Mantle. We move now into the bottom of the fifth.

The Yankees went out in the fifth and the Dodgers came up for the sixth. It was still 1-0 in favor of the Yankees and the Dodger fans in the crowd were pulling for a Brooklyn rally. Games were tied 2-2 and the Dodgers wanted this one to get ahead so they could win at Ebbets Field with a victory in the last two games. Carl Furillo, Roy Campanella and Sal Maglie went out easily. The Yankees rallied again in the bottom of the sixth. Andy Carey started it with a single. Larsen bunted him to second.

Bauer is the batter against Maglie. The righthander delivers . . . a line drive to right field . . . base hit . . . Carey's coming around third and in to score as Furillo throws the ball to second base. The Yankees lead, 2-0.

Before the inning ended I mentioned that the crowd was becoming increasingly aware that the Yankees had supplied the only offense so far—two runs and four hits—while the Dodgers had been going down in order. The Dodgers were now coming to bat in the seventh. I focused my attention on the play-by-play. Gilliam grounded out, Gil McDougald to Collins. One out. Reese hit an easy fly ball to Mantle in centerfield. Two out. Duke Snider swung late on Larsen's fast ball and lofted a fly ball to left. Three out.

No runs for the Dodgers in the top of the seventh. Larsen has retired 21 straight men. The Yankees have four hits. That's all there are in the game.

Now the crowd's response became part of the drama. They were restless through the Yankee seventh. They wanted the Dodgers to bat. They wanted to see Larsen pitch again. They wanted to see if such a feat were really possible. As soon as Jackie Robinson came to bat, the crowd grew still. They were no longer just rooting for a game. They were rooting for themselves. I have always believed people root for no-hitters almost as much for their own part in it as witnesses as for the pitcher's part.

Jackie Robinson up, Larsen ready, the pitch . . . right back to the mound. Larsen has it, throws to Collins, one out. Here comes Gil

Hodges. Outfield shaded toward left. Last time up, Hodges was out on a wicked line drive to left center in the fifth inning.

The crowd was more tense than ever. This was the man who had threatened Larsen the most. Hodges was an imposing figure at the plate, a big man, deep in the box, his cap pulled down well over his forehead.

Hodges swings . . . a line drive . . . right to Carey. Two out. Amoros up. Larsen looks in, gets the sign, delivers, Amoros swings, there's a fly ball to centerfield, Mantle is there, under it . . . he has it. The Dodgers are out in the eighth inning with nothing across . . . and their totals remain blank in the ball game. Larsen has retired 24 straight Dodgers as we await the final chapter. The Yankees have two runs, four hits and no errors.

The Yankees couldn't go out fast enough in their half of the eighth inning. It was as if they were as anxious as the fans to see if Larsen could do it. Now it was the ninth inning. The scheduled hitters were Carl Furillo, Roy Campanella and Maglie. There would certainly be a pinch-hitter for Maglie.

Larsen was ready to pitch to Furillo. The pitcher took a deep breath and threw his last warm-up pitch. Now the Dodger right fielder dug in at home plate. The crowd was still. There was very little movement or sound anywhere.

Furillo, 34 years old, a Dodger for 11 seasons, kicked some dirt off his shoes, pumped his bat at Larsen and looked out at the pitcher. Larsen bent low to study Yogi Berra's sign.

Now he's ready . . . the pitch . . . there's a foul back behind home plate . . . strike one.

The roar was intense . . . louder than anything in the previous inning. The crowd was in the game as much as Larsen. Emotions were running deep. There was no longer any rooting for winning or losing. There was rooting only for the historical moment. Don Larsen was on the threshold.

The pitch . . . ball one.

Groans. Gasps. Some boos. Furillo removing more dirt from his shoes. Larsen standing on the rubber, a tall figure, bent over, his eyes on Berra's stubby fingers . . . one finger down . . . Larsen, a deep breath. . . .

Furillo swings . . . a fly ball to right field . . . not too deep . . . Bauer getting under it . . . has it . . . listen to that crowd. . . . One question consumes them all . . . is it possible? . . . can it happen? . . . With one out Larsen goes to the resin bag . . . now looks in . . . here comes Campy.

Bob Wolff

The Dodger catcher, a stocky figure, moved slowly to the plate. He swung a heavy bat, dropped it and picked up his regular bat. He was 34 years old and had been with the Dodgers since 1948. He had been playing professional baseball since 1936 when he started in Philadelphia in the Negro leagues as a 15-year-old. He had played with Josh Gibson and caught Satchel Paige. He had caught games in three different towns on the same day as a youngster. He was growing old now. He had batted only .219 but had hit 20 home runs with 73 RBIs. He was still an outstanding hitter when he got his pitch.

Larsen looks in at Berra and gets the sign . . . now he's ready . . . rocks and delivers to Campanella . . . there's a ground ball to second . . . Billy Martin has it . . . over to first . . . Campanella is out. Two down . . . the crowd is going wild . . . the fans are yelling, shouting, cheering, imploring Larsen to come through . . . what a moment . . . what a game.

Everybody was standing now with Dale Mitchell coming out of the on-deck circle to hit for Maglie. The Dodgers were down to their last out and they had called on Mitchell to pinch-hit.

"My job was to get on base any way I could," Mitchell would recall years later. "It was still a 2-0 game and if I could get on I could bring the tying run to the plate. I was just looking for a pitch I could handle."

Mitchell had hit .300 in six seasons for the Cleveland Indians. At 35, he had been an effective pinch-hitter for the Dodgers. Now he was the man between Larsen and the greatest pitching feat in World Series history. Mitchell was a left-handed hitter standing 6-1, weighing 195 pounds, with a stance slightly bent over. He had faced Larsen many times before in the American League. The only thing different now was Larsen's no-windup style. That, and the 26 straight outs.

Mitchell steps in. Larsen's ready . . . the pitch . . . Larsen fires a fastball just off the plate . . . ball one.

Babe Pinelli was the home plate umpire. He had announced before the Series that this would be his last year of umpiring. This would be the last time he would umpire a major league game behind home plate.

Larsen looks in . . . here's the pitch . . . a strike called . . . a fastball . . . one and one the count on pinch-hitter Dale Mitchell.

The crowd noise was deafening . . . a rising sound which reverberated through Yankee Stadium . . . all eyes were on Larsen, studying his every move, his back bent as he waited for Berra's sign . . . then suddenly the silence, the almost unbearable moment of suspense as the pitch was on its way.

Larsen throws. . . . Mitchell swings and fouls it back . . . one and two count . . . ninth inning . . . two out . . . ball one, strike two to Mitchell.

Larsen took off his cap and rubbed at his forehead. Now he put the cap back on and bent low again for the sign. Berra wiggled his stubby finger. Larsen began to pivot his body.

Here comes the pitch.

Babe Pinelli stood immobile at home plate. The baseball was in Berra's glove but there was no sign. Pinelli had waited a long instant. It seemed very long. It seemed as if all the world had suddenly been frozen in its place for that fraction of a second. And then Pinelli's right hand began moving up from his side, the fist clenched tightly, now at his head, now over his head, now stretched to its full reach.

Strike three called . . . a NO-HITTER . . . he's done it . . . a perfect game for Don Larsen . . . Yogi Berra runs out there, he leaps on Larsen . . . and he's swarmed by his teammates . . . listen to this crowd roar . . . Don Larsen has retired all 27 Dodger batters in a row. He has pitched a perfect no-hit, no-run game and the Yankees win the fifth game of the Series, 2-0. . . .

There were 64,519 people standing and shouting and waving and laughing. They had been part of history. As Larsen had completed his masterpiece, they were guaranteed a small piece of fame. They had been there. They had seen it with their own eyes. No one could ever take this game away from them.

I never realized how tense I was as I broadcast this game to sixty million people until it was over. Then I couldn't lift my right arm. It ached for 24 hours. I had thrown every pitch with Larsen.

Letters and telegrams poured in from people all over the country and throughout the world who told me how thrilled they were with the broadcast of this great game. With all the kind words, I will probably remember best the man driving his car that afternoon in Idaho. He had lost control of his vehicle and crashed into a railroad car at a crossing. When the judge asked him what had happened he said, "I wasn't concentrating on my driving, your honor, I was too busy listening to Bob Wolff describe Larsen's perfect game."

The case was dismissed.

Ray Scott

19

In the Clutch...
Green Bay

**RAY
SCOTT**

A COACH named Vince Lombardi, a quarterback named Bart Starr and a broadcaster named Ray Scott spanned an era considered by many the most significant in professional football history.

Scott televised the games of Lombardi's Green Bay Packers, led by the magnificent Starr, for more than a decade. It was during this time that Green Bay, under Lombardi, changed from a struggling team to one of the greatest in the game's history.

Scott was assigned to do the Green Bay games by the Columbia Broadcasting System in 1956. The Packers were still a poor team.

"CBS was almost apologetic about giving me the Green Bay games," said Scott, "but it certainly turned into a great break."

Scott's deep-throated, concise descriptions of the Packer games were as much a trademark of the team to the television viewing public as Starr, Paul Hornung, Jimmy Taylor, Jerry Kramer and all the rest of the Packers.

CBS began shifting broadcasters on a rotating basis so there is no longer personal identification with any single team, but for more than a decade Ray Scott meant Packer football.

Scott began his career for $55 a month at a small station in his home town of Johnstown, Pennsylvania, in 1937. For that princely sum, he also wrote copy, sold advertising time and picked up a loose broom.

A year later he began his play-by-play career with high school football and basketball games in Western Pennsylvania.

After time out for Army duty during World War II, Scott returned to WJAC in Johnstown. He then moved to WCAE in Pittsburgh and did Carnegie Tech football on a suburban radio station.

Two years later he left broadcasting to take a job with the advertising agency that handled the sponsorship of the college games, doing freelance announcing at the same time.

"It was about this time that television was making inroads on sports," Scott said, "and I recognized that this would make it a whole new ball game."

Through his ad agency connections, Scott helped sell the idea of professional football coverage to the Westinghouse Electric Corporation and the games were carried on the Dumont Television Network. He began doing NFL games in 1953 with Herman Hickman as the halftime entertainer and analyst. Betty Furness was at the height of her career at the same time as the girl who opened the Westinghouse refrigerators on television.

"We had professional football on in prime time on Saturday nights against programs like the "Show of Shows" with Sid Caesar and Jackie Gleason's show. A second game was televised on Sunday afternoon," he said.

In the 1956 Sugar Bowl, Scott was involved in one of the most dramatic moments of broadcasting history.

"I was doing the Pittsburgh-Georgia Tech football game on ABC," Scott said. "This was the first time a Negro college football player was to play in the Sugar Bowl."

That would have had enough impact by itself. But the drama increased when Scott's broadcasting partner, Bill Stern, became ill.

"After a couple of plays it was obvious Bill couldn't manage," Scott said. "They took him off the air and I did the game myself. The game dramatically hinged on an interference call against the Negro back for Pitt which led to the game's only score and a 7-0 Georgia Tech victory."

Scott began broadcasting the Green Bay games the following season. He now does pro football with Pat Summerall, broadcasts the Washington Senators' televised games, college bowl games, west coast basketball games and various golf tournaments. In addition to his CBS duties,

Scott works for the Hughes Sports Network and goes wherever Dick Bailey, president of Hughes Sports Network, sends him.

Scott makes his home in Scottsdale, Arizona, where he lives with his wife, Eda, and their five children. One boy is with the Marines in Vietnam.

Here Scott is at the Cotton Bowl in Dallas, Texas, as the Green Bay Packers meet the Dallas Cowboys. It is January 1, 1967, and the winner will represent the NFL in the first Super Bowl.

Ray Scott

THE old year was running out. I had been with the Green Bay Packers since 1956. It seemed fitting that I spend New Year's Day in 1967 with them as Vince Lombardi's team tried to win its fourth National Football League title in the last six years. Few teams have ever dominated a sport as conclusively as Green Bay dominated the NFL in the Lombardi era.

I arrived in Dallas late Friday afternoon for the NFL championship game on Sunday between Green Bay and the Dallas Cowboys. Seven years after they entered the league, coach Tom Landry had the Dallas club in a championship game. They were young, strong and enthusiastic. They played the tough defense Landry knew as a player with the New York Giants and coach of the Cowboys.

Dallas was led by flamboyant Don Meredith. He would be a good contrast at quarterback to smooth, poised, skilled Bart Starr.

Starr had led the Packers to three championships, 1961, 1962, 1965, and was now trying for his fourth as Packer quarterback.

My old friend, Bill Kelley, a television executive from Pittsburgh, was with me at the game as he had been ever since our friendship started when I worked in Pittsburgh. He would serve as my spotter for the championship game.

We had a quiet dinner together Friday night after some long meetings with the CBS television people. After breakfast Saturday we attended another meeting with the production people. There would be some 40,000,000 people watching over television and we wanted to make sure everything was ready.

I'm an early riser so Sunday morning I was up just after the crack of dawn for the final NFL game of the 1966 season—or the first of 1967, if one wanted to be technical.

For the first time in professional football history, this game had an added significance. Kansas City and Buffalo were meeting for the AFL championship the same day in Buffalo and the winner of that game would get a chance for the first time to challenge the winner of the NFL championship game in what people were beginning to call the Super Bowl.

Bill Kelley and I had our breakfast and took off for the Cotton Bowl shortly after 10:00 o'clock. I was a little nervous. I guess you have to be a little nervous when you know that that many people are going to be watching you.

We got to the ball park as the crowds began to gather and we went first to the Green Bay dressing room. I checked on the condition of the players, wished Coach Lombardi good luck, said hello to a few of the players and left. Then I made another quick visit to say hello to Tom Landry, wish him well and greet some of his players.

The weather was perfect and it was good to be out in the warm air after so many months of the long, cold Green Bay winter. This game would be settled on the field. Unlike so many games in Green Bay, weather would be no factor.

I was in the booth now. We had all our charts and all our scorecards ready. I would have an entire half to get ready. Jack Buck was to broadcast the first half of the game and I would do the second half. I had been doing television games since 1952 and I was prepared. I knew that the picture carries the action and the job of the broadcaster is something like the sophisticated writing of captions. I had been with Green Bay all season so I had to make sure I never lost sight of the main objective, to give a fair and equal description of the game. A good play is a good play no matter who makes it.

There were 75,504 people in the Cotton Bowl and all of them seemed to be standing and shouting as Danny Villanueva of Dallas approached the football for the opening kickoff. He boomed the ball down to the end zone and the NFL championship game was on.

The smooth machine of the Packers immediately went to work. With Starr mixing his passes with runs by Elijah Pitts and Jimmy Taylor, the Packers drove relentlessly downfield. They were across midfield into Dallas territory before two minutes of the game were gone. With a little more than four minutes to go the Packers had a first down on the Dallas 17-yard line.

Dallas moved its secondary up close as they expected Starr to begin smashing out the yardage. The Packers lined up in a tight T. The wide receivers, Carroll Dale and Boyd Dowler, were split toward their respective sidelines. Starr noticed the bunched-in Dallas defense and called an automatic at the line of scrimmage. He sent running back Elijah Pitts through the middle of the line, across the Dallas secondary and toward the left corner. Pitts turned and Starr's pass floated into his arms. Babe Chandler kicked the point and the Green Bay Packers led, 7-0, in the NFL championship game.

The crowd sat down subdued after watching the Packers score. They had high hopes for their young Dallas team but Starr, the master craftsman, had dashed them in this very first drive.

It was so early it really didn't matter. Dallas was a good team and one touchdown shouldn't have worried them. But soon it was two.

Green Bay kicked off to Dallas and Mel Renfro camped under the ball at the Dallas 20. Bob Brown, the huge defensive tackle of the Packers, struck him a smashing tackle and the ball squirted free. Jim Grabowski, along with Donny Anderson considered the richest pair of rookie running backs in professional football history, scooped up the loose football on the 19-yard line and raced in without a Dallas player getting near him for the second Green Bay touchdown. The Packers led, 14-0, after Chandler's kick and there seemed to be a collective gasp from the Dallas crowd. Green Bay had scored 14 points in 12 seconds.

With a little less than eight minutes remaining in the first quarter, Dallas started another drive. This time they held onto the ball and moved well. They began to puncture small holes in the Green Bay front. Dan Reeves and Don Perkins, two hard-running backs, were ripping off surprising yardage through the Green Bay line. Meredith was hitting his vital third-down passes. Landry was standing coolly on the sidelines. Lombardi was marching up and down in front of the Green Bay bench.

Dallas was on the three-yard line. Meredith handed off to Dan Reeves. I remember seeing the huge number 30 going across the goal line as the crowd let out its first huge sustained roar of the afternoon. Dallas was on the scoreboard and Green Bay's lead was cut to 14-7 as Villanueva split the uprights.

Now it was a lifted Dallas team that kicked off to Green Bay. The young Cowboys were back in business. They had a score, they were in the game again and their confidence was back. Could they upset the Packers?

With the first period running out they showed they had a marvelous chance. They tied the football game. Don Perkins split Green Bay's right side, flashed through the secondary and scored standing up from 23 yards out. Villanueva kicked the extra point through again and the score was 14-14.

Suddenly the momentum had shifted. The Cowboys had scored twice to tie the football game and Green Bay was on the defensive. The crowd was roaring. The period ended and the teams shifted sides. I had a cup of coffee and checked the charts again. I would be on the air in 15 minutes.

Defense was now the important thing. Green Bay had the ball and couldn't move. Dallas got the ball back but they were stalled. Now it was the Packers again. Starr was fading back to pass. I looked downfield quickly. I saw Carroll Dale all alone. I had seen this play a thousand times before. There wasn't a defender within 20 yards of him. Starr lofted the ball high and Dale caught it easily and jogged in for another Green Bay touchdown. Chandler kicked it through again and the Packers led, 21-14. It wasn't enough for Lombardi. He continued to pace the sidelines.

Shortly before the first half ended, Dallas scored again. This time it was Villanueva on a field goal from 11 yards out and Green Bay's lead shrunk to 21-17.

The gun sounded. The Packers were ahead but the young Cowboys were not about to quit. There was still plenty of time left for almost anything to happen in the second half.

This is Ray Scott from the Cotton Bowl in Dallas, Texas, where we are about to begin the second half with Green Bay leading the Cowboys, 21-17.

Now I could relax and call the game. Once those first words are out you feel comfortable. You get a little bit of a running start when you do the second half instead of the first but you still have to get going. Now it was just a question of seeing that I had the right numbers on the right men.

Dallas ball, fourth and 32. Villanueva in to try his second field goal. Meredith waiting for the snap from center, the ball is touched down . . . up . . . and good. Dallas scores. The lead is now cut to one point. The Packers lead 21-20, three minutes left in the third period and the entire fourth quarter to go.

The pace was heating up. You could feel the tension. The crowd sat silently watching each play until they knew whether or not to cheer it. If Dallas gained, they cheered. If Green Bay held, they sat almost still.

Green Bay moved downfield again as the third period was almost gone. Starr worked his backs and Dallas pinched in their defense. Now Starr was ready to exploit a weakness. He had spotted Dallas moving closer to the line. It was time to put the ball in the air again. Somehow, Starr had that sense of timing all the great ones need. He could feel instinctively, almost, when it was time to put the ball in the air.

Starr back to pass.

I wonder how many times in my life I have said that? *Starr back to pass.* It was a marvelous picture of an artist at work. Starr had come out of Alabama without a very big reputation. He had been with the Packers as a journeyman backup quarterback for a couple of years before Lombardi took over in 1959. Lombardi chose him over the other quarterbacks and he had become Lombardi's alter ego on the field. His play calling was masterful, his inspirational field leadership vital to Packer success and his passing clever.

. . . He looks downfield . . . he's got Dowler . . . touchdown Green Bay! The Packers lead, 27-20. Bart Starr has hit Boyd Dowler for 16 yards and a Green Bay score. Now here's the kick by Chandler . . . good . . . Green Bay 28, Dallas 20.

The third period ended that way. Dallas couldn't move the first time it had the ball and Green Bay had it back. The Packers drove downfield again. And again, it was Starr back to pass.

McGee on the right side, all alone . . . touchdown! Green Bay. Bart Starr has passed to Max McGee for 28 yards and a touchdown. Green Bay leads 34-20. Chandler in to kick. The ball is down . . . the kick . . . no good . . . wide to the right. The score is 34-20 with a little more than 13 minutes left to play in the National Football League championship game.

I guess I thought it was over right there. Maybe everybody did. Few teams had caught Green Bay from behind in the fourth quarter since I had been there. But I just reported the action. I didn't want to say anything that I would regret. I had seen too many football games turn too quickly. But 14 points in the last quarter? It seemed impossible.

Dallas had the ball with five minutes to go. They trailed by 14 points and had to score quickly. They moved into formation and ran a couple of plays in the Green Bay line. Now it was third down for the Cowboys. They needed a big play if they were to stay alive. They got it. They stayed alive.

Dallas out of the huddle. Meredith over the ball. Meredith back to pass . . . he's got good protection . . . throws . . . he's got Clarke all alone at midfield . . . he's got it . . . Frank Clarke goes in for a Dallas score . . . Dallas has come back again . . . Green Bay leads 34-26 . . . Villanueva's kick . . . is good . . . Green Bay leads 34-27.

Suddenly, a game that appeared over, was now alive again. So was the crowd. They were standing and shouting. They were imploring the Cowboys to get the ball one more time, to take one more shot at tying this game, to push it into an overtime and upset the Packers.

The clock was moving. Green Bay had the ball. Fourth and two. Lombardi sent Chandler in to punt. The crowd was screaming. Chandler stood on his own 31. The pass from center was a little off to the side. Chandler had trouble controlling it. When he finally grabbed the ball it wiggled off the side of his foot as he let it go. The ball traveled all of 16 yards. Dallas had a big break. The Cowboys had the ball on the Green Bay 47-yard line. Two and a half minutes remained.

Meredith moved for the tying score. He spotted Reeves free on the left side of the field and threw the football to him. Dave Robinson and Tom Brown moved over and sandwiched Reeves before he knew what hit him. The ball flew free and Reeves got up very slowly from the ground and walked back to the huddle.

Incomplete. Second down and ten for Dallas on the Green Bay 47. Meredith back to pass again. He's got good protection this time, throws downfield to Frank Clarke . . . complete on the Green Bay 26. First down, Dallas. One minute, thirty seconds left in the game and the clock is running. One-twenty-nine . . . 1:28 . . . 1:27 . . . 1:26 . . . Meredith back again . . . looking downfield . . . under pressure . . . throws . . .

The ball was thrown high and far. It was leading Clarke as he cut across the field and raced toward the right sideline. He was almost free at the five as the ball floated over his head and his arms reached out. And then he was down. And the flags were all over and the crowd was screaming hysterically. Clarke had been scissored by Dave Robinson and Tom Brown two yards from the end zone before he had a chance to catch the football. Robinson had pulled him back and Brown had actually tackled him without the ball.

"I had to grab," Brown said later, "it was the only way to stop him. He was gone and I had to take my chances on a penalty. He had me beat and he was going into the end zone for the football. I did what I could to stop him."

Clarke bounced off the ground screaming and the referees quickly assured him they had seen the play. In an instant they were calling for the football, lining up the ball at the two-yard line and giving the signal for interference.

First down, Dallas. From the two. Green Bay leads 34-27. Dallas at the line of scrimmage. Meredith gives to Reeves . . . he's smothered at the line of scrimmage . . . maybe gained a yard . . . they're unpiling slowly . . . second and one for Dallas from the one.

Reeves was hit hard on that play. He had been hit hard on the previous play to him. It was to be very costly to Dallas in a few more moments. Now they came back again to the line of scrimmage. Second and one from the one. The clock showed less than a minute to play in the football game. Dallas was a yard away from tying Green Bay for the championship of the NFL. The teams were a minute away from what might be the second "sudden death" overtime in championship history.

Meredith back to pass. He throws to Pettis Norman. He drops the ball. A flag on the play. Meredith threw to his tight end but Norman dropped the ball and the penalty appears to be against . . . Dallas . . . offside Dallas . . . the ball will go back to the six.

The crowd booed the play more out of frustration than disagreement. Left tackle Jim Boeke had clearly jumped the play and had been caught. Now Meredith had to do it all over again from the six-yard line.

Second down and six now. Meredith back to pass. He's got Reeves in the flat. He drops the ball. Incomplete. Third down. There are 48 seconds left in the game.

This is the play that cost the Dallas Cowboys. Reeves was alone and the ball was thrown right to him. He was groggy from the battering he had taken and never controlled the football. Now Meredith had one or two more plays left and 75,000 people were standing to see them. I kept reminding myself in the booth to stay calm, stay coherent, just be objective, just report those plays. The emotion was staggering. When a crowd catches fire like that Dallas crowd it is hard not to be swept up with the tide.

Third down. Meredith back again . . . he's got Norman . . . he's down on the two-yard line. Fourth and goal from the two for Dallas. There are 22 seconds left to play.

Now the whole season for Dallas was wrapped up in this final play. A touchdown would tie and give Dallas a chance to beat Green Bay in the overtime. Anything less would give the Packers another championship in Vince Lombardi's brilliant career.

In the huddle Meredith bent down in front of his team and in a clear voice said, "Fire 90, on set, let's go." That was all that was left of their season. "Fire 90" was a rollout to the right, Meredith carrying himself, with the option of going in from the two if he could or passing to a free man. It was a brave call. All the burden would be on the quarterback who had taken the team this far.

Dallas out of the huddle, Meredith over the center . . . Meredith keeps it . . . rolls out . . . under pressure . . . throws . . . intercepted by Tom Brown at the goal line. Green Bay has the ball. They have held off the Cowboys.

Meredith had rolled to his right, all alone, in an attempt to fake the Green Bay defense to his left. Dave Robinson, not to be faked, came up from his linebacker position and crashed into Meredith just before he released the ball. It went wobbling a few yards downfield in the general direction of Bob Hayes but it never got there. Brown pulled it out of the Green Bay crowd.

"I saw Hayes," said Meredith, "but I couldn't get it to him. Robinson had his hand in my face. Give him a lot of credit."

Three seconds . . . two . . . one . . . there's the gun. The Green Bay Packers are the champions of the National Football League. Green Bay wins 34-27.

There may have never been anything like it. The last two minutes of that football game, with the young Cowboys driving and the veteran Packers holding firm, was a spectacle as breathless as anything I had ever seen.

Lombardi and his team had been brilliant again. Starr had been the perfect quarterback, cool, capable, always ready with the right play at the right time. He had thrown four touchdown passes and gained 304 yards. It was some work day.

Meredith, who had brought the Cowboys from a weak expansion team to within one minute of tying for the NFL championship in regulation time, had been outstanding, too. His clutch touchdown pass to Clarke that closed the gap had shocked the Packers and awakened the crowd.

But somehow, they will all judge him on the last few seconds, instead of the previous 58 minutes. It was to Meredith's credit that Dallas came that far. Most people will forget that. They will only remember that he couldn't get the football across the Green Bay goal line from two yards out with five chances to do it.

Ray Scott and Bart Starr.

Fred Capossela

20

By a Nose

FRED CAPOSSELA

"It is now post time . . . the crowd approaches the rail . . . the horses are at the starting gate . . . *and they're off!*"

The sound of those words sends shivers of excitement through every racing fan in America as the horses charge out of the gate in the rush to gold and glory.

Only one man, Fred Capossela, who has called 70,000 races in 36 years, remains calm. While all hell is breaking loose on the track in front of him, Cappy continues to call the race clearly and carefully with his only interest in the outcome being the accuracy of his call.

"I never made a bet in my life," says Capossela. "I couldn't do it and still maintain my objectivity about the race."

The peppery little man, who is the chief announcer at the New York tracks, admits that he has mixed up his horses a couple of times in his thousands of races.

"It happens so rarely that I remember them," he says. "I once had a horse named Aching Back and I called him Aching Feet. I had another horse named Nashville. For some reason I kept calling him Louisville."

Capossela's fantastic memory is one of the wonders of the modern world. He sits in his booth, high above the track at Aqueduct or Belmont, memorizes the colors of the silks, repeats it over and over to himself out loud, calls the race and wipes the colors out of his mind.

"Five minutes after the race is over," he says, "I don't have the slightest idea of who ran in it or who won."

Capossela, born in Brooklyn some 68 years ago, graduated from Boys High School and went to work in the sports department of the Brooklyn *Eagle*. His first job was handling the horse racing entries. It was the accidental beginning of an exciting career.

Four years later he became racing editor of the New York *Post* and stayed in that job eight years.

"The late Bryan Field was the race announcer in New York," said Cappy, "and he also worked at Delaware Park. He would take the train down at night and I would get to do the last race in New York and I would hold the fort until he got back the next day for the second race. I would usually get a race a day that way, at least, and sometimes more if the train was late."

When Field left his announcing post to become general manager at Delaware Park, Capossela became the voice of the New York tracks in 1943. He has been there ever since.

In addition to his calling of the races at the track, Capossela has broadcast most of the feature races on radio and television for more than 20 years, including the Kentucky Derby, the Preakness, the Belmont, the Saratoga Stakes and many, many others.

It is August 18, 1962. Fred Capossela describes the most exciting horse race he ever saw.

Fred Capossela

THE lovely ladies in their stylish summer dresses, the handsome men in their flashy sports clothes and the incredibly beautiful horses. Each August, under the cool shade of Upper New York State, the racing season switches to Saratoga.

The $2 bettors are the heart of the racing business in New York, commuting by subway and car to Aqueduct and Belmont, for a chance at their fortune. But in Saratoga, each summer, the leisure class comes to enjoy the fresh air, delight in a beautiful track and cash some big bets if they are lucky.

It is at a track like Saratoga, where the racing is run over a manicured surface, that horse racing became the Sport of Kings.

They come here in chauffeured limousines and the drivers sit in the sun reading *The Racing Form* all afternoon and sneaking in for a few $2 bets, while the master of the house sits in his private box, and enjoys the thrills of the day.

No racing fan, whether he was a $2 bettor of infrequent appearance, or a regular $100 bettor, will ever forget the feature race at Saratoga on the afternoon of August 18, 1962.

The day was perfect. The sky was clear and blue and a capacity crowd was on hand for the running of the Travers Stakes at Saratoga over a mile and a quarter. This was the 93rd running of the oldest stakes race for three-year-olds in America. Much of the excitement of a race comes from the tradition. Add to the tradition a big crowd, a fine day and some marvelous horses and there is nothing that can match it.

Although I don't bet, I do read the racing pages, of course. The stories that day told of the excitement being generated by the match-up of the two finest three-year-olds in the country that season.

Two horses, Jaipur and Ridan, were causing all of the excitement. Rarely have two horses ever been so evenly matched going into a race.

Jaipur, son of the famed Nasrullah and Rare Perfume, had won five of six races that season, including a victory in the Belmont Stakes. Willie Shoemaker was on Jaipur.

His opponent, Ridan, owned by Mrs. Mood Jolley and trained by her son, Leroy, had finished second to Greek Money in the prestigious Preakness in Maryland. Manuel Ycaza was up. Each horse carried 126 pounds.

These were the class horses in the field as I drove into Saratoga, parked my car and walked to the booth shortly after 11:00 o'clock that day.

Shortly before noon I got on the public address system in the park to give the changes for the first race that day. There may be a last-minute jockey change or a change in weight or a scratch. I make these announcements quickly and clearly and allow the early bettors to think more deeply about their selection.

After calling the first six races of the day I prepared for the feature race, the Travers Stakes, by memorizing the silks.

It is a system I have worked out over the years. It has never failed me yet. I do not memorize the numbers or the color of the horse or a long or short tail or a strange, awkward gait. I just memorize the colors of the silks. The silks can be similar for several races but are never similar in the same race. It is an infallible system.

"John Jones, yellow and black . . . John Jones, yellow and black . . . John Jones, yellow and black . . ."

Over and over and over again I repeat the colors and the name of the horse. I know then, when the race begins, I can see the colors and automatically call the horse. I can't do it five minutes after the race is over but I always do it perfectly while the race is on.

There are 10 minutes to go before the big race and I am looking down the track. There they are! A burst of excitement rushes through me. After all these years, after all these races, after all the sounds and colors and noises, the appearance of the horses on the track fills me with anticipation.

The horses are on the track.

I have made my announcement and the fans study the numbers and their charts and the fastest way to make a buck. I am too busy memorizing horses and their silks.

Jaipur, light blue and dark blue . . . Jaipur, light blue and dark blue . . . Jaipur, light blue and dark blue . . .

Ridan, black and white . . . Ridan, black and white . . . Ridan, black and white . . .

Military Plume, pink and yellow hoops . . . Military Plume, pink and yellow hoops . . . Military Plume, pink and yellow hoops . . .

Now I have the horses memorized as they exercise before the race. I watch them through my binoculars, calling them out as they run back and forth, to myself.

Five minutes to post time.

You can feel the tremors in the stands. The final five minutes before the race is the most active time for the fans. They are busy with their last-minute calculations, busy exchanging sage advice with their friends, busy selecting what they know is a certain winner.

The fans rush to the windows, change their minds seven times before the race is run and finally bet the way the stranger in front of them bets.

"Number seven, three times," they say. They have finally decided on number seven because they were married October 7. It is as good a system as any.

Two minutes to post time. Two minutes.

Now the horses are all being urged into the starting gate. Some move slowly. Others walk right in, their heads high, proud, ready to run as they have trained hard these many months to perform. Their owners sit in their boxes anxiously eyeing their horses as one would a child at his first school play. The bettors rush off to the windows certain they have seen something to convince them they now have the right horses.

One minute to post time. One minute.

Now I move close to the microphone. I clear my throat and sip some water. After calling more than 70,000 races I have never had any trouble with my throat. My voice sounds high and excited to some people but that is my natural voice. I had to laugh one day when an actor tried to imitate my voice on the Ed Sullivan Show. I was certain he was straining terribly and would have a sore throat for a week.

There is that silent instant when the horses are in the gate, when the gate is locked, when the jockeys are anxious, when the horse can certainly understand the tension of the moment. They are ready and anxious to blast out of the gate and still the gate is locked. Now they are all lined up. The crowd is still. The owners cross their fingers. The fans check their programs for the final time. The gate crashes open. There is an explosive roar. The horses rush out. What a moment!

They're off.

More than 70,000 times I have said that and it still fills me with excitement. It is as if all the juices in my body began to flow at once as I search out the track for my memorized colors.

Ridan and Jaipur are nose and nose in the lead. Military Plume is two lengths behind them. Cicada is fourth . . .

I go through the entire field but I somehow manage to keep one eye on the leaders. It is still Ridan and Jaipur nose and nose as they approach the first turn.

The race is a mile and a quarter and rarely will two horses ever stay that close together out of the gate for very long. But this race seems different. The two favorites have broken from the gate together, almost stride for stride, as they approach the first turn. They are the class horses and they have already pulled well ahead of the other horses in the field. The crowd is beginning to sense a very special race as the two horses charge into the first turn.

Shoemaker is urging his horse to move ahead and Ycaza is staying stride for stride with him on Ridan.

At the first turn it's still Jaipur and Ridan nose and nose . . . Military Plume is third . . . Cicada is fourth . . .

Fred Capossela

The noise is beginning to build as they race on the straightaway on the opposite side of the track. I look through my glasses and it is as if there was one horse with eight legs. I can see the legs as they bounce up and down the track but I can see only one head.

Now they are thundering toward the far turn just beyond the halfway point of the race. I have never seen anything like this. Not a hair has separated the two horses as they have run neck and neck, nose and nose for more than three-quarters of a mile. The crowd is screaming wildly as the two horses stay together at the turn.

At the halfway pole it is Ridan and Jaipur, Jaipur and Ridan . . . Military Plume is third . . . Cicada is fourth . . .

I lean forward just a little more in the booth, hold my binoculars a little tighter on my face as the two horses roar around the turn. There is no separating them.

It has become an impossible race to call. There is no way to separate the horses. The crowd is on its feet urging one or the other of their favorites on. The rest of the field is now strung out, three, four, five lengths behind the leaders.

Shoemaker, one of the greatest jockeys of all time, has gone to his whip as they reach the final turn. His horse has answered with all he has. It should be enough to shake Ridan but Ycaza is giving his horse the ride of its life. Both jocks have now gone to the whip as they reach the final turn. It doesn't seem to be separating them.

At the final pole it is still Ridan and Jaipur, Jaipur and Ridan . . . Cicada coming on the outside at Military Plume for third.

The rest of the field is strung out now way back. Military Plume is holding on to third but all eyes are on the two horses at the head of the stretch, still running nose and nose, head and head, stride for stride.

In the stretch it is Jaipur and Ridan, Jaipur and Ridan . . . Military Plume has third . . .

With 30 yards to go I am certain it is going to be a photo finish. It is too close to call but I finally think I see a little daylight. I think I see Jaipur's nose edging just a trifle ahead of Ridan as they race those final yards.

Now they are racing to the finish line right beneath me, I am certain I see some daylight. I call it that way. I wait until their noses hit the finish and I decide to gamble.

At the finish it's Jaipur by a nose in a photo with Ridan . . . Military Plume is third . . . Cicada is fourth . . .

Now comes the waiting. The two horses have run nose and nose for one and a quarter miles. At the last few yards there is daylight and I catch it. I want to be able to give the fans the winner if I can but I don't want to be wrong. The photo will be the official word but I feel certain I have called the right winner. There is buzzing throughout the track. The arguments are loud as people near the finish all decide how they've seen the race. After all these years I have learned that the people who have bet on a race cannot see it accurately. They are too busy searching the track for all the horses.

The judges are viewing the photo. It is sometimes impossible to pick a race that close from the booth but it is easy to pick it with the photo. Even a fraction of an inch of the horse's nose can look like a great difference in the photo. Now they make their decision and the result is flashed on the board.

The roar is evenly divided among people who had bet on Ridan and people who had backed Jaipur. The photo proves me correct.

The winner is Jaipur. Jaipur is the winner. Ridan is second and Military Plume is third.

The prices were placed on the board and the favorite, Jaipur, hadn't paid too much to the bettors but had thrilled them with the most exciting race they probably had ever seen in their lifetimes.

I covered most of the races won by Whirlaway and they were thrilling because of Whirlaway's special style of coming from behind and finishing with a rush to win his race.

I don't fall in love with horses. I am too busy remembering their colors as they run and forgetting them as soon as they finish running. But one horse always stands out in my mind. That was Count Fleet, the horse of the year in 1943. He was one of the few horses I had ever seen who could run equally as well under any conditions. He could run on muddy tracks or hard ones, he could run on blistering hot days and cool ones. He could run in crowded races or in uncrowded races. He was just a very special horse.

As the Travers Stakes ended that day, I watched the winner, Jaipur, prance into the circle where his owner, George Widener, waited for him. The owner patted the horse several times and congratulated the jockey. They had just won $53,722 in the stakes race but that didn't seem to be the reason for all the smiles. There was something much more important than money in winning a race like this. Most of the people who own horses aren't in it for the money. They usually have enough. They are in it because they love the sport, they love the competition and they love the excitement.

Fred Capossela

There can hardly be anything more exciting in sports than being the owner of a horse on a day it wins a big race.

It is like the thrill of being the track announcer in a nose-to-nose finish of a race and getting the right horse.

Five minutes after the race was over that day I had forgotten the names of all the horses in the race. I was busy memorizing the names and colors of the horses in the next race.

But now it is so many years later and I can still see those two horses, Jaipur and Ridan, Ridan and Jaipur, pounding down the stretch in that marvelous finish.

The race lasted two minutes, one and three-fifths seconds, but it seemed like a lifetime of thrills was packed into that short period of time.

Jaipur and Ridan. Ridan and Jaipur. Separated by a nose. I guess I'll always be happy that I had the right nose.

Portrait of the master at work.

Bill Stern

21

Rote vs. Notre Dame

BILL STERN

*Bill Stern, the Colgate Shave Cream
man is on the air,
Bill Stern, the Colgate Shave Cream
man with stories rare,
Take his advice and you'll look keen
You'll get a shave that's nice and clean.*

HARDLY a radio fan in the 1940s and 1950s
will forget the opening jingle for the Bill
Stern Sports Newsreel, a regular Friday night
feature when radio presented word pictures
of all the major events in the exciting world
of sports.

Stern's show, in which he dramatically re-
created the major sports events of the time
and brought to life the personalities of the
day, combined drama, excitement and tension.

". . . and that man's name," Stern would
say and then pause, "was Lou Gehrig." The
impact would sink in and while the listener
was almost breathless from the excitement
Stern would say, "That's the three-oh mark
for tonight."

A generation of young sports fans became

familiar with the journalese 30, or three-oh, for the end, through the drama of Stern's show.

Stern, who was born in Rochester, New York, went to high school in Rochester, prep school in Tarrytown, New York, and college in Chester, Pennsylvania.

He started his broadcasting career in 1925 at a small station in Rochester for $11 per week.

"I was quickly fired," Stern says. "I was called in by the fellow who runs the station and advised, 'Get out of the business. You'll never make it.' That fellow still has the same job. I get a Christmas card from him every year. He always writes the same thing. 'I still think I'm right.' He's a real great guy."

Stern went to work at Radio City Music Hall in New York as a stage manager but pestered officials at the National Broadcasting Company across the street until they gave him a chance at announcing.

"I thought announcing would be an easy way to make money," Stern says.

Stern was working later for a Texas radio station, doing the University of Texas football games on Saturday, when he was involved in a serious auto accident. He suffered a compound fracture of the left leg. When the break wasn't set properly, gangrene set in and Stern suffered the loss of his left leg. He was 28 years old at the time.

While Stern was in the hospital in New York, NBC program director John Royal came to visit him.

"He thought I was dying," said Stern, "so he offered me a job broadcasting football."

Six months later Stern walked in to NBC, shocked John Royal with his vitality and was hired to broadcast football.

Stern became the biggest name in football broadcasting, doing almost every big football game carried by NBC. His fast-paced, dramatic descriptions of college games became a standard for every budding broadcaster around the country. Most of the football broadcasters of the day were influenced by his style.

While Stern was considered the biggest name in sports broadcasting, he was fighting a highly personal and dramatic battle.

Because of continued trouble with his leg, Stern became medically addicted to morphine. He spent more than 15 years battling the problem. It finally culminated with an on-the-air breakdown during the Sugar Bowl game between Navy and Mississippi in 1955.

He was hospitalized at the Institute of Living in Hartford, Connecticut, for six months.

Stern resumed his career after his recovery on a much lower key and now does a sports show for the Mutual Broadcasting Network out of New York City carried by several hundred stations across the nation.

His voice is the same, his style as exciting and fluid as ever. In the traditional position of a sports broadcaster, his hand cupped against the crowd noises over one ear, Bill Stern still is as exciting as ever.

Now it is December 3, 1949, and Bill Stern is at the Cotton Bowl where Notre Dame and Southern Methodist University are the opposing teams.

Bill Stern

THE Fighting Irish of Notre Dame had dominated the college football picture for four straight seasons. Since their titanic tie with the Army team of Blanchard, Davis and Tucker, saved by the shoestring tackle of Johnny Lujack, in the 0-0 battle at Yankee Stadium, they had been tied once and won every other game.

From 1946 through this day in 1949, December 3, the final game of the season, Notre Dame had won 38 games, tied two and lost none.

There was little chance they would lose anything this day.

Their opponents were the Mustangs of Southern Methodist University, the home team from Dallas, but an unlikely challenger for any national crown.

The oddsmakers had established Notre Dame as 28-point favorites and that seemed a wee bit generous after the SMU game the previous Saturday. All-American Doak Walker, the talented triple threat back, was now on the sidelines with a leg injury. Walker would not even be in uniform this afternoon but would lend what moral support he could to the Mustang cause in street clothes.

It hardly seemed to matter.

The Irish were deep, talented and resourceful. Their cast included All-American end Leon Hart, who would double at fullback when some precious yards were needed; charging runner Emil (Six-Yard) Sitko, nicknamed for his skill in shaking tacklers off until he gained at least six yards; quarterback Bob Williams; fleet receiver Bill Wrightkin; and the typical Notre Dame depth in the line and defensive backfield.

The Mustangs, without Walker, who could run, pass and kick with the best of them, presented little problem. They were typical of most of the teams in the Southwest Conference. They depended on the forward pass and would throw the ball 30, 40 or 50 times a game and think nothing of it.

On this cloudy afternoon in Dallas they would not have Walker. Their best receiver, Johnny Champion, small and swift, would be looking to a relative unknown for his forward passes. The tailback in the wide spreading Southern Methodist system would be Kyle Rote, a junior, who had been used mostly as a running back. If the Mustangs were going to do anything this day they would have to get some passing from Rote.

Rote had done some passing in high school, but at SMU, with Walker available, he had been a runner and a receiver. Now he would have to get the ball in the air if they were going to challenge the huge Notre Dame team.

Early Saturday morning I got up early, went down to breakfast in the hotel, studied the Dallas papers for any last-minute information and went over the names and numbers of the players.

It is much easier to do a game when you have the numbers firmly fixed in your mind and don't have to depend on the spotters. One slow action by the spotters can foul up a pretty exciting play.

I took a cab from the hotel to the Cotton Bowl. There I visited with both teams. Frank Leahy, the Notre Dame coach, assured me that his team was in fine physical shape. He was worried about overconfidence.

"I think everyone is selling this Southern Methodist team short," he said. "They are a real fine ball club. I am sure they are going to give us a very good game. They can put the ball in the air. The teams from down here always can."

Like all coaches, Leahy was being overly pessimistic. Everyone knew that the Mustangs really didn't belong on the same field with Notre Dame that day. But, of course, nobody really knows what a passing team can do on a hot day. Could a junior running back suddenly become an accurate passer against the murderous charge of the Notre Dame line and their fantastic pass defense?

There were 75,457 people in the stands that afternoon to find out. We went over the final small details, checked the time and prepared for the signal that we were on the air.

From the Cotton Bowl in Dallas, Texas, the Fighting Irish of Notre Dame against the Mustangs of Southern Methodist University. . . . Good afternoon, everyone, this is Bill Stern . . .

Now the bands were marching on to the field, their bright uniforms freshly pressed for this big game. We gave the lineups and waited for the bandmaster to raise his arms at the 50-yard line. We looked out over the field, watched the bandsmen and announced the National Anthem. The anthem was over and now we were ready to start the football game.

Steve Oracko approaches the ball for Notre Dame. There's the kick, a beauty, sailing high and far into the Southern Methodist end zone. The Mustangs will start from the 20-yard line, first down and ten.

I looked down on the field and announced the offensive lineup for Southern Methodist and the defensive lineup for Notre Dame. It almost seemed like a high school team against a college team, or a college team against a professional team. Most of the SMU players seemed tall and thin while all of the Notre Dame players appeared to be tall and husky and hard. Maybe I was just focusing on Leon Hart, the huge end of the Fighting Irish, who was their defensive star as well as an offensive end and part-time fullback.

SMU couldn't move with the ball and had to kick to the Fighting Irish. Notre Dame took over on its own 26-yard line. Notre Dame tried a couple of ground plays, gained a few yards and had to kick back to SMU. With the ball for the second time, SMU still couldn't move against the Irish. With six minutes gone in the first period Notre Dame got the football again.

This time they moved. Williams handed off to Sitko and the hard-running fullback charged the middle of the SMU line for, naturally, six yards. Williams passed to Hart for 12. Now Williams had a first down in SMU territory.

First and ten for Notre Dame on the SMU 42. Williams over the center, takes the handoff, back to pass, looks downfield . . . throws to the left corner . . . touchdown Notre Dame . . . Williams hits Bill Wrightkin for 42 yards and the score. . . Notre Dame leads, 6-0.

The Irish had scored the second time they had their hands on the ball. Steve Oracko came into the game for the extra-point try.

Williams puts the ball down, the kick is up by Oracko . . . and good. Notre Dame leads 7-0.

The Irish kicked off to Southern Methodist and the huge, hometown crowd groaned as the Mustangs tried two runs, gained only three yards, tried a pass which was battered down, and kicked back to the Irish.

Williams took the Irish downfield again. Three running plays, a short Williams pass over the middle and a 17-yard running play by Sitko put the ball on the Mustang 27.

First down for the Irish on the SMU 27. Williams going back to pass again, he has good protection . . . throws . . . the ball is battered around downfield . . . up in the air . . . and . . . caught by Ernie Zalejski at the goal line for a touchdown. Williams has his second touchdown, this one a 27-yard touchdown pass to Zalejski.

Now it seemed that on top of everything else the Mustangs weren't going to get a break. They had batted Williams' pass around at the goal line and the ball had floated softly down into the hands of a Notre Dame receiver. The Irish were not only good, they were lucky.

The score was 13-0 in the second period and the crowd seemed pleased that the out-weighed, out-manned Southern Methodist team was holding the National Champions to such a small margin of victory. The small SMU boys were fighting hard to keep the game under control.

SMU got the ball again in the middle of the second period, and put on a fine drive They took the ball on their own 39-yard line after a Notre Dame punt and began to move on the ground.

Rote takes the ball over the right side of the Notre Dame line . . . he's to the 40, the 45, across midfield into Notre Dame territory . . . first down SMU. Kyle Rote has carried the ball into Irish territory. . . . Now it's Rote again from the 48 . . . he breaks over the middle, cuts to his left, fights off one tackler, gets away from another . . . before he's pulled down by two Notre Dame men at the 31. Notre Dame leads 13-0 but the Mustangs are driving.

The crowd was on its feet cheering itself hoarse. Kyle Rote was carrying the fight to the Irish. On the sidelines, Doak Walker stood against the bench and yelled encouragement to his teammates. The Mustang bench was alive and the crowd was going mad as Rote called the next play.

Rote again . . . he's up to the 25, the 20 . . . the 15 . . . 12-yard line before he's down . . .

Rote had suddenly taken charge of the game. Except for 17 yards gained on a pass and one other run, Rote had carried 10 times in 12 plays. Now the ball was on the Notre Dame three. First down for Southern Methodist with the score 13-0 and the Mustangs driving.

Rote has the ball again, he is over the right side of the Notre Dame line . . . touchdown Southern Methodist. Rote has gone in standing up for the first SMU score. Notre Dame leads 13-6 but now it's a ball game.

On the opposite side of the field the Irish seemed confused. This wasn't how the script was supposed to go. Notre Dame, the national champion, was supposed to be running the Mustangs out of the Cotton Bowl. Instead, SMU trailed by only six points.

At halftime, coach Matty Bell of Southern Methodist told his team that they had played brilliantly and that he was very proud of them.

"I'm not willing to settle for just playing well or tying them," he said. "I think we can beat them. Now let's go out there and play tough football."

Bell had decided this was the time to shift his attack. His team had tried to run on Notre Dame in the first half. That was their best bet with Rote. Now they would try to put the ball into the air, the last thing Notre Dame was now expecting.

"Kyle," said Bell, "I know you can do it. Let's throw the ball over them."

Southern Methodist had the ball deep in its own territory. Rote thought about the call. A run would be the expected play but Coach Bell thought the Irish were ready to be passed on.

"Pass left, Champion on three, let's go," Rote said in the huddle.

The Mustangs would send receiver Johnny Champion deep in the left side of the field and Rote would try to hit him going away. It was a long, breakaway gambling play.

Now Rote went back to pass and Champion raced down field. The Irish line charged hard and Rote was rushed.

Rote looking for a receiver, he's in trouble, gets the ball away deep to Champion on the left side . . . intercepted . . . by Jim Mutscheller . . .

The pass play had backfired. Notre Dame had charged Rote and now was in possession of the ball deep in Mustang territory. On the first play from scrimmage Williams handed off to Bill Barrett and the halfback thrust over the right side of the Mustang line for a touchdown. The Fighting Irish led the Mustangs, 20-7, and all the joy of the afternoon seemed gone for the SMU fans.

They couldn't know that the game was really just about to begin.

Rote took the next kick and ran it back to the SMU 39-yard line. There were five minutes left in the third period.

Rote back to pass again . . . he looks downfield . . . he has Champion on the left side of the field . . . a long pass . . . Champion has

it . . . he's knocked out of bounds . . . on the one-yard line. . . .
Rote has completed a 60-yard pass to Johnny Champion, a spectacu-
lar play . . . on the one-yard line from the SMU 39-yard line.

Now the crowd was on its feet. The noise was deafening. Notre
Dame wasn't going to have an easy game after all. The underdog
Mustangs were fighting as hard as they could. Rote was a yard away
from the score. Now he took the football himself, drove through
the right side of the Notre Dame line and scored. Notre Dame led
20-14 after Billy Sullivan kicked the point.

The crowd started hoping for a miracle. Notre Dame had the ball
but seemed to lose its poise. The Mustangs had the ball again.
They now had a chance to tie the score. They could go ahead with
a touchdown and the extra point.

Rote passed to Champion for 12. Rote drove the center of the
SMU line for six. Rote drove to the Notre Dame 36. In eight plays
the Mustangs were on the Notre Dame three-yard line. The noise
was everywhere as we tried to hear ourselves think in the booth.

Kyle Rote, the incredible junior halfback for Southern Methodist,
has taken the Mustangs down to Notre Dame's doorstep again . . .
first down on the three . . . Notre Dame leads by six points . . . he
is . . . in . . . another touchdown for Kyle Rote . . . the score is tied.

Programs and paper bags and banners and pennants and hats and
ties and a few jackets went flying from the stands at the huge Cotton
Bowl. Kyle Rote had just scored his third straight touchdown for
the Mustangs and the score was tied. SMU, with four losses on the
season, and Notre Dame, without a loss in four years, were dead-
locked with 4:42 to go in the game.

Now Billy Sullivan was in the game to try for the extra point.
The kick would put the Mustangs ahead of Notre Dame and set
off another massive demonstration of loyalty to the Southern Methodist side. Not a person in the park could sit still. I leaned forward
in the booth, zeroed in on Sullivan and watched the ball placed
down.

The kick is . . . blocked . . . Notre Dame has blocked the kick
. . . the score is still tied. . . .

The whole left side of the Irish line had charged through a gaping
hole and stopped Sullivan's kick as the ball left his feet. He never
had a chance.

Now the score was 20-20 as the Mustangs kicked off to Notre
Dame. Time was a factor. The clock was running out. Notre Dame
didn't want a tie to mar their perfect record on the season. Southern

Methodist didn't want a tie, either. They were on the field to beat the national champions.

The blocked kick was the break Notre Dame needed. They regained their composure and went after the victory. They had the ball at midfield. Williams passed for six to Hart. Francis Spaniel carried through the middle of the Mustang line for four. Sitko made only five this time. Now the Irish needed another first down. They moved Hart back from his end position and gave him the football. First down, Notre Dame.

Williams studied the clock and moved the Irish carefully. He wanted the winning score but he wanted it with very little time left to play. Rote had become too dangerous a factor in the game.

Notre Dame on the six. Two and a half minutes left to play. Williams calling the play. He is over the center.

Williams gives to Bill Barrett, who goes around left end . . . touchdown . . . touchdown Notre Dame . . . the Irish lead 26-20. Bill Barrett circled his own left end for the score. The Mustangs were looking for a play up the middle and the Irish completely fooled them. A great call by Bob Williams.

Steve Oracko kicked the extra point and the undefeated Notre Damers leaped for joy on their bench. They had gone ahead with less than two minutes left in the game.

On the SMU side, Kyle Rote sagged on the bench and Doak Walker, in his civilian clothes, walked the entire length of the SMU bench kicking the dirt with his good leg and looking at the sky.

There was still more than a minute left when Rote called another pass play. It was first down from the 47. Rote went back to pass. The Notre Dame line charged.

Rote being rushed . . . being rushed . . . looks for a receiver . . . he's hit hard by Leon Hart and knocked down . . . he's out . . . Rote is out cold on the ground.

The crowd was still. They saw Rote trying to get to his feet, finally being helped off the field by his teammates, staggering under the force of the blow.

Fred Benners, a sophomore replaced Rote, and called for a long pass play. It was incomplete. On third down he called a short pass. This time he hit his man for six yards.

Now Benners is down at midfield . . . Leon Hart again . . . the big end knocked Rote cold and now has knocked Benners down. . . . He's being helped to his feet and taken out of the game. . . . Who will replace him?

237

From the sidelines a figure got off the bench and pulled on his helmet. He jogged slowly on to the field, favoring a leg, rubbing at the side of his face, pulling on his chin strap.

Ladies and gentlemen, we are seeing one of the greatest displays of courage I have ever seen in my long years of broadcasting football games. Kyle Rote, who was knocked silly by Leon Hart, is coming back on the field for SMU. He looks pretty groggy but he is out there.

There were 22 seconds left to play. SMU had a fourth down on the Notre Dame 41. The crowd was thundering its applause. Rote went back to pass again. This would be SMU's last play of the game. They had no time outs left. They needed a touchdown to tie the game.

It's Rote back to pass . . . Champion is racing downfield. . . . Rote is hit . . . lets the ball go . . . Champion in a crowd . . . reaches up . . . it's being fought for and grabbed away by two Notre Dame defenders. . . . Notre Dame has intercepted Rote's pass. . . .

Seconds later the gun sounded and Notre Dame had its streak intact with a 27-20 victory.

Kyle Rote, who was to go on to a brilliant career with the New York Giants, had played the greatest game of his life. He had completed 10 of 24 passes against a massive Notre Dame line for 146 yards. He had gained 115 yards himself on the ground. He had punted for an average of 48 yards. He had scored all three SMU touchdowns and had the Irish backed to their own end zone on the very last play, despite throwing off a bad foot.

The accolades came from every member of the Notre Dame team and from coach Frank Leahy.

"Rote is the most underrated back in the country," said Leahy.

"Rote is the wildest thing I've ever tried to tie on to," said Emil Sitko.

None of Rote's feats surprised the local folk. They had seen Rote do the same thing in high school and now he was coming into his own in college. He would gain 1,809 yards all by himself in his senior year at SMU by rushing, passing, catching passes and running kickoffs back.

Sportswriter Bill Rives knew Rote well. "Rote always wins at whatever he does," said Rives. "You can have him down nine holes in a golf match and he will win the next nine holes and beat you on the extra hole."

That day in the Cotton Bowl, Rote wasn't able to beat the

national champions by himself but he played one of the greatest games these old eyes ever saw.

Bill Stern gags it up in an era long gone.

239